THE DIARY

OF

WILLIAM HEDGES, ESQ.

THE DIARY

OF

WILLIAM HEDGES, ESQ.

(AFTERWARDS SIR WILLIAM HEDGES),

DURING HIS AGENCY IN BENGAL;

AS WELL AS ON HIS VOYAGE OUT AND RETURN OVERLAND
(1681 - 1687).

TRANSCRIBED FOR THE PRESS, WITH INTRODUCTORY
NOTES. ETC.,

BY

R. BARLOW, ESQ.

AND ILLUSTRATED BY COPIOUS EXTRACTS FROM
UNPUBLISHED RECORDS, ETC.,

BY

COLONEL HENRY YULE, R.E., C.B., LL.D.,

PRESIDENT OF THE HAKLUYT SOCIETY.

VOL. 1.

THE DIARY, WITH INDEX.

First Published in 1887
Indian Reprint in 2017

Published by

Kalpaz Publications
C-30, Satyawati Nagar,
Delhi – 110052
E-mail: kalpaz@hotmail.com
Website: kalpazpublications.com
Ph.: +91-9212142040

Cataloging in Publication Data—DK
Courtesy: D.K. Agencies (P) Ltd. <docinfo@dkagencies.com>

Hedges, William, *Sir,* 1632-1701, **author.**
The diary of William Hedges, esq. (afterwards Sir William Hedges), during his agency in Bengal : as well as on his voyage out and return overland (1681-1697) / transcribed for the press, with introductory notes, etc., by R. Barlow, esq., and illustrated by copious extracts from unpublished records, etc., by Colonel Henry Yule.
volumes cm
"First published in 1887"—Title page verso.
Contents: vol. 1. The diary, with index
ISBN 9789351284758 (HB)

1. East India Company—Early works to 1800. 2. India—History—1526-1765. 3. Hedges, William, Sir, 1632-1701—Diaries. 4. Hedges, William, Sir, 1632-1701—Travel—India—Bengal. I. Title.

LCC DS485.B46H43 2017 | DDC 915.4140425 23

DIARY OF SIR WILLIAM HEDGES.

PREFACE.

The work now issued to the Society requires some prefatory explanation as to the manner in which it is presented, and some information also regarding the Diarist beyond what has been supplied in Mr. Barlow's "Introductory Notes".

A transcript of the Diary was brought to my notice some years ago by the Rev. James Long, to whom it had been lent by Mr. Barlow. How the Diary itself fell into this gentleman's hands may best be told by an extract from a letter with which he has favoured me:

"I was living near Broadstairs, and not unfrequently visited Canterbury. There was a bookseller in the High Street, named Bohn, from whom I had made purchases on one or two occasions, and on September 20th, 1875 (so I find from my log-book), in answer to my usual inquiry for old Voyages and Travels, he mentioned that he had an old manuscript which perhaps might interest me. A glance showed me that its author, William Hedges, must be the same gentleman whom Bruce (*Annals of the E. I. Company*, ii, pp. 467-505) mentions as the first 'Governor', as well as 'Agent', for the Bengal Factories. So I bought it at once.

"There was no mark, nor stamp, nor line of any description to indicate the previous owner, but I understood from Mr. Bohn that he had it as part of a lot at a sale; and my impression is that he said a sale of some things belonging to Lord Sondes,[1]—and this is all I know about the book's history. The condition proved that it had been very lightly esteemed. . . . . I copied it carefully, and I think accurately, intending to get it printed. But I discovered that the half-dozen copies I intended to distribute among my few friends, as an amusing 'illustration' of early trade under difficulties, would cost nearly as much as an entire edition, whilst it would probably really not interest a single modern individual, so I gave up the idea. Mr. Long, however, happened to call one day, and thought with myself that it conveyed a good insight into the inner life and habits of some of the Honourable Company's servants, so I lent him the transcript."

---

[1] The fourth Baron Sondes died in 1874.

There can be little doubt, I think, that the document came originally from the India House, and possibly it formed an item among the papers which were carted away to be destroyed under a certain order issued by the Secretary of State in Council, at the time when the seat of that body was transferred from the old House in Leadenhall Street to Westminster. If so, it is probably not the first of the records then dealt with, perhaps too hastily, which our Society has made accessible to readers; for the quaint and curious Diary of Richard Cocks, of the English factory in Japan, which was so ably edited for us in 1883 by Mr. Edward Maunde Thompson of the British Museum, may likewise have been one of those unnaturally exposed foundlings.[1]

On a cursory reading of Mr. Barlow's transcript it seemed to me that, though not a document of very high value, its interest was great enough to render it worthy of being printed by our Society, and would be felt by a greater number of readers than its owner anticipated, especially as published information regarding

[1] Probably, however the culpable disposal of the present document occurred at an earlier date; for further acquaintance with the old India records has made me aware of the vast masses of correspondence from India that had disappeared, apparently before the beginning of this century. With regard to the more recent destruction of documents, it is recorded, on 15th May 1859, that the Committee of the India Office, dealing with such matters, had "reason to apprehend that official documents, sold as waste-paper for the purpose of remanufacture had, notwithstanding the engagement to the contrary entered into by the purchasers, been otherwise disposed of." And it was directed that in future an officer of the Record Department should witness the mutilation of the papers. In February 1860 it was directed by the Secretary of State in Council that all useless records at Cannon Row (Board of Control) and Leadenhall Street should be destroyed. It was determined that this destruction should embrace: (1) Duplicate records in the Registrar's Department; (2) Factory journals and ledgers from the three Presidencies, with the import and export warehouse books; (3) The Proceedings of the Board of Trade (I do not know what these were); (4) Proceedings of the Medical Board; (5) The Durbar accounts; (6) "Cutcherry and Admiralty Proceedings"; (7) Interest accounts, and contingent bills, with a number of miscellaneous books of account that were never consulted; (8) The Madras military disbursements, which had never been journalised (about thirty-five immense volumes each year). Also an immense mass of papers in "Mr. Hornidge's Department". It was estimated that the whole would amount to some 500 tons! But it did not eventually prove to be so much.

the early settlements of the Company in Bengal is scanty. The proposal to print it was accordingly adopted by the Council.

The *Diary* had been furnished by Mr. Barlow with the brief "Introductory Notes" (comprising also a Table of Contents) already alluded to, as well as with a few useful foot-notes,[1] and for the further necessary editing was placed in the hands of a gentleman who appeared to be interested in the subject. Nothing, however, came of this. The first sheet was printed off without my cognizance, or I should have suggested some modification of form. But in passing the rest of the work through the press nearly all the correction, with the insertion of necessary additional foot-notes, fell upon me. And eventually it became evident that whatever further editing the book required must also be provided by me, if the work was in any degree to assume such form as I deem necessary for the reputation of the Society over which I have the honour to preside. To complete such form an index was required, which I have supplied.

But it was obviously desirable also to obtain, if possible, more information regarding William Hedges and his connections than Mr. Barlow had found in Bruce's *Annals*. The search for this gradually led me to extend my researches in the MS. Records of the India Office, the British Museum, and elsewhere, till I found that a volume was growing under my hands. Much of this is in type, but there is much yet to complete; and some curious questions have suggested themselves which require a little time and further research to solve. It has been decided, therefore, to issue the *Diary* itself with Mr. Barlow's Introductory Notices, and my Index, as Vol. i, whilst Vol. ii will contain copious biographical and historical details regarding Hedges and most of the persons named in his *Diary*, compiled from the various sources indicated above, and will be separately indexed.

[1] Foot-notes at pp. 17-32, 36-41, 60-61, 64, 67, 69, 99-100, 107, 133, 141, 158, 177, 180, 182, 194, 200 (note 2), and 250, were supplied by Mr. Barlow. For the remainder I am responsible.

Some of the corrections made now in the *Errata* ought properly to have been made in the correction of proofs. But when correcting the proofs I did not consider that the office of Editor had devolved on me, and had not made the research which I have since undertaken.

I should add before closing this preface that, since the *Diary* was printed Mr. Barlow has liberally presented the original (much of which is in Hedges' holograph)[1] to the India Office.

H. YULE.

[1] *I.e.*, from the beginning to July 3rd, 1682 (p. 28), and again from the words, "This Diary was thus far", etc. (p. 147), to the end. The intermediate portion is in the writing of copyists.

ERRATA.

At p. 5 and *passim*, *for* Nathanael Letter, *read* Nathanael Letten; and my footnote (2 at p. 174) is wrong.

At p. 33 and *passim*, *for* Richard Frenchfeild, *read* Richard Trenchfeild.

(These two names had been misread by the transcriber of the copy for the press.)

At p. 13, terminal note in parenthesis. The chief facts of Sir Wm. Hedges' subsequent career will be given in Vol. ii, as well as those of his nephew Robert, who *was* the chairman of Council, and at a later date President, in Bengal.

Page 7, line 20, *for* Muvadavad, *read* Muxadavad.

" 8, line 19, *for* Dustuchs, *read* Dustucks.

" 12, line 8, *for* Kergavar, *read* Kengavar.

" 17, footnote is erroneous. President Beard who died at Madras was this John Beard's son, as will be detailed in Vol. ii.

" 32, in footnote, *for* Masters, *read* Master.

" 40, second line from foot of note. Fyre *should be* Eyre *or* Eyres. See Vol. ii.

" 41, regarding Mr. Catchpoole's history see Vol. ii.

" 65, line 20, *purga* or *pyrgo* seems to represent a local Balasore term for a small boat or canoe.

" 68, note. "A generall" was an official letter usually signed by all members of the local council.

" 87, line 10, *for* Emir Pussick, *read* Emir Tussick, *i.e.* the *Mir-tozak*, "Master of the Ceremonies".

" 122, line 1, *for* Hohun, *read* Mohun.

" 136, line 26, *for* Impost, *read* Imprest.

" 147, line 8, *for* Lowdon, *read* Sowdon.

determined, on taking into consideration the evils resulting from the dependency of the Bengal Factories on the Fort, to constitute the Agency at Hooghly a distinct and separate Factory from Fort St. George. But, in an affair of such importance, that they might act with certain knowledge, the Court appointed Mr. Hedges, a member of their Committees (or what in modern times would be termed a Director of the East India Company), with special powers, to be Agent and Governor of their affairs in the Bay of Bengal, and of the Factories subordinate to it, or Cossimbuzar, Patna, Balasore, Malda, and Dacca; and directed that the Stock of £230,000, appropriated for Bengal, should be distributed as follows: viz., £140,000 to be sent to Cossimbuzar; £14,500 to Patna; £32,000 to Ballasore; £15,000 to Malda; £16,500 to Dacca; and £12,000 to remain at Hooghly. After specifying the Silks, Cloths, and other articles expected from each of these Factories to form the investment of the season, the Court repeated their orders against the Interlopers, and directed that a corporal of approved fidelity and courage, with twenty soldiers, should proceed from the Fort to be a guard to the Agent's person and the Factory of Hooghly, and to act against the Interlopers. Such was the foundation of the Company's government in Bengal, or what became, in the sequel, the centre of commerce, and the seat of government in British India."

. . . . "It appears", [by letters from the Agent and Council at Hooghly, and the Agents at the subordinate Factories in Bengal, 27th May, 14th and 18th July, and Sept. 2, 1682] "that Mr. Hedges the Director had arrived at Hooghly,[1] and intimated his commission and the new plan of commercial administration with which he was intrusted. But that he had found both Hooghly and the subordinate Factories disturbed by an order which had come from the Mogul for levying $3\frac{1}{2}$ per cent. Customs. The Agents at

[1] He landed there July 24, 1682.

Cossimbuzar, Ballasore, etc., were struggling to be exempted from this tax, and making such purchases as would meet the Company's orders."[1] . . . .

It appears from Mr. Hedge's *Diary* that he decided to visit the then Nuwab, Shaista Khan, at Dacca, to obtain remission of this tax of 3½ per cent., and left Hooghly about Oct. 10, 1682, for this purpose, *viâ* Cossimbuzar, so as to consult with Mr. Charnock, the Agent there. He was politely received by the Nuwab on October 29, at Dacca, three days after his arrival, and it appears that the acquaintance he displayed with Turkish and Arabic made a favourable impression. He was accompanied by a Vakeel, James Price, to interpret apparently, but, completely failing to obtain any thing but conditional promises, left Dacca about December 15.

As early as Dec. 1, Mr. Hedges had listened to scandal—possibly true—as to Job Charnock's *moral* character, and every little trifle from this time seems to have embittered his dislike. A second visit to Cossimbuzar, April 15, 1683, brought about an open rupture; and Mr. Hedges, who could not understand the *suaviter in modo*, commenced with a *fortiter in re* examination into several discreditable abuses on the part of subordinates, and became unpopular, and worse. He was unquestionably a zealous and (pecuniarily) honest man; but his dislike to Mr. Charnock became so notorious, that [April 26] even the native officials found their advantage in fomenting disputes, by which, of course, the Hon. Company were sufferers in the end, and themselves gainers; and after Oct. 12, 1683, the feud assumed a character of hopeless antagonism.

There is an hiatus in the Diary from Jan. 12, 1684, till July 2nd of that year, in consequence, it is stated, of his sending *this very diary home* by "ye *Herbert*, Capt. Henry Udall", "to my brother Sambrooke"; and on July 17, Mr. Hedges

[1] Bruce's *Annals of the East India Company*, vol. ii, 492.

received private information, by a ship from Madras, that he had been dismissed by the Court.

1684.—In explanation of this dismissal, Bruce states:—

"As Mr. Hedges had been appointed by the Court to be Agent, with a Council, at Bengal, independently of any subordination to Fort St. George, it is material to look at the proceedings of this supervisor and at the effect of his measures on the sales and export from Madras, as well as on the general interests of both establishments.

"It might have been expected that Mr. Hedges, from his former rank, would have been fully acquainted with the opinions of the Court, that an undue influence had been exercised by the Government of Madras over the agency in Bengal to favour the private trade of the Members, ... or . . . . . that the Agents in Bengal, independently of this control, had taken advantage of the Company's Stock, and employed it to promote their particular speculations; and, therefore, that he would have executed the trust reposed in him, or examined the sources of those evils, and acted on public grounds; but it appears that, instead of fulfilling the expectations entertained of his prudence and exertions, he had considered himself as the only person entrusted with the confidence of the Court: and in the application of this power had involved their affairs: for, by intercepting and opening letters from the Members of Council to Sir Josiah Child, the Governor or Chairman of the East India Company, he not only lost the confidence of the Court, but the opportunity of controlling their servants abroad—and, therefore, he was dismissed from the service.

"This circumstance induced the Court to recede from the plan of rendering Bengal independent of Fort St. George, and to appoint Mr. Gyfford, the Agent at the Fort, to be Agent at Bengal, with the title of President over both settlements."[1]

Mr. Gyfford assumed formal charge at Hooghly Factory

[1] *Bruce*, vol. ii, 504, 505.

Aug. 30, 1684, and certain entries in Mr. Hedges' Diary, under date Sep. 1, 1684, and Feb. 6, 1685, sufficiently prove that Mr. Bruce was correct as to the "opening letters".

Mr. Hedges remained at Hooghly, after his supersession, until Christmas 1684, when he somewhat precipitately quitted, and joined the *Recovery*, a barque which he had apparently chartered, and loaded for a voyage to Gombroon.

Accompanied by his nephew, Mr. Robert Hedges, Mr. Nathanael Letter, and Mr. Robert Dowglasse, "chirurgeon", Mr. Hedges left "Barnagore" on Dec. 31, 1684, reached Balasore Road, Jan. 10, 1685, receiving there a severe protest from Mr. John Beard, "Agent at Hooghly", for abducting a Mr. Gough from his duties, etc. The *Recovery* proceeded, however, the same night, and reached Madras Feb. 2. Mr. Gyfford happened to be in the Fort, and received Mr. Hedges politely with a "salute of 15 guns".

Leaving Madras Feb. 7, 1685, the *Recovery* had a tedious passage, and was in danger among the Maldive Islands on March 6, 7, and 8. She reached Muscat April 29, and left for Gombroon May 15, 1685; did not, however, go there, because a squadron of seven or eight Dutch ships were in the Port. He steered for Cong, arriving there May 27, 1685; and here Mr. Hedges left to travel thence by Lar, Ispahan, Bagdat, Mosul, Diabekir, Aleppo, Iscandroon, Tunis, Sardinia, Toulon, Paris, and Calais, to Dover, arriving at the latter port on April 4, 1687, after a journey of two years and three months from Bengal. The actual time Mr. Hedges held office in Bengal was:—

From July 21, 1682
Till August 30, 1684

2 years 1 month.

CONTENTS.

N.B.—There seem at this time to have been 7 *Sloops*, used as occasion required, for Cargo, Passage, or Piloting.

Goodhope	George Heron, master.
Madapollain	John Hampton.
Arrivall	
Thomas	Mr. How, Mr. Scott (April 4, 1683)
Ganges	
Lilly	afterward Lost on Balasore bar, June 24, 1683.

	1683.	
Thomas Haggerston absconds from Surat with 50,000 Rupees	July	2
Mr. John Byam, Chief at Balasore, died July 8.		
Change of Members of Council at Cossimbuzar	,,	9
Mr. Hill, Chief of Maulda Mint—and Nephew Hedges 2nd	,,	9
Permesuradass received a present for civility (R. 1,500, 500)	,,	11
Ships *Henry* and *William*, and *Hare* come up to Hooghly; *Herbert* does not.		
Shaista Khan's excellent letter on the Duties and Customs	,,	18
Hedges holds secret audience with the dismissed James Harding	,,	20
Mr. Wm. Rushworth died at Cossimbuzar	,,	28
Nephew Hedges resigns Englesavad. Mr. Peachie appointed	Aug.	27
3 Interlopers—*Lumley Castle* (Alley), *Con. Merch.* (Smith), ———— (Aubany), arrived at Madras on 30 July.		
Commencement of a dispute with Mr. Charnock about Dustucks	,,	27
Goolaub Ray promised a present if the Emperor grants Freedom from Duty	,,	31
Private entries of irritated feelings	Sept.	2
Letter of complaint—S. Langley *v.* Watson	,,	3
Mr. Charnock involved in the paper squabble	,,	12
Mr. Watson suspended (Mr. Beard dissents)	,,	24
Mr. Beard considers that Mr. Ellis should be reinstated	,,	26
Report that the Dutch intend to close the Straits of Sunda and Malacca	,,	26
Capt. Alley, an Interloper, visits Hooghly in state	,,	26
Mr. Hedges reprimands Mr. Charnock	,,	26
Letter from Mr. Ellis, remonstrating on his dismissal	,,	28
Tattle about Mr. Charnock	Oct.	2
Capt. Alley visits the Phousdar of Hooghly in state	,,	8
Letter from Mr. Charnock, dated Oct. 6.		
Mr. Hedges' private opinion thereon	,,	12
A Dutch "Directore" with great powers	,,	22
Mr. Hedges reflects upon the characters of Interlopers and his Council	,,	27
A visit from Bulchund. Mr. Hedges gives him a Persian horse	,,	30
Mr. Hedges thinks that a Fort on Saugor Island is required	,,	31
Permesuradas dismissed by order of the Nuwab	Nov.	5
Mr. Hedges orders Capt. Hayward to carry the Flag as Admiral	,,	6

	1684.	
Dutch Governor [Martinus Huysman] pays a polite visit -	Nov.	6
Haggerston claims Rupees 197,998 8a. from Mr. Hedges -	„	11
Bullubdos tells a trading tale of President Gyfford -	„	13
Mr. Richard Gough hints that Mr. H.'s Voyage to Persia will be estopped - - - -	„	13
Appeal to Mr. Beard in the affair of Haggerston -	„	14
The Dutch power. Fear of an embargo of Pilgrim Ships	„	17
Mr. Rd. Gough proposes to accompany Mr. H. through Persia	„	22
A Cyclone? - - - - -	„	23
Correspondence about Mr. Gough resigning.		
Mr. Francis Ellis (evidently readmitted to the Service and to Council) signs after Mr. Gyfford, and Mr. Beard -	„	28
Some Remarks on Mr. Beard - - -	Dec.	6
President Gyfford annoyed by some Dutch Ships at Hooghly enquiring of Capt. Richardson and his soldiers, when passing in a boat "If they were going to Bantam?"[1] - - - -	„	8
Mr. Hedges' private opinion of President Gyfford -	„	8
A singular statement about Saugor Island and Kedgeree -	„	15
All hope of avoiding payment of the 3½ per cent. abandoned	„	23
Mr. Hedges requests the Dutch Governor to grant him a Pilot to conduct his ship, through the New Deepe by the Island of Saugor, to sea - - -	„	23
Mr. Hedges learns that the Nuwab requires himself or Mr. Beard to come before him—on the Haggerston complaint - - - - - -	„	25
See July 21, 1682.		
Mr. Hedges quits Hooghly and goes on board *Recovery*, the ship he had chartered for Persia—at Barnagore -	„	26
Calls on the Dutch Padre for his interest to procure a Dutch flag to fly in his Budgero. The Dutch "Directore" declines to permit such an innovation -		
The *Recovery* drops down to Great Tannah - -	„	31
	1685.	
Reached Hidgellee - - - -	Jan.	8
Rows in the Budgero round the "Island" of Kedgeree.		
Recovery anchors off the Brace, and presents Mr. George Heron with 50 Rupees for piloting service.		
Sailed into Balasore Road, and received cargo - -	„	10

[1] The English were expelled from Bantam by the Dutch on Aug. 30, 1682.

	1685.
Mr. Hedges hires 125 camels and 13 Mules - -	Dec. 1
In comp. with his Nephew, Mr. Douglas, and Mr. Letter, starts from Ispahan - - - - -	,, 13
Compelled to remain two days at Cogga, because a camel broke its leg - - - - -	,, 20
	1686.
A sick camel driver supposed to be frozen to death at Feraspa - - - - - -	Jan. 5
A Robbery of silk and money at Kergauar - -	,, 6
Detained at Kirmansha for Duties, etc. - -	Jan. 11 to 22
Bread of barley and acorns at Aslan Chesmesi -	Jan. 30
Much snow, succeeded by torrents of rain, at Chamsura	Feb. 10
In danger of losing goods, and lies in the gullies.	
Reach Bagdad after 71 days from Ispahan[1] - -	,, 21
Takes a house, and receives a Phirmaund to be treated with respect - - - - -	,, 23
Heavy custom duties, and reflections.	
Curious arrangements for the journey to Aleppo.	
Remain at Bagdad 50 days, till - - -	April 11
Visit the Birs el Nimrood - - - - -	,, 14
Engage Usier-Beg, for 550 dollars, to supply 50 horsemen as a guard as far as Mosul - - -	,, 19
Pitched near the Zab - - - - -	,, 28
Arrive at Mosul (about 195 Geog. miles N., 18° W. from Bagdad) - - - - - -	,, 33
Cousin Letter leaves on a raft on the Tigris for Bagdad (Stay at Mosul 25 days.)	May 12
Leaves Mosul and ferries over the Tigris *en route* to Diarbekir - - - - - -	,, 26
Description of Gizra - - - -	June 3
The Pasha of Kirkooke - - - - -	,, 10
Extortion of Mehmet Usier - - -	,, 13
Reach Diarbekir (about 176 Geog. miles from Mosul) - Remained 16 days.	,, 19
Theft and Justice - - - - -	July 2
Leaves Diarbekir for Aleppo (51° W., dist. 159 G. miles) -	,, 6
Severe illness on the road, and remedy - -	,, 11
Reach Aleppo (just 12 miles from Cong) - -	,, 29
(Remained in extreme ill health 84 days.)	
Quits Aleppo for Scanderoon (N. 67°, W. 53 Geog. miles)	Oct. 26

[1] Distance not stated; it is about 380 geographical miles as the crow flies.

	1686.	
Leaves Scanderoon, with Nephew Hedges, in a French "Provincial" ship for Marseilles - - -	Nov.	6
Touches at "Solinus" (Cyprus) - - -	,,	9
Left Cyprus - - - - -	,,	18
Gale off Candia - - - - -	Dec.	7
Pass on eastern side of Sardinia - - -	,,	19
Abreast of Corsica, and run South in a Northerly gale -	,,	21
Take refuge in Tunis Bay - - - -	,,	24
Leave and put back again. Kindnesses.		
	1687.	
Quit Tunis finally - - - -	Jan.	16
Anchored for refuge in Palma de Sol (Sardinia, West side) Left and returned three times.	,,	17
Hard gale—drove—so cut away mainmast - -	,,	28
Resigned passage, and embarked in a Settee - -	,,	31
An occurrence at St. Pietro, and at Orestano (Sardinia) -	Feb.	1
Reached Toulon (and went into Quarantine) - -	,,	9
Released, and arrived at Marseilles - - -	,,	20
Set out for Lyons Feb. 28; arrived - - -	March	6
Reached Paris March 13, and left - - -	,,	26
Reached "Callis" March 29, and embarked for Dover 2 P.M.	Ap.	3
Landed at Dover - - - 1 A.M.	,,	4
Interview with Lord High Chancellor Jefferys - -	,,	7
Married - - - - -	July	21
	1688.	
Knighted - - - - .	March	6

(Subsequent career unknown; but a Mr. Hedges, possibly the nephew Robert, was Chairman of the "English" Company, or President on *alternate weeks* with Mr. Halsey, of the "London" Company. See *Bruce*, vol. iii, 50.)

A Journall kept by WILLIAM HEDGES from ye day of his receiving a Com'ission from ye Right Worpll ye Govr., Depty, and Comittees of ye Honble. English East India Compy to be their Agent and Govr. for their affaires in ye Bay of Bengall and in the East Indies. Viz.

THE LOG TO BENGAL.

1681.

November 25, 1681, my com'ission was given to me by ye Right Worshfull Sr Josia Child, Bart, being then Govr, and Thomas Papillon, Esqre, Deputy.

Nov. 30.—Departed from London towards Deal.

Dec. 2.—Arrived at Deal.

Dec. 3.—The *Defence*, Capt. Wm Heath, Commandr, on whom I was ordered by ye Honble Compy to take my passage, with my wife and family, arrived in ye Downs, whereof I gave ye Compy notice by letter from my selfe and Mr John Beard. The same night I recd the Company's dispatches to me by Mr Zinzan.

Dec. 19.—The *Resolution*, Captn Francis Wilshaw, Com'andr, arrived in the Downes.

1682. *Jan.* 4.—The shippe *Expectation*, Capt. Ally, Com'andr, an Interloper, arrived in ye Downes from Porto Novo.

Jan. 13.—The *Eagle*, *President*, and *Berkeley Castle* arrived in ye Downes from ye Coast and ye Bay of Bengall. The *Society*, *Persia Merchant*, and *Barnadiston* from Bantam.

Jan. 28.—The *Resolution* and *Defence*, about 4 o'clock in ye afternoon sailed out of ye Downes with a fair wind.

Jan. 29.—About 2 in ye afternoon, we came up with ye Isle of Wight.

Jan. 30.—By 12 o'clock at noon we got up with ye Lizard. The Gale continuing to freshen, we ran 9 knots.

Feb. 2.—It pleased God to take out of this world M[r] John Richards, appointed Chief of Balasore.

Feb. 3.—By observation were in y[e] Latitude of 42 Degrees.

Feb. 6.—This day little wind. By observation were in y[e] Lat. of 39½.

Feb. 8.—Were in Lati[de] of 38° 30′ by observation.

Feb. 10.—We had a good observation, and were in y[e] Lat[de] of 35° 40′.

Feb. 11 and 12.—Calme.

Feb. 13.—We were in y[e] Lat[de] of 33½, but saw neither Porto Santo nor y[e] Madera Islands.

Feb. 14.—Lay becalm'd.

Feb. 15.—We were in y[e] Lat[de] of 31°.

Feb. 16.—We saw y[e] Pike of Teneriffe.

Feb. 18.—We gott up with y[e] Island of Teneriffe.

Feb. 20.—Little wind, but were gott into y[e] Lat[de] of 26° 30′ N.

Feb. 21.—The wind began to freshen at N.E. and N.E. and b N.

Feb. 22.—From yesterday noon to this day noon we had a fine fresh gale at N.W.; by our log we had run 117 miles. Our course S.W. and by S. and were in y[e] Lat. of 24° N. This afternoon, the gale freshening at N.N.W., we steered S.S.W., and by 8 o'clock this night judged ourselves within y[e] Tropic of Cancer.

Feb. 23.—These 24 houres y[e] gale continued fresh. By y[e] log we ran 158 miles; our course S.S.W. The wind at N.E. and N.N.E., our Lat[de] 21° 30′ N.

Feb. 24.—These 24 houres a fresh gale. Have run by our Log 165 miles, our course S.S.W.; wind N.E. and N.E. by E., Lat[de] by observation, 18° 50′ N.

Feb. 25.—These 24 houres y[e] gale continued. Have run 163 miles, our course S. b W., and y[e] wind N.E. b E., Lat[de] by observation, 16° 14′ N.

Feb. 26.—We saw y[e] Isle of May [Mayo], being in y[e] Lat. of 15° 7′ N.

Feb. 27.—By 7 o'clock in y[e] morning it pleased God to bring us in safety to S[t] Jago, being y[e] thirteenth day since we came out of y[e] Downes. Here we met with y[e] *Barbadoes Merchant*, a small vessel of Plymouth, James Cock, Master, bound for Barbadoes, laden with Salt, mules, and Africos, bought at y[e] Isle of "May", by whom we wrott the following letter to y[e] Honorable Comp[y], viz.:—

"From aboard y[e] *Defence*, at S[t] Jago,
27th Feb[y] 1681.

"May it please your Honors,—

"On y[e] 28 Ult[o] this shippe and y[e] *Resolution* set sail out of y[e] Downes, with a fair wind, w[ch] continued so prosperous to us y[t] on the 30th by Noon we were up with the Lizard. And on the 2nd Instant it pleased God to take to himselfe M[r] John Richards, occasioned by a slip of his foot in his cabbin 3 nights before, which we apprehend (by y[e] great effusion of blood out of his mouth and nose before he died) broke something within him. God prepare us all for y[e] like change!

"The Wind continuing still in our favour, on y[e] 3rd Instant we gott into y[e] Latitude of 42°. On y[e] 13th Detto we were in 33½ degrees, but so far to y[e] Eastward of Porto Santo and y[e] Madera Islands, that we saw them not. Here we were so troubled with calmes and contrary winds, y[t] it was y[e] 18th Detto before we came up with Teneriffe; and this morning (God be praised) both our Shippes and men arrived here in safety, all in good health, with y[e] losse only of one of y[e] *Resolution's* sailors, Thomas Coops, who dyed the 16th Instant.

"In Port we mett y[e] *Barbadoes Merchant*, a small Shippe of Plymouth, James Cock, Master, bound this night for Barbadoes, by whom this is intended. After us, this morning, came in a small Dutch Shippe, bound for Saranam, who shall carry its duplicate. Our business here being only to water and recruit ourselves with fresh provisions, we shall hasten its despatch (what possibly we can) to proceed on our Voyage with all expedition, which we pray God may have an end no lesse prosperous and gracefull than it has a beginning.

"These 2 Shippes sail so much alike y[t] we cannot say which sails best. We designe, God willing, to goe *Without* Madagascar.

"This being all that has happened to us remarkable in this voyage, we com'it you, your affaires, and ourselves to y[e] Divine Protection, resolving always to approve ourselves,

"Your Honors'

"Most humble, faithfull, and obedient Servants,

"FFRAN[S] WILSHAW. WM. HEDGES.

"WM. HEATH. JOHN BEARD."[1]

March 4.—This morning, between 10 and 11 o'clock (having supplyed ourselves wth water and fresh provisions), we sett sail from S[t] Jago.

March 5.—From y[e] time of our departure yesterday from S[t] Jago to 12 o'clock this day, we have run, by our log, 157 miles; our course S.E. by S.; the wind at N.E.; our latitude, by observation, 12° 38′ N.

March 6.—These 24 hours fair weather and fine fresh gale. Run 120 miles, course S.E. b. S.; wind, N.E.; latitude by observation, 10° 56′ N.

March 7.—These 24 hours fair weather, a gentle gale. Run 93 miles, course S.E. b. S., wind N.E., latitude, by observation, 9° 30′ N.

March 8.—These 24 hours fair weather, gentle gale. Run 88 miles; course S.E. b. S.; wind N.E.; latitude observed, 8° 13′ N.

---

1 John Beard. Mr. Beard, after a service in India of twenty-four years, died at Madras July 7, 1706.—See Bruce, *Annals*, vol. iii, 602.

March 9.—These 24 hours fair weather, little wind. Run 67 miles; course S.E. b. S.; wind, N.E.; latitude per observ[n], 7° 12′ N.

March 10.—These 24 hours fair weather, little wind, much lightning in y[e] morning. Run about 53 miles; course S.E. b. S.; wind N.N.W.; latitude 6° 31′ N.

March 11.—These 24 hours fair weather, little wind, much lightning in y[e] night. Run 35 miles; course S.E. b. S.; wind N.N.W.; Lat. 6° 0′ N.

March 12.—These 24 hours most part calme, much thunder and lightning in y[e] night, with divers showers of rain.

March 13.—These 24 hours very little wind, some smart showers of raine. Run these two days but 27 miles; course and wind various; lat[de] 5° 9′ N.

March 14.—These 24 hours little wind, much thunder and lightning, with great showers of raine. Run 41 miles; course S.E. b. S.; wind N.N.W., 4° 37′ N.

March 15.—These 24 hours fair weather, little wind. Run 39 miles; course S.E. b. S.; wind S.W. and S.S.W.; lat. 4° 5′ N.

March 16.—These 24 hours fair weather, very little wind. Run 25 miles; course and wind very variable; the sun, so near our zenith, could take no observation; latitude, by estimation, 3° 48′ N.

March 17.—These 24 hours fair weather, little wind. Run 22 miles; course S.E. b. E. and S.S.E.; wind variable; latitude, by account, 3° 38′ N.

March 18.—These 24 hours fair weather, a pretty fresh gale, but directly contrary. Run 57 miles; course W. b. S. to S.E.; wind variable; by calculation we have gott but 22 miles to the S[d]; lat., by judgem[nt], 3° 16′ N. The Sun being this day in our Zenith.

March 19.—These 24 hours much rain, with some gusts in y[e] night, but a smooth sea. Run 64 miles; divers courses from S.E. to E.S.E.; the wind variable from S.W. to S.S.W.; lat., by acc[nt], 2° 47′ N.

March 20.—These 24 hours much rain and great gusts—soon over. Run 59 miles; course from S.E. b. E. to S. b. W.; wind variable; lat., by Judgem[nt], 2° 3′. N.

March 21.—These 24 hours fair weather, fine gale and a smooth sea. Run 68 miles; course from S. to E.S.E.; wind variable. Latitude, by account, 1° 18′ N.

March 22.—These 24 hours fair weather, little wind. Run 30 miles, course E.S.E.; wind at south; lat., by judgement, 1° 5′ N.

March 23.—These 24 hours fair weather, little wind. Run 45 miles; course from E.S.E. to W.S.W.; wind S. and S.S.W.; latitude, by observation, 1° 16′ N.

This being the first day we could observe since the 15th instant, by which we find ourselves mistaken in our account 11 minutes, besides what we have gained to y[e] southward since yesterday noon.

March 24.—These 24 hours fair weather, smooth sea, and fine fresh breeze. Run 83 miles; course from S.W. to W.S.W.; wind S. and S.S.E.; lat. obs[d], 0° 40′ N.

March 25.—These 24 hours fair weather and fine fresh gale, and moderate heat. Run 110 miles; course from S.W. b. W. to S.W.; wind S. b. E. and S.S E. By observation we find ourselves just under y[e] Equinoctiall Line at noon, the Sun's Declination being 5° 57′. Our Meridian Distance from y[e] Lizard, 6° 38′ to y[e] westward, and from S[t] Jago, the place of our last departure, 6° 32′ to the eastward, where we crossed the Line.

March 26.—These 24 hours fair weather, smooth water, and fine fresh gale. Run 72 miles; course S.W. b. S. and S.W.; wind S. b. E. to S.S.E.; lat., by obs[n], 0° 36′ to y[e] southward.

March 27.—These 24 hours fair weather, little wind. Run 56 miles; course from S.S.W. to W.S.W.; wind from S.S.E. to S.; lat[de], by observation, 0° 45′ S.

March 28.—These 24 hours quite calme.

March 29.—These 24 hours quite calme. We putt out our boat, and found we had a current, which sett us near two miles an houre to the westward, so that these 2 days past we may reasonably believe ourselves about 90 miles farther to y[e] Westward than we expected.

March 30.—These 24 hours calme. Run, by y[e] log, but 9 miles; course S.W.; wind S.E. b. S.; latitude, by observation, but 51 minutes S.

March 31.—These 24 hours fair weather, a fine fresh gale. Run 65 miles; course S.S.W. and S.W. b. S.; wind S.E.; lat. 1° 39′ S.

April 1.—These 24 hours fair weather and a fresh gale. Run 97 miles; course S.S.W. and S.W. b. S.; wind S.E. and S.S.E.; latitude, per obs[n], 2° 43′ S.

April 2.—These 24 hours fair weather, little wind. Run 61 miles; course S.S.W. and S.W. b. S.; wind S.E. and S.S.E.; lat[de], by judgement, 3° 28′. Weather being cloudy, could take no obs[n].

April 3.—These 24 hours fair weather and a fresh gale. Run 102 miles; course S.S.W.; wind S.E.; lat. 5° 13′ S.

April 4.—These 24 hours fair weather and a very fresh gale. Run 122 miles; course S.S.W. and S.W. by S.; wind S.E.; latitude 7° 1′ S.

April 5.—These 24 hours fair weather and a fresh gale. Run 120 miles; course S. and S. b. W.; wind E.S.E. and S.E. b. E.; lat. 8° 49′ S.

April 6.—These 24 hours a fine fresh gale. Run 90 miles; course South and S. b. E.; wind E. b. S. and E.S.E.; latitude 10° 9′ S.

April 7.—These 24 hours fair weather and a fine gale. Run 85 miles; course S., S. b. E., and S.E. b. S.; wind E.S.E., E. b. S., and East. No obs., but, by account, lat. 11° 31′ S.

April 8.—These 24 hours fair weather and a fresh gale. Run 112 miles; course S.S.E.; wind E.N.E.; latitude, 13° 3′ S.

C 2

April 9.—These 24 hours fair weather, little wind. Run 73 miles; course S.E. b. S.; wind E.N.E. and E. by N.; lat. 14° 10′ S.

April 10.—These 24 hours fair weather, little wind. Run 74 miles; course S.E. b. S.; wind E.N.E. and N.E.; lat. 15° 12′ S.

April 11.—From yesterday noon to this day noon fair weather, little wind. Run 59 miles; course S.E. b. S.; wind N.E. b. E.; latitude 16° 2′ S.

April 12.—These 24 houres fair weather but very little wind. Run 28 miles; course S.E. b. S.; wind E.N.E. and N.E.; lat. 16° 26′ S.

April 13.—These 24 houres fair weather but very little wind. Run 30 miles; course S.E. b. S.; wind (as seldom seen in these parts) at North and N. b. W.; lat. 16° 59′ S.

April 14.—These 24 hours fair weather and a fine gale. Run 95 miles; course S.E.; wind N.W.; latitude 18° 5′ S.

April 15.—From yesterday noon till 8 o'clock this morning fair weather and a fresh gale—having then much rain and gusty weather; and being in ye latitude of Saint Martin de Vaz and two other Islands, we lay by till 5 in ye morning, at which time we made sail, but saw no land. Run 116 miles; course S.E. b. E.; wind N.W.; latitude 19° 41′ S.[1]

April 16.—These 24 hours very little wind. Run but 23 miles; course S. b. E. and S.S.E.; wind N.W. b. N. and S.W.; lat., by judgmnt, 19° 41, (?) weather cloudy these 2 days past; had no observation.

April 17.—These 24 hours fair weather and little wind. Run 50 miles; course from ye S.S.W. to S.W. b. W.; wind from S.E. to S.S.E.; latitude, by observation, 20° 27′ S.

This morning we saw a sail about 4 leagues to leeward of us; about 5 in ye afternoone we spake with her. She proved to be the *Crowne*, Capt Dorrel comr, an interloper. She wanted [was less than] 2 months from England. Came not through ye Downes, but went on the Backside of ye Goodwin Sands. They told us plainly they were bound for Hugley. Mr Pitts and two or three passengers more were aboard of her. After saluting each other, we all made ye best of our way, but, she sailing best, was almost out of sight next morning.[2]

April 18.—These 24 hours fair weather, with a fine fresh gale. Run 105 miles; course from S. b. W. to S.W. b. S.; wind from E.S.E. to S.E. b. S.; latitude, by judgment, 21° 37′ S.

This afternoon, at 4 o'clock, Captn Wilshaw, sailing better than our shippe, desired to part company, and tooke his leave of us, making ye best of his way after ye Interloper.

---

[1] "Martin Vas" is in long. about 28° 51′ W., lat. about 20° 28′ S.—R. F. B.

[2] See *Bruce*, vol. ii, p. 466.

April 19.—These 24 hours fair weather—a gentle gale. Run 85 miles; course S. b. W. to S.S.W.; wind from y[e] S.E. b. E. to E.S.E.; latitude, by judgement, 22° 50′ S.

April 20.—These 24 hours fair weather and little wind. Run 45 miles; course S. b. W.; wind S.E. b. E.; lat. 23° 31′, by which account we are past y[e] Tropic of Capricorne.

April 21.—These 24 hours fair weather and a fine gale. Run 81 miles; course from y[e] S. to y[e] S.S.E. and S.W.; wind variable from W. to S.S.E.; lat 24° 18′ S. Capt[n] Wilshaw still in sight.

April 22.—These 24 hours fair weather, very little wind, but a great rolling sea. Run 38 miles; course S.S.W. and S.W. b. S.; wind S.S.E. and S.E. b. S.; lat. 24° 32′ S. Capt. Wilshaw in sight.

April 23.—These 24 hours fair weather and very little wind. Have run but 19 miles; course from E.S.E to S.S.E.; wind from S. to W.; latitude 24° 47′ S.

April 24.—These 24 hours fair weather—a small gale. Run 65 miles; wind W. and W.N.W.; lat. 25° 50′ S.

April 25.—These 24 hours gusty foul weather, with much rain and lightning. Run 123 miles; course S.S.E. and S.E.; wind from W.N.W. to S. b. W.; lat. 27° 18′ S. This morning our main top gallant mast broke. Capt. Wilshaw not above 3 leagues ahead of us.

April 26.—These 24 hours gusty weather, with showers of rain. Run 79 miles; course E.S.E. and S.E. b. E.; wind S. W. b. S. to W.; lat. 27° 56′ S.

April 27.—These 24 hours a fresh gale, with great gusts of wind and showers of rain. Run 130 miles; course S.E. b. E.; wind from S.W. b. S. to W.; lat. 29° 14′ S.

April 28.—These 24 hours wind continuing very fresh, with some violent gusts and showers of rain. We have run 165 miles; course S.E. b. E.; wind W. to W.S.W.; lat[de] 30° 53′ S.

April 29.—These 24 hours it blew for the most part very fresh. Run 150 miles; course S.E. b. E.; wind N.W. b. W.; latitude, by judgment, 32° 32′ S.

April 30.—These 24 hours it hath blowen very fresh, with great gusts and showers of rain. We have run 185 miles; course E.S.E.; wind N.W. to W.; lat., by judg[nt], 33° 57′ S.

May 1.—These 24 hours it hath blowen very hard. Yesterday in y[e] afternoon we ran 11 knotts 6 fathom, with our top gallant sails standing, which were no sooner taken in but our fore topmast broke, and y[e] storme increased to y[t] violence, that till midnight we could carry no more sail than our fore course and sprit-sail: the wind being then something abated, we sett our main-sail and main-top-sail, and have run 180 miles; course E. b. S. and E.S.E.; wind W. to W. b. S.; lat., by obs., 34° 16′ S. We judge y[e] aire here as sharpe and cold as it is at any time in y[e] month of March in England.

May 2.—These 24 hours we have had a fine moderate gale, and have run 120 miles; course E. b. S. and E.S.E.; wind S.S.W. to S.W.; lat. 34° 31′. (The last night we gott up our new fore-top-mast, and sett ye sail.)

May 3.—These 24 hours fair weather and a gentle gale. Distance run 109 miles; course E.S.E.; wind W.S.W.; lat., by judg^{nt}, 35° 12′. Our long^{de} from ye merid. of Lizard is 20° to ye W^d of ye cape.

May 4.—From 12 o'clock yesterday till 5 in ye afternoon was quite calme, and then it began to rain most violently as it hath still continued with little or no intermission till this day noon, always blowing so hard that we could carry no more sail than our two courses. This is ye greatest storme we have had (God be praised for it) since we left ye Downes. Wind at S. b. E. and S.S.E.; course E. and E. b. N. We judge the violence of this storme has driven us back 15 or 20 miles to ye Northward; lat., by judg^{nt}, is 34° 59′. Distance run 35 miles.

May 5.—From yesterday noon till towards midnight it continued raining exceeding hard. but ye storme nothing abated till 8 o'clock this morning, since which time we have carryed our fore-top-sail, halfe mast high. We have run 90 miles; course E. b. N. to N.E. b. E.; wind S.E. b. E. to S.S.E.; latitude 34° 37′ S.

May 6.—These 24 hours it hath blowen very hard, without rain. We have run 75 miles; course from S.S.W. to S.S.E.; wind S.E. to E.; lat., by judgment, 35° 15′ S.

May 7.—These 24 hours ye storme hath continued so violent that we lay under a main-course till 8 o'clock this morning, since which we have sett our *other two* courses: the wind still blowing very hard, with drizzling rain. We have run 54 miles; course E.S.E. and E. b. S.; wind at N.E. and N.E. b. N.; lat^{de}, by judgment, 36° 14′ S.

May 8.—These 24 hours we have had more rain than wind. Distance run but 53 miles; course E. b. S. and E. b. N.; wind N.N.E. to N.E. b. N.; lat., by judgment, 36° 28′ S.

May 9.—These 24 hours have had but little wind, except what came in gusts, with lightning and rain. Distance run 44 miles; course E. b. S. to E. b N.; wind N.N.E. to N.N.W.; lat., by judgement (having seen no sun for obs^n since ye 2nd instant), 36° 40′ S.

May 10.—These 24 hours we have had very tempestuous and gusty weather. Distance run is 72 miles; course from E.N.E. to N.E. b. E.; wind from E. to S.E.; latitude, by judgement, 36° 1′ S.

May 11.—These 24 hours the storme has increased to that violence, y^t for the most part we have layen a-try, with a mainsail and mizen only abroad, ye sea being exceeding great, so y^t we continue still driving to ye northward. Our distance run is 32 miles; course E. b. N. and E.N.E.; wind S.E. b. S. and S.E.; lat., by judgment, 35° 21′ S.

May 12.—From yesterday noon to 8 o'clock this morning (ye storme increasing) we lay under a main-course, and since have sett our mainsail [fore sail?] and mizen. Distance run is 19 miles; course E. and E. b. S.; wind S. b. E.; lat., by acc[ot], 34° 52′ S.

May 13.—These 24 hours we have had little wind, with a great rolling sea. Distance run 47 miles; course E. b. N.; wind S.S.E.; latitude, by observation, 34° 42′ S.; so since y[e] 9th instant we have been driven back two degrees (except 2 minutes) to the northward.

May 14.—These 24 hours we have had very little wind. Distance run 33 miles; y[e] course E.S.E.; wind W. and S.W.; latitude 34° 44′ S.

May 15.—Yesterday about 5 in y[e] afternoon a fresh gale sprung up at S.W., and continued freshening to y[e] degree that, between 4 and 5 this morning, it broke our main top-mast. This is y[e] second topmast we have lost in a fortnight's time, besides 2 top-gallant masts. Our dist. run is 130; course E.S.E.; wind S.W. b. S. to S.W.; lat[de], by observation, 35° 10′ S.

May 16.—These 24 hours y[e] gale being fresh we have run 146 miles; course E. b. S. to E.S.E.; latitude, by judg., 35° 15′ S. About 12 last night we gott up our main top-mast, and sett its sail.

May 17.—A small gale. Run 79 miles; course E. to E.N.E.; wind S.S.E. to S.E.; lat., by account, 35° 40′ S.

May 18.—These 24 hours for y[e] most part a small gale, but accompanyed by great and sudden gusts and darke cloudy weather. Run 88 miles; course E. b. N. to E. S. E.; wind S. E. b. S. to S.; lat. obs[d] 34° 23′.

May 19.—These 24 hours it hath blowne exceeding hard, especially since morning, being able to carry no more sail than our courses, which hath driven us considerably to y[e] northward. We esteem ourselves here within 100 leagues of y[e] Cape; at this time of y[e] yeare it is counted strange not to have a fair wind to weather it, but such is our misfortune to have had more calmes and contrary winds (since we left St. Jago) than has been known by our most experienced mariners. Our distance run is 108 miles; course E. to E.S.E.; wind S.S.E. to S.; lat., by observation, 34° 7′ S.

May 20.—These 24 hours y[e] wind still blowing contrary a very fresh gale at S.E. b. E., course S. b. W. Dist. run 60 miles; lat., by obs[n], 34° 5′; variation of y[e] compass this morning being 8° 40′,[1] going S. b. W. 3 points leeway to W[d], yet they imagine from the Mag. var. they are 50 leagues to S.: we judge ourselves about 40 or 50 leagues to y[e] westward of y[e] Cape.[2]

---

[1] *Note.*—Variation 8° 40′. It does not appear whether East or West; probably Westerly, because in Sir Thomas Roe's *Journal* (1615) it was 3° E. It is now about 28° West.

[2] Mag. Var.—In vol. iii of Astley's *Voyages* (Lond., 1746), p. 336, de-

May 21.—Gale moderate. Run 74 miles; course S. b. W. and S.S.W.; wind S.E. and S.E. b. E.; lat., by obs., 35° 0′ South.

May 22.—From 6 o'clock yesterday afternoone it hath blowne hard and made a great sea. Our dist. run is 89 miles; course E. and E. b. N.; wind S.S.E. and S.E. b. S. lat.; by obs^{n}, 34° 16′ S.; so that in these 24 hours past we have been driven back 44 miles to ye northward. 'Tis bad plying to windward when ye sea runs very high, and ye wind blows so hard, that the topsails can hardly be carried up half ye mast.

May 23.—These 24 hours we have had a constant fresh gale. Run 84 miles; course S. and S.S.W.; wind E.S.E. to S.E.; lat., by obs^{n}, 34° 48′ S.; so that notwithstanding ye distance run of 84 miles, ye sea and current are both so forcible against us, that we have gott but 32 miles these 24 hours, to the southward.

May 24.—These 24 hours the gale has been moderate; this morning it sprung up fair at N.N.E. Our distance run is 65 miles; course S. to E. b. S.; wind E.S.E. to N.E. b. N.; lat., obs^{n}, 35° 56′ S.

May 25.—From 10 last night till noon this day it hath blowne exceeding fresh. Our dist. run 129 miles; course E. to E.N.E.; wind N. b. E. to N.N.W.; lat., by obs^{n}, 35° 31′ S. Having this day seen many sea-weeds, a seal (?), and some such birds as appear only about ye Cape, at 4 o'clock this afternoon we hoisted out our boat, and casting ye lead, struck ground at 49 Fathom depth, which by ye tallow was white, and hard as chalke. We judge Cape de Agullias bears North, at 40 miles distant. Blessed be God we are come thus far on our voyage in perfect health and safety, not having lost a man (except Mr. Richards), either by sickness or any other accident, since we left England, which wants but 3 days of 4 months, and is just 2 months this day since we passed ye Equinoctial Line.

May 26.—These 24 hours it has blowne very hard; at 7 o'clock this morning we sounded again and struck ground (of a whitish sand) at 90 fathom. Distance run 159 m.; course E. b. N., E. b. S. and E. S.E.; wind from N.N.W. to ye W.; lat., by obs^{n}, 35° 20′ S.

May 27.—Gale continued very fresh. Run 156 miles; course E.S.E.; wind W.N.W.; lat. obs^{d} 39° 59′ S.

May 28.—These 24 hours it has blowne exceeding fresh, with very great sea. Our distance run is 149 miles; course E.S.E., wind W.N.W.; lat. obs. 36° 18′ S.; 4 months since we left the Downes this day.

---

scriptive of the Cape of Good Hope, "the declination of the needle has much varied here. According to authors it was 6 *degrees* N.E., about a century ago. The Missioners, in 1685, found it to be 0° 11′ 30″ N.W. Mr. Kolben, in 1705, observed it (0° 11′ 55″) the same way." The Admiralty Chart of 1867, corrected to 1879, makes the variation 30° 9′ W. (increasing 0° 1′ 30″ annually).

May 29.—These 24 hours it has blown very hard, and from 8 o'clock last night to 8 this morning it has blowne a storme. Run 186 miles; course E.S.E.; wind N.W. and to ye N^d^; lat., by obs^n^, 36° 27′ S.

May 30.—Very gusty weather, with a great sea. Dist. 160 miles; course E.S.E.; wind W.N.W.; lat. obs. 36° 58′.

May 31.—These 24 hours gale has been more moderate, but ye sea great. Distance run 127 miles; course E. b. S.; wind W.N.W. to S.W.; lat., by judgement, 36° 30′ S.

June 1.—These 24 hours little wind, and for ye most part contrary, with a great sea from S.W. Dist. 62 miles; course E., N.E., S. b. E., E. b. S., E. b. N. to N.; very variable; lat., by judgement (ye weather being exceedingly foggy and drizzling) 36° 54′ S.

June 2.—Fresh gale N. b. W. to W.N.W., thunder and much lightning, with darke cloudy weather, course E.S.E. Distance run 138 miles, latitude, by judgement, 36° 54′ S.

June 3.—These 24 hours it has blowne an exceeding great storme, and so continues, with much lightning and frequent violent gusts of rain and hail, which putts us from all our sailes, except the fore sail; ye seas very great and lofty. Our distance run by log 197 miles, but by ye variation 'tis judged we have run neer 220 miles; course E.S.E., E. b. S. and E.; wind W. and W.S.W.; lat., by an imperfect obs^n^, 36° 0′ S.

June 4.—These 24 hours ye storme has and does still continue with ye same violence and rage as it did yesterday, with terrible gusts and showers of rain, and seas running mountains high, which made us roll exceedingly. Dist. run 195 miles, but conceive we have gone much farther; course E.S.E.; wind from S.W. b. W. to W.N.W.; latitude, by judgement, 35° 36′ S.

June 5.—These 24 hours ye storme has encreased (and still continues) to be a mere frett of wind, ye whole sea being like a perfect breach, with most violent gusts every ¼ or ½ hour, accompanied with fierce showers of hail and rain. The last night we shipped 4 seas in ye great cabbin, two from a port (which it forced open) over ye head of ye rudder, and 2 more from one of ye gallery windows. We had only a foresail and spritsail abroad; ye latter broke its sheet, and could not be sett again till ye morning. Our dist. run by log is 214 miles; course E.S.E. and E. b. S.; wind W.; lat., by obs., 34° 54′ S.

June 6.—From yesterday noon till 12 o'clock last night ye storme continued in its full force, as it has been for these 3 days past, and then abated so gradually that at 8 o'clock this morning we ran but after the rate of 2 miles an hour, with both topsails abroad. Distance run 134 miles; course E.S.E.; wind S.W. and S.W. b. W.; lat., by judgement, 34° 45′ S.

June 7.—From yesterday noon till 7 or 8 o'clock at night ye gale continued increasing very gradually, when, for divers hours following, we ran 10 or 11 miles an hour. Our dist. run is 194 miles; course S.E. b. E. and E.S.E.; wind W. b. N. to N.N.W.; lat., by judgement, 34° 59′ S.

June 8.—From yesternoon till 12 at night yᵉ gale continued exceeding fresh, in which time only we ran 119 miles, and then it fainted away, so that in these 24 hours our distance ran in yᵉ whole is but 170 miles; course E.S.E.; wind N.W. to W.; lat., by obsⁿ, 34° 35′ S.

June 9.—These 24 hours fair weather (more than we have had this month), and a fine gentle gale, with smooth water. Run 78 miles; course E. b. S.; wind W.N.W.; lat. obs. 34° 14′ S.

June 10.—Fine, pleasant weather these 24 hours; smooth water, and steady fresh gale. Dist. run 141 miles; course E. and E. b. N.; wind N. to N.W.; lat., by obs., 33° 20′ S.

June 11.—Fair, fresh, steady gale, smooth water. Dist. 177 miles; course, E. b. N.; wind N.N.W.; lat. 31° 57′.

June 12.—Little wind, smooth sea, dark cloudy weather. Dist. run 74 miles; course from E.N.E. to E.S.E.; wind from N. to N.E.; lat., by judgement, 39° 21′ S.

June 13.—These 24 hours wind has been contrary, a fresh gale and dark cloudy weather. Run 84 miles; course N.N.W. to S.E. b. E.; wind E.N.E. to N.E.; lat., by judgeⁿᵗ, 31° 55′.

June 14.—Wind has continued contrary, very fresh gale from N. to N.E. b. E., with much rain and dark cloudy weather. Run 73 miles; course N. W. to E.N.E.; latᵈᵉ, by account, 32° 5′ S.

June 15.—From noon yesterday to midnight, little wind; from that time it has blowne very hard, with continued rain (more or lesse), and exceeding dark cloudy weather, and, which is worst of all, yᵉ wind still continues contrary. Our dist. run is 63 miles; course N.E. to E. b. N.; wind N.N.W. to N. b. E.; latitude, by judgement, 31° 39′ S.

This day we threw Robert Pattison, one of our Quarter Masters, overboard. He is the first mariner that has dyed in this shippe, and lay many days sick of scurvy.

June 16.—Between 11 and 12 o'clock last night yᵉ wind came up fair, and so it continues. Our distance run is 93 miles. A great sea and dark cloudy weather; course E.N.E. to N.E. b. N.; wind N. to S.W. b. S.; lat., by obsⁿ, 30° 8′ S.

June 17.—These 24 hours yᵉ gale has been very fresh; a great sea, with dark cloudy weather. Distance 157 miles; course N.E. b. N. and N.E.; wind S.S.W. and S.W. b. S.; latᵈᵉ, by observation, 27° 50′ S. We judge ourselves this day 1000 leagues from yᵉ Cape, which (considering yᵉ contrary winds we have had) is esteemed a very good run from yᵉ 25ᵗʰ ultimo.

June 18.—These 24 hours fair. Run 154 miles; course N.E.; wind S.S.W. to S.E.; lat., by obs., 25° 8′ South.

June 19.—These 24 hours fresh gale at S.E. b. S. to E.S.E.. with darke cloudy weather. Dist. run 154 miles; lat., by judgement, 22° 57′ S. This morning we are passed yᵉ Tropick of Capricorne in 50° 35′ merid. distance to eastward of yᵉ Cape,[1] and in 16° degrees variation.[2]

June 20.—These 24 hours the gale has been very fresh, E. b. S. and E.S.E., but, going close-hauled yᵉ distance run is no more than 124 miles; course N.E.; lat., by obs., 21° S. Variation 14° this morn.

June 21.—These 24 hours it has blowne so hard from yᵉ E. b. S. to S.E. that sometimes we have been forced to hand both our topsails. This morning our fore-topsail split, and going close hauled. Our distance run is but 133 miles; course N.E. to N.N.E.; lat., by obs. 18° 49′ S.

June 22.—These 24 hours it has blown exceeding hard, especially in gusts with raine, which were very violent, contrary to our expectation so far within yᵉ Tropick, we have carried no more saile than our courses and *fore*-topsail, reefed, upon yᵉ cap. Our distance run 123 miles; course N.E. b. N.; wind E. b. S. and E.S.E.; lat., by obs., 17° 4′ S. Yesterday in yᵉ afternoone our *fore* topsail was split a second time.

June 23.—These 24 hours for yᵉ most part it hath blowne a storme from E. b. S. and E.S.E., with exceeding hard and frequent gusts of drizzling rain. Till 8 o'clock this morning we have not been able to sett our topsails, reefed ⅓ of y mast; yᵉ weather extream darke and cloudy, with a very great sea. Dist. run 97 miles; course N.E. b. N. and N.E.; lat., by obsⁿ, 15° 29′ S.

June 24.—These 24 hours it has blowne hard, with dark cloudy weather; the main-top sail handed all right.[3] Run 106 m.; course N.E. b. N. to N.E. b. E.; wind E.S.E. to S.E. b. E.; lat. obs. 13° 54′ S. Var. 11°.

June 25.—Very fresh gale at E.S.E., with divers great gusts and raine, dark cloudy weather, and a great sea. Dist. run 136 miles; course N.E. by N.; lat., by obsⁿ, 12° 0′ S.

June 26.—These 24 hours yᵉ gale has continued E.S.E., very fresh, with frequent great gusts and violent showers of raine, with little intermission, the weather exceeding darke and cloudy. Dist. run 133 miles; course N.E. b. N.; lat., by judgement, 9° 54′ S.

June 27.—These 24 hours yᵉ rain has been so violent that it has seemed (in a manner) one continued showre, the wind blowing hard by gusts from E.S.E. to S.E., and weather so dark and cloudy that we have not seen the sun, either for observation of latitude at noon, or amplitude at night or morning, these 2 days. Distance run 108 miles; course N.E. b. N.; latitude, by judgement, 8° 6′ S.

June 28.—From yesterday noone till 5 o'clock this morning, darke

---

1 Reckoned from Lizard. 2 Mag. var., 1875, 13° W.

3 Furled.

cloudy weather, with frequent gusts and raine. At 3 this morning we tacked for fear of ye Islands of Candi and Ady,[1] and stood to ye Southward till towards break of day, supposing ourselves in 7 degrees—the latitude of these Islands. Dist. run 93 miles; course N.E. by N. and S. b. E.; wind S. b. E., E.N.E., and N,E.; lat., by obs., 7° 19′ S.

June 29.—These 24 hours fair weather, a fine fresh gale E. b. S. and E., and smooth water. Dist. run 119 miles; course N.E. b. N. and N.N.E. This morn^g^, by amplitude, ye varia^n^ was 8°; lat., 5° 31′ S., course now altered to N. b. E.

June 30.—From noon yesterday to 6 this morning, fine gentle gale; since then, calme, darke, cloudy weather, with much rain, thunder, and lightning. Distance run 85 miles; courses N. b. E. and North; wind E. b. S. and E.S.E.; lat^de^, by judgement, 4° 6′ S.

July 1.—These 24 hours very little wind, and that sometimes contrary, ye weather exceedingly dark and cloudy, with great showers of raine. Distance run 57 miles; course from East to N. b. E.; wind N.N.E. to N.W. b. N.; lat., by judgement, 3° 27′ S.

July 2.—These 24 hours dark cloudy weather, little wind and smooth water. Dist. run 83 miles; course N. b. E.; wind S.W. and S.S.W.; lat., by obs., 1° 56′ S. Variation this morning, by amplitude, 7 degrees. The like var. of 7 degrees this evening, which has caused us to steer N.

July 3.—These 24 hours fair weather, little wind from S. b. W. and S.S.W., smooth water, but ye weather darke and cloudy. Distance run 80 miles; course North; lat., by obs., 0° 28′ S. This night, about 9 o'clock, we judged ourselves past ye Equinoctiall Line.

July 4.—These 24 hours fair weather and fine fresh gale, especially since 8 o'clock last night, and smooth water. Distance run 118 miles; course N.; wind S. to S.W. b. S.; lat., by obs^n^, 1° 30′ to the Northward of the line. Variation this morning 7° 48′.

July 5.—These 24 hours fine fresh gale, S. b. W. and S.S.W., smooth water, but dark cloudy weather. Distance run 103 miles; course N. and N. b. E.; Lat., by judgement, 3° 13′ N.

July 6.—These 24 hours fresh gale W. b. S. and W.S.W., with great gusts of rain and dark cloudy weather. Distance run 146 miles; course North; lat^de^, by obs., 5° 13′ N.; and ye longitude or meridian distance from ye Cape, 55° 1′. No azimuth nor amplitude these two days to know ye variation.

July 7.—From yesterday noon to 6 o'clock at night, a fresh gale and dark cloudy weather, in which time having run 35 miles North without seeing Zeilon (Ceylon), and judgeing our selves to ye Westward of ye Island, we steered East all the night. By 5 o'clock this morning we saw land about 4 leagues off, and so continued sailing ye same distance

---

[1] Query, Diego Garcia—in lat. 7° 25′ S., long. 72° 30′ E.?

for y[e] shore; course E. b. N.; wind at W. and W.S.W. A fine, fresh gale this morning. We sounded, and had ground in 30 fathoms. The sun afforded us no observation.

July 8.—From yesterday noon till 1 o'clock this morning we steered East, and then lay to till 5 o'clock this morning, when, making sail, we steered N., N. b. E., N.N.E., and North by East again. Y[e] whole distance run 106 miles; wind at W. and S.W. b. S.; lat[de], by obs[n], 6° 33′ N. The gale continues fresh, with indifferent weather. This night a Dutch sloop came off to us from Batticalo Fort, Zeilon.

July 9.—This morning y[e] Dutch sloop left us, assuring us he saw not, and believed no English ship was yet passed by this Island. These 24 hours a fair and a moderate gale. Distance run 100 miles; course N.N.E., N. b. E., and N.; wind S.W., b. S.; lat., by obs., 7° 56′ N.

July 10.—These 24 hours fair weather but little wind, and a very great rolling sea, which makes us believe here is a great current, that sets against us to y[e] South[d], in regard our distance run (being 69 miles by our Log), is more than twice as much as we find we have really run by our observation, which is 8° 30′ N.; course N. b. E.; wind at S.S.W. and S.W.

July 11.—From yesterday noon till 8 at night little wind; then it came up very fresh; which makes our distance run 153 miles; but finding, by our observations, we have not advanced to the North[d] full two degrees, we are forced to cut off 33 miles of our log, concluding a very strong current setts against us to the S[d]; course N. b. W. and North; wind W.S.W. and W. b. S.; lat., by obs., 10° 47′ N.

July 12.—These 24 hours very fresh gale and great sea. Dist. run 173 miles; course N. and N. b. W.; wind W. and W. b. S.; lat., by obs., 13° 5′ N.

July 13.—These 24 hours hath rather smooth water, and a fair moderate gale. Distance run 116 miles; course N.E. b. N. and N.N.E.; wind W. b. S. and W.N.W.; lat., by obs., 14° 56′ N. We judge y[e] current now setts for us.

July 14.—This 24 hours it hath blown hard, with exceeding dark, cloudy weather. Between 11 and 12 o'clock last night we were suddenly a back-stays (taken aback) with a violent gust of wind and rain, accompanyed with much lightning and thunder. Our distance run 143 miles; course in y[e] night N.E.; before night yesterday, in y[e] afternoon, N.; this morning, by break of day, N.N.W.; wind from y[e] W.S.W. to y[e] W.N.W.; latitude, by judgement, 16° 37′ N.

About 2 o'clock this afternoon we saw y[e] Main Land, and sailed within 7 leagues of it till night, steering N.E. and N.E. b. E.

July 15.—These 24 hours fair weather and a fresh gale. Dist. run 145 miles; course from y[e] N.N.W. to y[e] E.N.E.; wind from y[e] West to y[e] W.S.W.; lat., by obs., 18° 10′ N.

July 16.—These 24 hours it has blown very fresh, with hard gusts of rain and dark cloudy weather. We lay by all last night till 10 o'clock this morning, yᵉ Captain being desirous to see yᵉ Jagernot Pagodas, for his better satisfaction, which we discovered this morning about 8 o'clock. Distance run 106 miles; course from yᵉ N.N.E. to E. b. S.; wind from yᵉ South to yᵉ W. and S.W.; lat., by judgement, yᵉ sun being in our zenith, 19° 50′ N.

July 17.—These 24 hours a fresh gale, with gusts of rain, and very dark cloudy weather. From 7 o'clock last night till 5 this morning we lay at anchor in 18 fathoms water, and then made sail. Dist. run, 73 miles; course N. b. E. to E.; wind W. and S.W.

About 2 in yᵉ afternoon we doubled yₑ Point of Palmiras, and between 6 and 7 in yᵉ evening we came to an anchor in yᵉ Bay.

July 18.—About 8 in yᵉ morning we had gott out our Long boat, and weighed our Anchor. At 11 o'clock this morning we anchored again, about 8 or 10 miles distant from a Ship and 5 small vessels we saw in yᵉ Road, and 15 or 16 miles from yᵉ shore; however, soon after we came to an anchor I sent away Capt. Raynes in yᵉ *Pinnace*, ashore with a letter to yᵉ Chief and Council of yᵉ English Factory at Ballasore; and Mʳ Garret (one of our Mates) in the Yall to yᵉ Master of yᵉ first Yacht he can speak with, to come off to us, and Pilot our Ship into yᵉ Road.

Yᵉ Copy of yᵉ letter wrote to yᵉ Factory is as follows:—

"Aboard of yᵉ *Defence* in Ballasore Road,
"Sirs, "July 18, 1682.

"The Honᵇˡᵉ E. India Company have made yᵉ severall Factories in this Bay a distinct Agency from that of Fort Sᵗ George, and having sent us hither for yᵉ Government of their affairs, We desire the Chief and Second (at least) of your Factory, to come off as soon as may be, to consult with us concerning yᵉ management of their business; and that you would dispatch yᵉ Sloops to us with all expedition, wherein you will not only do an acceptable piece of Service to y Company but likewise oblige,

"Sirs, Your most humble Servants,
"William Hedges. Joseph Dodd.
"John Beard. William Johnson.

"To yᵉ Chief and Councell of the
English Factory in Ballasore."

July 19.—We weighed anchor again, and bore down about 2 or 3 miles to 2 sloops which could not turn it up to us, and sending for ye Masters aboard, the one was y^e^ *Good Hope*, George Herne, Master; the other y^e^ *Madapollam*, John Hampton, Master. They told us the Ship we saw in Port was the *Crown*, Capt. Dorrell, with Mr Pitts, who had been here 11 days before. That Mr Pitts had hired a great house at Ballasore, carried divers Chests of money ashore, and was very busy in buying of goods. We were likewise informed that two other small Ships in our sight, over against Piply, were English vessels, arrived but 3 days before us; one of which was commanded by Capt. Say, of about 200 tons. The Commander's name of ye other Ship they did not know. but were informed they all wanted Pilots to carry them up the River to Hugly.

July 21.—About 1 o'clock in ye Afternoon I took my leave of Capt. Heath and all others on board y^e^ *Defence*, and embarked on ye Company's Sloop y^e^ *Good Hope*, of 100 tons burden, for Hugly, in company with y^e^ *Madapollam* (another Sloop) on which embarked Mr Beard and his Son, Mr Dodd, Mr Rushworth, Mr Leseley (ye Minister) and his Son, with 9 souldiers.

On our vessel were all my family, Mr Johnson, Capt. Heath, and Capt. Raines, besides Mr Byam of Ballasore, and Mr Hill, a young man sent down by Mr Vincent, with orders to the Company's Ships for the delivery of their goods. This night about 9 o'clock we anchored on ye Braces.

July 22.—This morning early we began to weigh our Anchor, but ye wind blowing hard and ye sea running high, and having broke our Windlace, were forced (not being able to weigh our Anchor) to cut off about 20 fathoms of our Cable. Whilst we were endeavouring to weigh, y^e^ *Madapollam* came up; she had broke her Cable and lost her Anchor. This morning the Sloop *Arrivall*, with Mrs Richards and her family, Mr Langly, Mr Bray, and Mr Ravenhill, came up with us. This Night we got up as far as a little Village called Rangamate, and there Anchored.

July 23.—This morning about 8 o'clock we weighed and sett sail with a small breeze, scarce stemming ye Current, but ye gale soon freshening we got up as high as a Village called Great Tanna,[1] by 12 o'clock, from whence I sent one of ye Boatmen with a letter to Mr Vincent at Hugly as follows:—

"From aboard of ye sloop *Good-hope*, off Great Tanna,

"July 23, 1682.

"The Honble E. India Company have thought good to make ye severall Factories in ye Bay of Bengall an agency distinct and independant from that of Fort St. George, and having sent us hither for ye management of their affaires, we request you to dispatch to us, with all convenient speed, ye Company's and some other boats, to carry us up to Hugly; being about 60 persons. Please to cause convenient accommodation to be made for our reception, and ye favour you shall show us herein will be thankfully acknowledged by

"Sirs, Your most humble Servants,

"W. H. and W. J."

This letter was signed only by myself and by Mr Wm Johnson (Mr Beard and Mr Dodd, on y^e^ *Madapollam*, not being in sight), and was directed—"To ye worsp^ll^ Mathias Vincent, Esqre, Chief for ye Honble E. India Comp^ys^ affairs in Bengall and Orixa, and Councell in Hugly."

July 24.—Early in ye Morning I was met by Mr Littleton, and most of ye Factory, near Hugly; and about 9 or 10

1 Great Tanna was built where now stands the house of the Superintendent of the Botanical Garden, about 3 miles below Calcutta, and distant from Hooghly about 20 miles by land. S. Masters writes in 1676:—"In Tannah stands an old ffort of mud walls, wch was built to prevent ye incursion of ye Arracaners, for it seems about ten or twelve years since that they were soe bold that none durst inhabit lower down the river than this place, the Arracaners usually taking the people of the shoares to sell them at Tiple (query Tipara ?)."

o'clock by Mr. Vincent near ye Dutch Garden, who came attended by severall Boats and Budgerows, guarded by 35 Firelocks, and about 50 Rashpoots and Peons well armed. He invited me to go ashoar with him to the Dutch Garden where he had provided an entertainment for me, and made preparation for my reception. I went along with him, and stayed till evening, expecting Mr. Beard's arrival in ye other sloop, who not coming in time, we went together to the Factory, and there parted company.

All transactions from this day to ye 10th October are entered in the publick Diary.

October 9.—The severall affronts, insolencies, and abuses dayly put upon us by Boolchund, our chief Customer (causing a generall stop of our trade), being grown insufferable, ye Agent and Councell for ye Honble E. India Compa affairs at Hugly resolved upon and made use of divers expedients for redress of their grievances; but all means proving ineffectual 'twas agreed and concluded in consultation that the only expedient now left was for the Agent to go himself in person to the Nabob and Duan at Decca[1] as well to make some settled adjustment concerning ye Customs, as to endeavor the preventing Interlopers trading in these parts for ye future; in order to which preparations were caused to be made. Mr. Richard Frenchfeild and Mr. William Johnson were appointed to go along with ye Agent to Decca. 'Twas also thought convenient to go by ye way of Merdadpore, a towne within 4 or 5 hours travell of Cassumbazar, to have ye opportunity to speak and consult with Mr. Charnock and some others of ye Councell there, what course is best to be taken in this exigency. Preparation of Budgerows and other Boats with Provisions, etc., being thus made, and notice of our resolution given to Permesuradas, ye said Bulchund's servant and chief customer here, and liberty granted by him to carry Presents, etc.

[1] *I.e.*, Dacca.

October 10.—The Agent with all his retinue, being 23 English men in Souldier's garb, and 15 Rashpoots and Peons, embarked on two Budgerows and divers small boats, between 6 and 7 o'clock at night, to go towards ye English Garden, to which place Permesuradas, contrary to his promise, sent privately divers armed boats to seize some of ours. This night they took one boat laden with 18 half-pieces of fine cloth, and carryed it with them so quietly, that we heard not of it till ye next morning. This evening I was followed to ye Garden by Mutoradass, who pretended he was sent by Permesuradass to adjust all differences betwixt us before my departure; and here in the presence of M^r. Bearde and the rest of ye Councell 'twas agreed on and concluded betwixt us, that for a present of 2,000 Rupees we should have free liberty to receive and send away all our goods, of which he was to accept our entrys without weighing or seeing them, we being obliged at the end of two Months to pay Custom for the said goods, if in that time we did not procure a Pherwanna from the Duan of Decca to excuse us from it.

October 11.—In the morning notice was given me that one of our boats with 18 half-pieces of cloth was stolen from us by Permesuradass his Servants. I then immediately despatched away M^r. Johnson, M^r. Frenchfeild, and my Nephew Hedges, with some Souldiers, ordering them to bring away ye boat from ye Mearbar,[1] or wheresoever else they should find her; which was handsomely performed, though with some threats from ye Governour's Servants; about noon we got 3 or 4 miles above ye English Garden, where we were overtaken by some horsemen ashore, and divers boats full of Armed men; and seeing the numbers ashore and by boat increasing every minute, we thought fit to pass over to ye other side of ye river out of Permesaradass his jurisdiction; but here we found ye stream so exceedingly rapid that our force was scarce able to stem it; here ye boats crowding

[1] *Mír-bahr*, customs or harbour master.

close upon us; and finding them not to be scared with ye bare presenting of Guns and Pistolls to their breasts without firing of them; (which was the only thing they desired that some person might be wounded or killed by us:) and the length of their lances secured them from Cudgells, we were prevailed upon to stay an hour in that place for ye Governour's answer. Before the expiration of this time we were overtaken by ye Caddies Neip,[1] ye Meerbar's deputy, and ye Dutch Director's Vakill (by the way 'tis observable ye Dutch omit no opportunity to do us all the prejudice that lyes in their power), who came from Permesuradass beseeching me to return to ye English Garden, where, they assured me with many oaths and protestations, Permesuradass should come to me to beg my pardon, and become friends again, which was all their design before I went to Decca, for fear of doing him prejudice there. If we refused to accept of this proffer, they assured us we should never proceed on our voyage without killing some of ye King's Souldiers, and what the ill consequence of that might be we were left to consider. But these men returning to Hugly without any promise of my going to ye Garden, about midnight, I attempted once more to force my way through three boats which lay athwart my boat, and sent my Nephew with some Souldiers to ye head of my boat, with a good Bamboo in one hand, and a Gun in ye other. Their lances prevented, as before, ye use of his Bamboo, and on presenting his Gun he had five lances clapped to his breast, bidding him take his choice which he would kill, and ye survivors of them would do ye like to him. During this scuffle the stream ran so strong that we fell near a mile astern towards Hugly, where we fastened our boat and lay the remainder of this night.

October 12.—This morning I returned to y^e English Garden and sent for M^r. Beard and M^r. Ellis to come and consult with

[1] *I.e.*, *Naib*, or Deputy.

us what course was now best to be taken for y^{e} Honourable Comp$^{ys.}$ most advantage. Here I was met again by y^{e} Cazee's "Neip", Muttradass, and an eminent Mogull Merchant; who with many oaths faithfully promised, if I would continue at y^{e} Garden this night, Permesuradass should come and cast himself at my feet, begging to be reconciled, and if I would grant him ye favour to accompany me to ye factory, I should return again with all my boats as soon, and to what place, I thought good, without any obstruction; and so we parted for this night, before which time it was resolved by ye Councell that if I should not prevail to go this way to Decca, I should attempt to do it with ye sloopes by way of the River of Rogues,[1] which goes through to y^{e} great River of Decca.

October 13.—This morning Permesuradass sent Muttradass again to excuse his not waiting on me this morning, "but he would not fail to do it to-morrow", which appearing to be only a trick to protract time, and (as we were credibly informed) that M$^{r.}$ Pitts (who was designed for Decca) might go before us, I caused all y^{e} boates to make what haste they could aboard of y^{e} sloopes, where we arrived about 4 or 5 o'clock in y^{e} afternoon. Here I was met again by y^{e} Cazee himself, with divers of y^{e} chief persons in towne, beseeching me not to stir this night, and to-morrow morning he would bring Permesuradass to me without fail. I gave little credit to these fair words, but ordered 2 sloops, the *Good Hope* and the *Lilly*, to be ready to sail ye next morning.

October 14.—Permesuradass sent divers persons to let me know he would visit me aboard my Budgero by ye sloops side, but would not go aboard ye sloop; desiring also that I would send a boat to bring him to me. When he was come to ye side of ye Budgero he sent to give me notice, and

[1] Rogue's River, now Channel Creek, was so called, from Portuguese outlaws using it as a station from whence they made piratical attacks on the shipping. They and the Mugs contributed to the desolation of the Sunderbunds.

desired I would come down out of ye sloop into ye Budgero. At my first coming down he embraced me with much respect before ye spectators. After mutual Salutes, ye Cazee and he used all ye arguments they could invent to persuade me to go ashore and make friends in the Factory, assuring me, with great protestations, if I would grant him that request he would not only permit me free liberty to go which way I pleased to Decca, without stopping ye boats with presents, but likewise write in my favor to Bulchund, his Master, at Cassambazar. I answered in fine to this frivolous request, not apprehending any advantage he could possibly receive by it, more than to delay my time; however, I went ashoar immediately, and took him in my hand, walking together in that posture from ye boats to ye Factory, he being guarded by Peons and Servants, and I by ye Souldiers and Peons of ye Factory, with most of all ye Englishmen in town. Being come home he had little more to say but to assure me of his respect and friendship for ye future, and that I might go which way I pleased, and that if I would send a servant with him, he would immediately send me ye letter promised in my favour, to his Master.

October 14.—As he went out of one of the factory doors I went out of the other, towards the Sloops, where resolution was taken for my going to Decca by way of Cassumbazar, as being ye most usuall,[1] though it is believed by others the voyage might be performed in less time through the River of Rogues. All things being put again into ye Budgerows, out of ye Sloops, and having waited till 5 o'clock in the Afternoon for Permesuradas's letter, I went aboard ye Budgero', and set forwards to Cassumbuzar; but I had almost forgotten to relate ye unjust and villainous practice used by Permesuradass towards our boatmen.

As many as he could take straggling, he beat and im-

[1] The rivers were deeper than they are now. The Jellinghee River in parts has silted up.

prisoned; the like he did to our Peons sent on our errands: and those Peons and Boatmen that he could not take, he sent for their wives and children or other near relations, beating and imprisoning them, that their Husbands and Fathers might leave our service; making also proclamation, by beat of Drum throughout the town, that if any Slave would run away from us he should be free, and liberty given to go where he or they pleased.

About 6 o'clock this night we got up to ye English Garden, where ye Servant I sent for Pernnesuradas's letter to Bulchund, met me, and told me he saw no hopes of getting ye letter, but was ordered by Permesuradass to tell me he would have me stay there till he sent to search my boats to see what was in them; and if I refused to stay there he would certainly stop me again at Trippany[1] some miles further up the River; but, resolving now to be abused no more in this manner, I sent all ye laden boats before, with Mr. Johnson to see them make all the haste that might be, and not to stop all night. Next to them went the Souldiers with ye other Budgero. I followed that, and 2 stout fellows, an Englishman and a Spaniard, in a light boat, came last of all.

About 2 hours within night a boat full of armed men came up very near to the Spaniard, who speaking ye language demanded who they were, and commanded them to stand; but those in ye boat returning no answer, nor regarding what he said, he fired his Musket in the Water, at which they fell astern. About an hour after, when we were got up as far as Trippany, the armed boat came up with ye Spaniard again, who commanded them to keep off, otherwise he would now

[1] The junction of three streams (Tri Beni) between Sooksagur and Chogdah. "Tribeny" ghaut is about two miles east of the present Muggra station on the railway; lat. 22° 59′ N. An article in the *Friend of India* for Dec. 3rd, 1857, mentions that the confluence of three rivers at Allahabad (Gunga, Jumna, and the imaginary Saraswati) is also called Tribeni, *i.e.*, three braids of hair.—*Friend of India*, p. 1168.

shoot amongst them though he shot at random the time before; so the boat fell astern, and perceiving that we resolved not to stay at that place, we saw them no more.

October 15.—Being Sunday we dined ashore at Pulia, under a great shady tree near Santapore,[1] where all our Saltpetre boats are ordered to stop, till we can have assurance from Permesuradass that we shall receive and send it on our Sloops, after entrys were made of it. At this place Mr. Wood, who has charge of ye said Petre Boats, came to me. I gave him a letter to Mr. Beard to be sent by an express to Hugly, and so proceeded on our Voyage.

October 16.—Early in ye morning we passed by a Village called Sinadghur, and by 5 o'clock this afternoon we got as far as Rewee, a small village belonging to Wooderay, a Jemadar, that owns all the country on that side of the water, almost as far as over against Hugly. It is reported by ye country people that he pays more than twenty Lack of Rupees per ann. to ye King, rent for what he possesses—and that about 2 years since he presented above a lack of rupees to ye Mogull and his favourites, to divert his intention of hunting and hawking in his country, for fear of his tenants being ruined and plundered by the Emperor's lawless and unruly followers. This is a fine pleasant situation, full of great shady trees, most of them Tamarins, well stored with peacocks and spotted Deer like our fallow-deer: we saw 2 of them near the River side at our first landing.

October 17.—This day about noon we got to a Village called Andoolee.

October 18.—We dined at Ballee,[2] and after a few hours repose, rowed on, and tracked all night.

[1] Now Santipur, lat. 23° 14′ N.; long. 88° 30′ E.

[2] There is a Balee on the Jellinghee River, in about lat. 23° 49′ N., long. 88° 30′ E.; about E. b. N., 10 miles from Plassey, on the Bhaghirathi.

October 19.—We rested about 5 o'clock at Uddumpoor, and lay till 12 at night, then rose and tracked all night as before. About 10 last night Mr. Johnson parted from us towards Meerdaudpoor with intention to go from thence to Cassumbazaar, and come with Mr. Charnock,[1] Mr. Catchpoole, and Mr. Rickman, to meet me at Meerdaudpoor aforesaid.

[1] Mr. Job Charnock was chief at Cossimbazar in 1680. Bruce first mentions him in 1680 (*Annals*, vol. ii, p. 450). Near the northern wall of St. John's Church, once the "cathedral" of Calcutta, is a rather oriental-looking open mausoleum, of black stone and brick, containing four upright memorial slabs within, viz., to Charnock; to his youngest daughter, Mrs. White, 1701; to Wm. Hamilton, surgeon, 1717; and to Mrs. Martha Eyles, 1743. There were twenty-eight inscribed slabs, lying nearly horizontally round the exterior in 1843.

According to Bruce (*Annals*, vol. ii, p. 450), Job Charnock's merits were handsomely acknowledged by the Court of Directors in 1680. In a letter to the Government of Fort St. George, the Court wrote that they "would rather dismiss the whole of their other Agents than that Mr. Charnock should not be the Chief of Cossimbuzar".

The slab is of an exceedingly black stone, and the inscription is in relief:

"D. O. M.
Jobus Charnock, Armig.
Anglus, et nup.: in hoc
Regno Bengalensi
Dignissim' Angloru'
Agens
Mortalitatis suæ exuvias
Sub hoc Marmore deposuit ut
In spe beatæ resurrectionis ad
Christi Judicis adventum
Obdormirent.
Qui postquam in solo non
Suo perigrinatus esset diu,
Reversus est domum suæ æter-
-nitatis decimo diei Januarii
1692."

"Pariter jacet
Maria Jobi primogenita
Caroli Fyre, Anglorum
hicce Præfecti

October 20.—About 10 o'clock this morning I arrived at Colcapoor, and at 6 this night Mr. Charnock, Mr. Catchpoole,[1] Mr. Barker, Mr. Rickman, Mr. Threder, and Mr. Harding came to me here. I consulted with those of Councell with me, and those of Cassumbazar, who all unanimously agreed that my speedy going to Decca and application to ye Nabob and Ministers there, was ye only probable means now left for redress of ye Honble Compys grievances, and recovery of their priviledges for ye future.

October 21.—We lay at Colcapoor, and about 5 o'clock this afternoon set forward towards Decca, and lay this night near ye mouth of ye Ganges, where ye River being broad and rapid with great shoals, we durst not adventure into it until daylight.

October 22.—We rowed down ye great river the most part of this morning. We went within a point of ye South, either East or West. In ye Afternoon we went much Northerly. Half an hour before Sunset we fastened our Budgeroes to ye shore to provide and dress our suppers. We reposed ourselves here till 12 at night, and then rowed on till morning.

October 23.—We continued rowing all day in ye most

Conjux carissima
Quæ obiit 19 die Feb'
A.D. 1696-7."

The adjoining slab, to the memory of the youngest daughter, who died in her first confinement, aged 21, is peculiar for a very well-worded (Latin) epitaph, in the course of which the writer drifted into Greek, describing her as "Τοῦ Μακαρίτου Jobi Charnoch, Filia Natu minima", etc.

Orme, who evidently is not partial to Charnock, speaks of him (vol. ii, p. 12, *Military Trans. in Hindostan*) as having been imprisoned and scourged by the Nabob; perhaps it was in the sense of having been *chastened*, that the writer of the above considered him *blessed*.

[1] Mr. Catchpoole continued in service, and was ultimately President of the Settlement on the Island of Pulo Condore, where he was murdered in a general mutiny of the Malay soldiers, March 2, 1705.—Bruce. *Annals of E. I. C.*, vol. iii, p. 606.

pleasant country that ever I saw in all my life. A little before Sunset we fastened to ye shore and reposed till mid-night, and then rowed on till morning.

October 24.—This morning we saw 4 men making a fire on ye shoar, and supposing it to be ye burning of a dead man, caused ye Budgeroe to row to ye shoar; found it to be a man half burnt up. Our course this morning has been from ye South-East to ye North-East. About 1 o'clock this afternoon we got to the Choukey of Jattrapoor from whence we were presently dismissed. At 5 this afternoon we went ashoar to dress our own and boatman's suppers, and reposed till 12 at night, and then rowed on till morning.

October 25.—By 12 o'clock this day we got to Chan Caun's garden, in sight of Decca, where we were met by ye Second and Third (ye First being lately dead) of ye Dutch Factory, in their Budgero; and by Mr. Pounset, Mr. Eyre, and Mr. Cross of our Factory. Mr. Hervy, their late chief, lying so weak after a fit of the Gout and Feaver that he was not able to come with them. We left this Garden between 3 and 4 o'clock, and got to the Factory at Decca by 6 in ye afternoon, this being the 11th day since we left Hugly.

October 26.—In the morning Mr. Pouncet and James Price, my Vakeel, went to acquaint Ray Nundelall, ye Nabob's Vizier, of my arrival last night, and desire that he would appoint a time when I might wait on him, and the Nabob; ye said Ray very courteously told them I might take my own time, so to-morrow in ye afternoon was agreed upon betwixt them. This afternoon a young Prince of ye Blood, Meerza Mazuffer Chan, whose mother and Orang Zeb (ye great Mogull's) were both sisters, and sisters to ye present Nabob Shah (Estah) Chan[1] of this place, came to give me a visit, and was entertained by me above two hours.

October 27.—An hour before Sunset I went to visit Ray Nundelall, ye Nabob's Duan, who gave me a most courteous

[1] Shaista Khan, Nawab.

reception, rising up and taking of me by ye hands, and ye like at my departure, which I am informed is a greater favour than he has ever shown to any Franke. He desired me not to visit the Nabob this night, but to stay till he sat in publick Durbar for a more fortunate hour, designing to show me ye greater respect, which would be on ye 29th in ye morning; to which I agreed with due acknowledgement for his respect and kindness to me.

October 29.—At 9 in ye morning I went to wait on ye Navab, who after ½ hour's attendance, sent officers to bring me into his presence, being sat under a large canopy of State made of crimson velvet richly embroidered with gold and silver, and deep gold and silver fringes, supported by 4 Bamboos plated over with gold. I was directed by ye Emir Tusuck, or Master of the Ceremonies, to sit over against ye Nabob, nearer ye canopy than his Duan or any other person. At my first entrance ye Nabob was very busy in despatching and vesting divers principal officers sent with all possible diligence with recruits for their army lately overthrown in Asham and Sillet, two large plentiful countries 8 days' journey distant from this City, which are all lost, except one little place held out and kept by 40 or 50 persons only; ye rest of ye Souldiers being all fled out of ye country. Amongst ye rest I saw a Portuguese who was to be Commander of 5 or 600 of his countrymen. This hurry of business continued ¾ of an hour. When it was done ye Navob called my Vekeel, James Price, and bid him tell me I was welcome into this Country; continuing his discourse and demanding questions of me for ¾ of an hour longer, as, How long it was since I left England? How many months of that time I had been at Sea; and, How many in this Country? Whether I was one of ye Company?—which he seemed very inquisitive to know, having twice asked about it,—and to be informed of my quality; highly commending ye Company for sending a person of credit to be their Agent. Whether I had been in Turkey and Arabia (as he was informed), and could speak those languages, in which I was immediately examined by a person placed (I suppose on purpose) near to me, to know whether yᵉ report was true or false; and for a good space after he was my Interpreter, with which they were pleased; and admired to hear from a Frenge (as they call us). He enquired also whether I had seen yᵉ Emperour of Germany? and in what part of yᵉ World yᵉ kingdom of Spain stood, and whether all yᵉ Dollars brought into those parts came out of this Country, with many more such like questions. When he gave me leave to depart (according to their customs) he rose up, and going away, stood still, and told me I should go first out of his Presence, which (I'm informed) is greater kindness than he has ever shewn before to any Christian.

This Afternoon I went to visit Haggi Sophee Chan, yᵉ King's Duan, where I was entertained with Coffee, and stayed about half an hour. He bade me welcome, and afterwards spoke to me himself in Arabick, demanding how I liked this country, and whether I thought it as good as my own, etc. This being yᵉ first visit, when matter of business is never mentioned, I took my leave and returned to yᵉ English Factory, which is at least 3 miles distant from this, or yᵉ Navob's Durbar, a most inconvenient situation for doing of business, being far from yᵉ Courts of Justice, Custom house, and yᵉ water side; for taking up or sending away of goods.

October 30.—I was visited by yᵉ three Dutch Factors in yᵉ Afternoon, viz., Jⁿᵒ Bonstoe, Alexander Urwin, and Jacob Smith, who supped with me. (31st) I sent to acquaint Haggi Sophee Chan, yᵉ King's Duan, I intended (God Willing) to wait on him in yᵉ afternoon. This day, at dinner time, yᵉ Navob sent his Chief Cook and Butler with 8 or 10 Dishes of meat (with a Compliment) from his own table, which I am told is intended for an extraordinary favour. Yᵉ Dishes and Covers were Silver and very Large.

A little before sunset I went to Haggi Sophee Chaun, who, after some few questions and discourse with me in Arabick promised me to renew my Phurwanna for ye free passing and receiving all our goods for ye remainder of ye Seaven Months formerly granted, and then invited me to stay and sup with him.

November 1.—This morning I sent all ye presents to ye Navob's Durbar by James Price, and followed them myself at 9 o'clock. When I was almost got thither, a Peon, sent by James Price, told me ye Presents were returning to ye Factory, Ray Nundelall being sick, without whose presence and assistance it would not be convenient to give them. So I went to Mierza Muzaffer's house, where I was this day invited by him to dinner, and returned to ye Factory again in ye Evening.

This Afternoon I sent James Price to mind Haggi Sophee Chan of ye Phurwanna which he promised, who assured him order should be given for the doing of it.

November 2.—I sent James Price to visit Ray Nundelall; before noon he brought me word ye Ray returned my salute, was much recovered of his distemper, and that I should be welcome to him to-morrow morning.

This afternoon I sent James Price again to press Haggi Sophee Chan for ye Phurwanna, who was put off till to-morrow. This night I received letters from Mr. Beard of ye 25th Ultimo, at Hugly, advising that on ye 20th detto, Ramgivan, our Vekeel there, was sent for by Permesuradass, Bulchund's Servant, who immediately clap't him in prison. Y^e^ same day [he] was brought forth and Slippered; the next day was beat on ye Soles of his feet, ye third day Chawbuct,[1] and ye 4th drub'd till he could not speak, and all to force a writing in our names to pay Rupees 50,000 for custome of ye Silver brought out this year. He hath given a writing for R^s^ 5,000,

[1] *Chawbuck't*, "flogged"; *chābūk*, "a whip".

yᵉ last message Mr. Brand recᵈ from Permesuradass was that if he sent not presently Rupees 50,000, he would beat Ramgivan to Death, so that unless speedy relief can be obtained at Decca, they must either pay Custome or yᵉ Ships cannot go home this year.

November 3.—I went in yᵉ morning early to inform Ray Nundelall of the injuries done us by Permesuradass, but he, being much indisposed at present, desired to be excused from yᵉ trouble of business. I acquainted his Chief Writer with all our concerns, who promised this afternoon to tell them all to his Master.

November 6.—Ray Nundelall, being so well recovered as to be able to go to yᵉ Durbar, I sent yᵉ presents this morning, and gave them to the Nabob, who told me he did not like so much cloth, but desired rather some rarities, which would be more acceptable to him. When yᵉ Durbar was over, I sent to know of yᵉ Ray when he would please to accept of his presents, who ordered them to be brought on yᵉ 9 Instant.

November 7.—I waited on Suffede Mahmud, Haggi Sophee Chan's Son, yᵉ Fousdar of Hugly (who would not admit me in yᵉ morning). After half an hour's discourse, with various entreaties and fair promises, he assured me he would use his best endeavors to procure yᵉ Perwanna so long promised, and accordingly went with me to his Father, where, after a long discourse betwixt them, yᵉ Fousdar told me his Father was out of power, a new Duan being on his way thither, and, therefore, he could not grant my Perwanna. I told him Permesuradass was not out of Power to do us mischief, and his authority was derived from him. At last, with many arguments and earnest entreatys to know the reason of this unkindness and breach of promise, he told me Bulchund had advised him and yᵉ Nabob, "if he trusted us and gave us time for payment of our custome in 7 Months", we would leave yᵉ Country and pay none at all.

To which I replied I would give security of Merchants in ye place (which was accepted), and to-morrow morning promised to bring them to him.

This night I was invited to sup with Coda Bux Chan, the Bucksi of this place, who is first Cousin to Orang Zeb, and marryed to this Nabob's daughter. He has assured me he will speak to ye Nabob for my dispatch, and favour me on all occasions what lyes in his power.

November 8.—I sent for some Gentu Merchants to be our security to ye Duan for our payment of Custome after 7 Months, if a Phirman be not procured in that time, which being a day, as also to-morrow, wherein their religion obliges them not to do any business, they desired to be excused till ye 10th instant, so [we] were forced to have patience till that time.

November 9.—I sent James Price to waite on Ray Nundelall, and to know when he would accept of his present, whose answer was, "When he would have it we should have notice to send it to him," and when he would permit me to discourse with him in private, for which last this afternoon was appointed: whilst my Vekeel was talking with ye Ray, a letter was brought him from Mr. Pitt.

This afternoon I waited upon Ray Nundelall, and discourst him fully concerning Bulchund and his Servant Permesuradass's villainous practices at Hugly. I told him, likewise, of my desire to have him procure me a new Phyrmaund, to which he returned this short reply, "Your business shall be done for you"; and appointed two of his Servants to treat with me concerning ye Price and Wording of ye Phirman.

November 10.—In ye morning I sent letters to Hugly and James Price to treat with y^e^ Nabob's Servants concerning y^e^ Phirman. All they did was to discourse of y^e^ former (?), and consider y^e^ best methods to go about it, and so parted. I treated with y^e^ Merchant for being our security, whose demands were so unreasonable, requiring an obligation for payment of $1\frac{1}{2}$ per cent., *per Mensem,* interest for so much money, and so long time as he should stand engaged for us, we were forced to send for another Merchant, whose demands were likewise very great. In fine, y^e necessity of closing with him, if we intended to take off y^e present stop on our trade, made me agree to ye lending of him Rupees 20,000 *gratis* for his security, and becoming obliged to him for payment of whatsoever sum ye Custome shall come to more than ye said Rupees 20,000, if a Phirman to clear us of Custome be not procured in 7 months' time.

November 11.—I send James Price, with our new security, to Haggi Sophee Chan for our promised Perwanna, and also to treat with ye Ray's servants about ye Phirman. This evening ye King's Duan granted an order (by his Son's mediation) to give us a Perwanna for passing our goods 7 Months from this day, upon our Entrys, without Payment of Custome.

November 13.—News being brought me last night that ye Nabob (in ye 82nd year of his age) had a Son born this day, and 'twas expected I should make him a visit, and give him a present, I went this morning to ye Durbar, and gave him 13 Gold Mohurs and 21 Rupees, which he accepted so kindly that I took ye opportunity to request his Perwanna in conformity to that granted by ye King's Duan; and that another Perwanna might also be sent, with two of his own Servants, to recover all the monies unduly and forcibly taken from us by Permesuradass at Hugly, which was likewise granted.

November 14.—I visited ye King's Duan and his Son, Sopheede Mahmood; ye Duan promised me a Perwanna for recovery of ye money paid to Permesuradass upon sight of that promised by ye Nabob.

November 15.—I sent away two Perwannahs to Cassumbazar to be shewne to Bulchund, and their Copy's to Hugly.

This afternoon Ray Nundelall sends me word ye Nabob would not give me his Perwanna on Permesuradass, to return yᵉ money forced from us, till I procured such a Perwanna first from yᵉ Duan. I sent James Price immediately to Haggi Sophee Chan, desiring him to grant me yᵉ said Perwanna, but as James was in yᵉ house, going to him, he was suddenly taken with such a violent fit of an Ague that he was forced to return home; *re infectâ.*

November 16.—The King's Duan not being to be spoken with at all in the morning, I wrote a letter to his Son, desiring him earnestly to solicit his Father for the said Perwanna, and facilitate his granting of it to me in the afternoon, when I intended to wait upon him; advising him, likewise, that Permesuradass was forcing Rupees 5,000 more from us at this time, and stopped the proceedings of our goods to Ballasore, giving all the furtherance he could to yᵉ Interlopers.

In the Afternoon I went to yᵉ Duan, where, after a long discourse with himself and his Son, he told me he durst not give his Perwanna for yᵉ recovery of any money that is once appropriated to yᵉ King; showing divers letters written him to that purpose by yᵉ King's order. Upon which I took leave, and went immediately to complain of this proceeding to Ray Nundelall, who told me yᵉ Duan did not deal so justly with me as he ought to do, and advised me to apply myself to yᵉ Nabob yᵉ next Durbar day (which is on yᵉ 18ᵗʰ Instant), and he would know yᵉ Nabob's pleasure in this business.

November 17.—This morning I received a letter of yᵉ 8ᵗʰ instant from Mʳ· Beard, advising me he was in so great fear yᵉ Ships would not go away this year, it had put him upon making yᵉ best terms he could with Permesuradass, to whom he had promised 4,000 Rupees, as a gratuity for Bulchund, to let our goods pass to and fro without molestation.

November 18.—I went to yᵉ Nabob, who, after a little pause, enquired of me how many ships Mʳ· Pitt had brought into this Country, to which I replied four or five. He then asked whether he belonged to ye Comp^y.^ I answered in ye negative. He further demanded whether it were usuall in this country for private Merchants to trade in these parts that were not of ye Company? I replyed No; at which an eminent person stood up and assured ye Nabob the contrary, and all I could say would not disswade from that opinion.

At last ye Nabob came to this resolution. If he were a private merchant, as I assured him, he should pay Custome, and give good security before he left ye Country that he would do no prejudice to any of ye Mogull's Subjects after his departure. As to my request for a Phirman "not to pay Custom" to be procured of the King, he told me it would be chargeable and tedious for him to get it, but he would willingly give me his letter in my favour, which, with a Servant of my own, would be sooner got on more reasonable terms.

That he would write to Bulchund to displace Permesuradass, and give me his Perwanna to cause all the money forcibly taken from us, to be paid into our Security's hands, till such time as it be known whether we can procure a Phirmaund from ye King in 7 Months. So we parted.

November 20.—I sent James Price to ye Nabob's Durbar, but Ray Nundelall's Uncle being dead, he could not be there; so no business was done for us.

This morning I agreed with a Merchant here to give him Dollers, to the value of 20,000 Rupees, to receive ye like sum in Hugly, Mr. Beard complaining he had not money in ye Factory to buy Victualls, and could not get any at interest. In ye Afternoon I went to ye King's Duan to know upon what terms we should send our money to ye Mint, who, after some difficulty, granted his Perwanna for ye payment of only 3½ per Cent. Custome, and that to be paid only at one of the two Mints of Decca or Rajemall, and in no other place, which has cut off Bulchund's pretences not only of Rup^s^ 50,000 for the treasure imported this year, but also ye arrears of ye 3 former years, which is very materiall if we should not have ye good fortune to obtain a Phirman to excuse our payment of Custome in 7 Months' time. Besides, I hope, upon showing this command to ye Nabob, he will grant his Perwanna to recover all the money forced from us by Permesuradass, at Hugly.

November 21.—I wrote to Mr. Beard, and sent him a bill of Exchange for 20,000 Rupees and a copy of ye Duan's Perwanna, that Gold and Silver are to pay but 3½ per Cent. Custome, at ye Mint only, and not to be demanded in any other place. This afternoon I sent copies of ye said Purwanna to Rajemall and Cassumbazar.

November 22.—This being ye Nabob's Birthday, when all persons that expect favour or respect at Court give him presents, 'twas thought convenient that I should do the like; and, being on ye way, a Peon was sent to me by Ray Nundelalls chief writer, desiring I would not go this day to visit ye Nabob, for reasons he did not then think fit to acquaint me. I sent James Price to speak with him, and returned to ye Factory.

November 23.—I went and presented ye Nabob with 21 Gold Mohurs and 50 rupees, and so returned; matters of business being not to be discourst on this day.

November 28.—This morning early news was brought me the new Duan was yesterday at Jattrapoor, one dayes journey from this place.

November 29.—This morning, notice being given me that ye new Duan was at a Garden near ye City, I went to give him a visit, and was respectfully and kindly received by him, with assurance of doing us justice upon all occasions, and furthering our trade what lyes in his power. In ye Afternoon I took my leave of Haggi Sophee Chan, ye late Duan.

November 30.—This being ye Moors feast of "little Byram", no business could be acted by me this day, so I sent James to ye Durbar to enquire whether Mr. Pitt and Capt. Dorrell were sent for hither, as Ray Nundelall had promised him yesterday. His answer was, that this being Byram, no business could be done till to-morrow morning.

December 1.—I sent James Price to Ray Nundelall's. This morning a Gentoo sent by Bulchund, Governour of Hugly and Cassumbazar, made complaint to me that Mr. Charnock did shamefully, to ye great scandall of our Nation, keep a Gentoo woman of his kindred, which he has had these 19 years; and that, if I would not cause him to turn her away, he would lament of it to the Nabob, which, to avoid further scandall to our Nation, with fair words I prevailed with ye poor fellow to be pacified for ye present.

I was further informed, by this and divers other persons, that when Mr. Charnock lived at Pattana, upon complaint made to ye Nabob that he kept a Gentoo's Wife (her husband being still living, or but lately dead), who was run away from her husband and stolen all his money and jewels to a great value, the said Nabob sent 12 Souldiers to seize Mr. Charnock; but he escaping (or bribing ye men) they took his Vekeel and kept him 2 months in prison, ye Souldiers lying all this while at ye Factory gate, till Mr. Charnock compounded the business for Rupees 3000 in money, 5 Pieces of Broad Cloth, and some sword-blades. Such troubles as these he has had divers times at Cassumbazar, as I am credibly informed; and whenever she or Mr. Charnock dyes, ye pretence will certainly lye heavy on ye Company.

This morning early I received a Genll from Hugly acknowledging ye receipt of ye Nabob's and Duan's Perwannas sent them for ye free passing of our goods, which Permesuradass would not obey, saying he was Bulchund's servant, and expected orders from him. I went immediately to Ray Nundelall and acquainted him how little ye Nabob's Perwannahs were regarded, who advised me to complain of it to ye Nabob, which I did, and received this answer: "That he would order Bulchund to suffer all our goods to pass freely for ye remainder of our 7 months, and to turn Permesuradass out of his service, and would order a tipstaff or messenger to go and see it put in execution"; so took leave and returned to ye Factory.

December 3.—I went to visit ye new Duan, after I had shewen all our old Phirmans and Perwannas in our favor for a free trade without payment of Custome, he told me these were once of value, but now signified nothing. The King having ordered that if Custome were not paid at Surrat it should be paid here, excepting ye respite given us of 7 months for ye procuring ye King's Phirman to the contrary. At present he confirmed the Nabob's (Haggi Sophi Chan's) Perwanna by his Chop, that no custome should be demanded for money, save at ye Mint, and that but 3½ per Cent.

December 4.—James Price brought me draughts of 3 Perwannas granted to me ye 2nd Instant. First, that Permesuradass should be turned out of his place; that ye money forced from us should be restored, and that our goods should pass free without interruption or payment of Custome; and that an Assole[1] or messenger, together with Bulchund's Vekeel, should be sent to see this perwanna put in execution. These 3 heads were put into one Perwanna.

The next Perwanna was directed to Bulchund and the Fousdar of Hugly, to seize M$^{r.}$ Pitts and Captain Dorrell, and bring them hither to give security not to use any hostility towards the Mogull's Subjects when they are gone out of port. If they come and appear, their voyages will be lost this year. If they abscond and go away, they will be esteemed villaines, and not permitted to come again hereafter.

The 3rd Perwanna granted was for relief of grievances at Maulda. These 3 Perwannas are promised to be signed to-morrow, w^{ch}, in such case, I will make a round proffer for a Phirman, and so make all the speed I can to see ye Company's

[1] *Assole* must mean *Yasāwal*, Turk. and Pers., a state messenger, a "Silver Stick".

affairs dispatched at Cassumbazar and Hugly for ye ship's departure.

December 5.—This being Tuesday, and no Durbar day, nothing could be done for obtaining the Perwanna.

December 6.—Received letters from M^r. Charnock, etc., returning the Nabob's and Haggi Sophi Chan's Perwanna, which Bulchund refused to obey.

December 7.—I went to ye present Duan's to desire a Perwanna for the free passing of our goods, who told me plainly we must pay Custome at Surrat or in this place, and would admit of no reasons to the contrary. When I alledged such practices would force us out of the Country, his answer was: "We might go when we pleased." I made complaint of this immediately to Ray Nundelall (in presence of Bulchund's 2 Vekeels), who advised me to acquaint ye Nabob with what I told him. I went directly to ye Nabob's Durbar, where I met with ye new Duan. I complained of Bulchund; the New Duan took his part, insisting upon our paying Custome. The Nabob [?] used divers arguments in our favor, and offering himself to be my security to ye Value of Rupees 50,000. At last he commanded ye Duan to give us his Perwanna for ye free passing of our goods the remainder of ye 7 months, saying he would write to ye King for a Phirman to free us from this Pretence, as we have been formerly. If M^r. Charnock had taken the paines to present these 2 Perwannas himself, 'tis probable, with a small present, he might have prevailed with Bulchund to have our goods freed. However, at this rate any pitifull Vekeel is as good to act ye Company's Service as himself.

December 8.—I wrote to Hugly and Cassumbazar by M^r. Johnson who went from Decca this evening.

December 9.—M^r. Beard, supposing me on my return to Hugly, wrote M^r. Pownset a letter dated ye 1st Instant advising that ye ship *Society* was safely arrived at Ballasore. She set sail out of ye Downes ye 30th May, and not touching at any place by ye way, lost 17 men of ye Scurvy.

This morning I went to ye new Duan, Emir Seid Amud, who made great difficulty to grant his Perwanna for ye free passage of our goods. At last he refused mine, and promised to accept of Gullab Ray's security, that if we did not produce ye King's Phirman in 6 months' time (1 month being expired), we should pay Custome immediately, according to our Talica[1] or entrys, and upon these terms he promised to give us his Perwanna in ye afternoon. So I left James Price and Goolab Ray to wait ye Duan's leisure, and get ye business effected, which they did, and brought ye said King's Duan's Perwanna accordingly.

December 10.—The Nabob sealed and signed all ye Perwannas, formerly [formally] granted, for ye free passing of our goods—turning out of Permesuradass,—and recovery of our money forced from us, appointing an Assole[2] or messenger, together with Bulchund's chief Vekeel, to carry ye Perwannas and see them put in execution. The Perwannas, for bringing up Pitts and Capt. Dorrell, were likewise sealed, and promised to be all given us to-morrow morning.

December 11.—This morning I sent away two Expresses; one to Cassumbazar, with ye King's Duan's Originall Perwanna and its copy, to be presented to Bulchund for taking off and freeing ye stop on our trade. The other Express was with ye copy of ye said Perwanna to M^r. Beard at Hugly.

December 12.—This morning I dispatched away two expresses more, with copys of ye Nabob's perwannas, "to Displace Permesuradass, and recover our money of him"; one to Cassumbazar, and ye other to Hugly, to give those Factories notice what I had done, that they might be sending their goods to ye ships at Ballasore.

As soon as these letters were sent away, I went immediately to Ray Nundelall's to have had ye Seapy, or Nabob's

[1] *Tálíkah* or *Ta'líka*, an inventory or invoice.

[2] See note, p. 53.

horseman, consigned to me, with order to see ye Perwanna put in execution; but, having thought better of it, ye Ray desired me to have patience till to-morrow morning. He would then present me to ye Nabob, whose commands to ye Seapy and Bulchund's Vekeel would be more powerfull and advantagious to me than his own. I took his advice and returned to the factory; after ye Ray had assured me at his house, he would prevail with ye Nabob to write to ye King for a Phirman for us, and our business should be all done according to my desire.

December 13.—I went to ye Rays in ye morning, and with him to ye Nabob's Durbar, where ye Nabob gave me ye Perwanna before mentioned, and called the Seapy and Bulchunds Vekeel commanding to see ye Perwanna carefully observed in every particular. I then desired him to undertake the procuring a Phirman of the King, who replied: "It was better for me to do it myself by a Vekeel which would cost less money, and be sooner got than if he sent for it", with which answer I took my leave of him.

This afternoon I took my leave of Coda Buxe and Mierza Maduffa, Orang Zeb's Sister's Sons, in return of the severall Visits they had made. The former is married to the Nabob's daughter, and ye latter to the Nabob's Eldest Son's daughter. Next I took my leave of ye new Duan, and, lastly, of ye Dutch Factory from whom I received divers Civillitys.

At night I received letters from Cassumbazar advising Bulchund's stomach was come down, promising Mr. Charnock to let our goods pass, and to be very good and friendly to me for ye future, his Vekeel here having advised him, ye Nabob was exceeding angry he disobeyed his Perwanna.

December 14.—This morning early I went to Ray Nundelall's with a letter from my self (in case his indisposition should prevent my speaking to him) to mind him of his promise to me divers times, "That the Nabob would write to ye King for our Phirman"; but, coming to his house, we found ye Ray's distemper so much increased upon him, that he commanded his Servants not to suffer him to be disturbed with any business. So I was forced to return home, and sent James Price to ye Ray's Deputy at ye Durbar, for our Maulda Perwanna, and for the copy of that Perwanna to bring up Mr. Pitts and Captn Dorrell.

In ye Afternoon I went again to visit ye Ray, and take my leave of him, who gave me great hopes of prevailing with ye Nabob to procure us a Phirman, assuring me, twice, he would (God willing) take the very first opportunity to acquaint the Nabob with my request, and to inform James Price with the Nabob's resolution, and for that purpose advised me to leave James Price behind me to take the Nabob's answer in case my occasions would not permit me to stay for it myself. I replied ye time was so far spent that ye Honble Compys occasions would not permit of my longer stay at this place, but I would leave my Vekeel and his present with Mr. Pownset at ye English Factory, and so took my leave of him. This night I received a letter from Mr. Hill at Rajemaul advising ye Droga [Darogah] of ye Mint would not obey a Copy, but required at least a sight of ye Originall, and that confirmed by ye new Duan, which shall be sent him to-morrow morning before I go from hence.

December 15.—This morning early I wrote my instructions to be left with James Price, and dispatched an express to Maulda and Rajemaul. To ye former I sent a Perwanna for the relief of all their grievances, and turning out of Jameshire Beigh, who had given them ye occasion of their laments. To Rajemaul I sent ye old Duan, Haggi Sophi Chan's, Perwanna, Chopt both by the Nabob and new Duan, for its confirmation, "That Custome of Money is to be demanded only at ye Mint, and there to pay but 3½ per cent."

After I had made these dispatches, I waited ye coming of Goolob Ray, who brought me a copy of the memorial sent unto ye Nabob by Ray Nundelall (his indisposition not suffering him to go in person), under ye Ray's own hand, of my proposals for a Phirman, not doubting of giving me a satisfactory account of ye Nabob's undertaking my business in two or three days at farthest. I gave Goolob Ray an obligation under hand and seal, to accept his bills on me as far as Rupees 6000, for Procuring a Phirman, and then took my leave of Decca and went aboard ye Budgero for Cassumbazar and Hugly, resolving (God willing) to make ye best of my way thither, having been 51 days since my first arrival at Decca.

Just as I was taking my leave of Decca City, I was visited by Mirza Maduffa (the King and he being Sisters' Children), who, seeing a glass of wine and water filled for me to drink to him, he desired to take it out of my hand, and drank part of it to me, telling and desiring that this might be a token betwixt us, as ye wine and water, although just now two distinct body's, were now inseparably united, and soe should our friendship be as long as we lived.

December 17.—About 12 o'clock at noon we got to ye Chowkee, where, after we had shown our Dustick and given our present, we were dismissed immediately.

December 18.—Bulchund's Vekeel not coming up with us according to ye Nabob's command, and his own promise, I sent away the Assole, with a Peon and ye Nabob's Perwanna, to be accompanied from thence by Mr. Charnock, etc., to Bulchund, and to require another Perwanna of him in conformity to ye Nabob's, to displace Permesuradass at Hugly before my arrival there.

December 20.—I received letters by a Cossid from Mr. Johnson and Mr. Catchpole, dated ye 18th Instant, from Muxoodavad,[1] Bulchund's residence, advising they had visited Bulchund, and got him to clear Mrs. Meverell's Budgero for Pattana, and Mr. Anthony's 4 boats for Rajemaull, who had lain there 2 days without hopes of being released. They likewise cleared 4 boats with ye Company's

[1] Now Moorshedabad.

treasure for Rajemaull, which [had] lain stopt before I passed by for Decca, and those boats which lay laden at Cassumbazar (which Bulchund declared he kept there so long, because no Englishman came to him for their proceeding to Hugly).

They prevailed also with Bulchund to write me a complementall obliging letter, assuring me 'twas Mr. Charnock's fault that ever he stopped our goods, or detained them so long; and that for the future he was resolved to court my Friendship to which I returned him an answer by the same express.

December 21.—One of Bulchund's Vekeels overtook me this morning, and after customary salutations, passed on to inform his Master of my coming.

December 23.—I wrote to Mr. Beard advising him of my arrivall this evening at Mierdaudpoor, and intention to visit Bulchund on my way to Cassumbazar.

December 25.—In ye night we lay a mile short of Muxoodavad. In ye afternoon I met with Mr. Johnson and Mr. Catchpool, coming to pay their respects.

December 26.—In ye morning I went to give Bulchund a visit according to his invitation, who rose up and embraced me when I came near him, enquired of my health and bid me welcome to Muxoodavad, assuring me of all ye friendship and kindness that lay in his power. And for my better satisfaction commanded divers Perwannas to be written directed to his several officers, requiring them not to give ye least trouble or disturbance to our trade, but to let all things pass with ye same freedom that ever it did. Bulchund told me he heard I had given Goolob Ray security for our payment of custom upon our entrys, in case a Phirman should not be procured; that he was now going himself to Decca; that he would take and bear my obligation, and be my security himself; and would not fail to get an order from the Nabob to settle a Mint at Hugly or at Cassumbazar, as I had formerly desired him. In recompence of which he requested me to remit one part of my Perwanna touching ye displacement of

Permesuradass, who, being thoroughly acquainted with his business, could not be turned out but to ye King's and his great prejudice. That he would command Permesuradass not to meddle in our affairs, that he should return all ye money forcibly taken from us, and would send another "Drogä" or Customer,[1] on purpose to take our Tallicas, and send them to him to be forwarded to Decca. These fair promises, together with ye consideration of ye time for lading and departure of our Ships was far spent, and if he should be cross and stubborn (as he is naturally inclined to be) ye lading of our Ships and their departure might be much delayed, I consented to his proposal; and as soon as I had despatched all my business here, and got ye Perwannas (which was not till after six at night), I went to Cassumbazar, where I arrived a little after 8 o'clock.[2]

December 27.—This day I spent wholly in seeing and examining what store of silk, &c., was now in ye Company's Godowns, where I found the quantity of more than 500 bales of silk not yet prized,[3] which I immediately caused to be brought out and prized whilst I was there, which was accordingly done, M^r. Charnock promising 500 great bales, and 200 chests of silk should follow me in 10 or 15 days at farthest. And this night about 9 o'clock we took boat for Hugly.

December 29.—We lay to at Nuddia, on ye Point of Cassumbazar Island, and after our boatmen had eaten, rowed all night, and ye next morning by 2 o'clock were past Sanctapoor.[4]

December 30.—By 8 o'clock in ye morning we got to Trippany, and dined at Hugly, where (God be praised) we arrived all in good health.

December 31.—Permesuradass ye Customar[5] sent 2 of his chief servants, desiring me to permit him to give me a visit, which I appointed him in ye afternoon. Being come, he ex-

[1] *I.e.*, Darogah or Customs official.

[2] About eight miles below Murshidabad.

[3] Priced.

[4] Santipore, about 81 miles.

[5] Comptroller of Customs.

pressed his great joy to see me so well returned from Decca, passing many compliments upon me. That he was a servant and did no more than his Master commanded him. That now, being otherwise directed, he would show me all ye respect and kindness imaginable, suffering all goods whatever to pass, that I desired him.

January 1683.

January 6.—This day I received a letter from Charles Crosse 3,[1] at Decca, whom I had ordered James Price my Vekeel to acquaint with all the Honble. Compy's. concerns, and to give me a constant advice of all his proceedings. Mr. Pownset having divers times declared if I left James Price behind me, he would give him 500 chawbuks[2] the next day after I was gone out of towne, and slipper him out of doors, so [I] was forced to order Mr. Pownset not to concern himself with James Price during his stay at Decca.

Mr. Crosse advises me that James Price had made an agreement with ye Nabob to procure us a Phirmaund from ye king; that whilst they were discoursing ye business, ye Nabob received a letter from Bulchund, advising him that ye Custome of this year's goods already registered (besides great quantities not yet come down) amounted to 75,000 Rupees, on which the Nabob demanded 3 years custome at that rate for procuring a Phirmaund; but this discourse passing over, ye Nabob began to talk of writing to ye king, and that he should be at great charge at court (to get our said Phirmaund) in Durbar expences, &c., which James finding no other remedy promised to pay; so ye Nabob ordered Goolob Ray our security to give him a Bill of Exchange payable to his Vekeel in Delly[3] for Rupees 10,000 for Court Expences. Besides which sum Cossadass ye Chief Secretary—Mutsuddies, and ye Nabob's

[1] *I.e.*, third in rank.
[2] Lashes.
[3] Delhi.

Chief Eunuch will be paid all their money before hand, as also ye Nabob Rupees 5000, and ye rest when ye Phirmaun arrives. Though this be chargeable, 't will be done effectually and money better given than ever was in this country.

For discharge of these for-going sums James Price has drawn his bill on me for Rupees 20,000, payable to Goolob Ray's Vekeel at 13 dayes sight, which I have accepted. Mr. Crosse further advises ye Nabob's letter to ye King is drawn out foul—when it is fair written, and James Price has seen it despatched, he intends to make all the haste he can to Hugly.

So that my going to Decca has in ye first place got 7 months time for procuring a Phirmaund; 2ndly, taken off wholly ye Pretence of 5 per cent. Custome, on all Treasûre imported this and ye 3 preceeding years, besides 1½ per cent of what [was] usually paid, at ye mint for some years past; 3rdly, procured ye general stop to be taken off all our trade, our Goods now passing as freely as ever they did formerly; 4ly, got a command to turn Permesuradass out of his place, and restore ye money forced from us; 5ly, and last, prevailed with ye Nabob to undertake ye procuring a Phirmaund for us from ye King, of which there being no great doubt to be made, I shall make this short estimate of the advantage we shall certainly receive from it this year:

6 per Cent. saved for Custome on £200,000 Treasure Imported is	£13,000
The Custome of £200,000 in Goods outwards at 3½ per Cent. is	7,000
In all	£20,000

besides great expence, not to be abused in ye valuing of our goods. If God gives me life to get this Phirmaund into my possession, ye Honble. Compy. shall never more be much troubled with Interlopers. I bless God for this great success I have had, beyond all men's expectations, in my voyage to Decca.

The two Perwannas procured to fetch up Mr. Pitt and Capt. Dorrell were compounded with Bulchund for a good sum of money, and 5 per cent paid by them for all their goods; with other great presents: though these men are so shameless as to deny it.

January 10.—This day I received letters from James Price at Decca, advising ye Nabob's letter to ye King for procuring our Phirmaun, was sent away to him some dayes since. Letters from Cassumbazar advised Thomas Bromly dyed ye 29 Ultimo.

January 21.—Ye Fousdar sent me word ye Perwannas taken out by me at Decca for ye seizing of Pitt and Dorrell were now come to his hands, and he was sending orders to seize them if possible at Ballasore. I shall not fail to give ye Nabob notice of this treachery in his officers.

January 22.—About 5 at night I went aboard ye *Madapollam* Sloop with the Honble. Compy's letters, Invoices, and Bills of lading for dispatch of ye *Defence* at Ballasore, which I resolved to go myself and see performed with more expedition. We got no further than over against ye Dutch factory by 8 oclock, when I received a letter from Mr. Beard, advising, I was no sooner put off from ye shore but Permesuradass began to play his old villainous tricks with us again; forcing away ye Master and all ye men of ye boat whereon ye remainder of our Decca fine cloth, and 28 Bales of Silk were laden, to complete ye *Defence's* Tonnage; so that Mr. Beard was constrained, with ye help of 6 or 7 Souldiers, whom I sent immediately to his assistance, to take all ye goods out of that boat and lade them in another Vessell, which I brought away with me.

January 23.—This day having little or no wind, we got no farther than Barnagur, though we rowed with our boat all ye way.

January 24.—By break of day we weighed anchor, and being a meer calm could get no farther than ye Ebb would carry us, which was not altogether so far as Jan Pardo. By ye way I met with y^e *Arrival* Sloop, who I hastened to bring away ye goods for y^e *Society.* Y^e tide being spent, and not a breath of wind stirring, were forced to come to an anchor, and lye here all night.

January 25.—This morning by daylight we weighed anchor and with so little wind that we could but just stem ye tide. About 11 oclock we met with y^e *Good-hope*, at an anchor in ye Narrows,[1] without Hugly River, and ordered him upon ye first of ye flood to weigh, and make all ye haste he could to Hugly, to take in what goods he found ready for y^e *Society.*

About 9 oclock this night we found y^e *Thomas* at an anchor, we hailed her, and commanded her Master to come aboard. But he not having a boat, we were forced to anchor by her, and send our boat for her Master, whom I ordered to take 28 Bales of Silk and some Bales of Cloth out of ye boat we brought from Hugly, and to bring them to me aboard of y^e *Defence,* with all possible diligence. We anchored this night on ye head of ye Diamond Sand.

January 26.—This morning early we weighed anchor with the tide of Ebb, but having little wind got no further than the Point of Kegaria Island, where, meeting with ye tide of Flood, were forced to drop our anchor. About 5 this afternoon y^e *Ganges* came up to us, whom I ordered to take in 588 Bags of Salt Petre that lay ready for him in two boats within Kejeria River, and make ye best of his way to deliver it aboard of y^e *Society;* and then to return to Hugly. This evening at 7 oclock we weighed, but growing calme, and being to pass through ye narrow sands of Point Ingelee, we chopt to an anchor and lay there all night.

[1] An old chart or eye-sketch, in the *English Pilot* of 1734, indicates that "the portion of the Hoogly river, now called Hoogly Bight, was then named the 'Narrows'." Above Hoogly Point the river was specially considered the River of Hoogly, in contradistinction to the Roopnarain, or "Old Ganges", up which, at a far earlier period, Chinese Junks may have traded to Tumlook.

January 27.—Before day this morning the Gale freshening in our favour we weighed, and after it was day, finding we could stem the tide, made ye best of our way towards ye Braces. About 1 oclock, as soon as we had got clear of them, both wind and tide failing of us, we dropped our anchor.

At 3 oclock ye Sea Breeze coming in, we weighed and made all sail till 9 at night, when ye wind proved contrary, so anchored again and lay till morning.

January 28.—At daylight we discovered the *Defence* and y^e *Society* about 2 leagues to windward of us. We made sail, and after 4 hours turning of it, we found we rather lost than gained, so came to an anchor. About 2 in the afternoon we weighed anchor with a small breeze. About 4 y^e *Defence* and *Society's* Pinnaces came and carried us aboard y^e *Defence*.

January 29.—The *Madapollam* Sloop delivered her lading, and was immediately dispatched away to Hugly.

January 30.—The *Thomas* arrived with ye 28 Bales of Silk taken out of the *Purga*, and was dispatched for Hugly ye same night.

January 31.—This day was taken up in comparing ye Boatswaines severall receipts with ye Bills of Lading, and at night I gave y^e *Defence* her Dispatches.

February 1683.

February 1.—This morning y^e *Defence* set sail for England, and by 3 oclock in ye afternoon was out of sight. Soon after y^e *Defence* was under sail I went aboard of y^e *Society*, and lay there this night.

February 2.—I came ashore in Capt. Gayer's Pinnace to ye Bankshall, about 7 miles from Ballasore, where I was met by M^r. Byam, and ye rest of our Factory, together with all of our Merchants that trade with us. The Fousdar, or Governor, sent his brother to salute and bid me welcome to these parts. Whilst I staid dinner at this place Capt. Dorrell and Mr. Pitt passed by in their Sloop, with 4 Guns and about 30 English Seamen to work ye vessel and row in ye *Crown's* pinnace, to tow ye sloop. About half an hour after 4 oclock I went in my Palenkeen for Ballasore, and arrived there about half an hour after 6.

February 5.—This morning ye *Crown* and ye other two Interlopers sailed out of ye road: together with Mr. Littleton in a sloop for Fort St. George.

February 10.—Mr. Tyler arrived in a vessel of his own, laden with Elephants from Tenassarim, advising me he met ye *Defence* ye 5th instant in 18 degrees with a fair and fresh gale of wind, steering due South.

February 26.—This night ye *Society* set sail out of Ballasore Road.

February 28.—I went to see Nilligree Hills. I went out of Ballasore at 7 in the morning, and got to ye tent, which was pitched by a Tank in a grove of trees, at ye foot of ye hill beyond ye town, by half an hour after 10.

March 1683.

March 1.—I went out a hunting with ye Ragea, who was attended with two or three hundred men, armed with bows and arrows, swords and targets, or javelins. I went with them beating ye woods till 11 o'clock: at which time finding ye Sun very hot, and having had no other sport than one hare killed with an arrow by a black fellow in ye woods, I returned to my tent. But Mr. Frenchfeild, and Capt. Raynes, resolving to see all that could be shown them, continued with ye Ragea in ye field. In ye afternoon they found a great Tiger, one of ye black men shot a barbed arrow into his Buttock. Mr. Frenchfeild and Capt. Raynes alighted off their horses and advanced towards the thicket where ye Tiger lay. The people making a great noise, ye Tiger flew out upon Mr. Frenchfeild, and he shot him with a brace of Bullets into ye breast: at which he made a great noise, and returned again to his den. The Black Men seeing of him wounded fell upon him, but the Tiger had so much strength as to kill 2 men, and wound a third before he died. At night ye Ragea sent me the Tiger.

March 2.—In ye morning early I went up the Nilligree Hill, where I had ye view of a most pleasant fruitful valley between ye hills, which they told me was 18 Course[1] long. Y^e^ Hills afford store of Iron, which furnishes all this country. Y^e^ Valleys are full of Rice, Gram, and divers sorts of Pulse. This evening I returned again to ye factory at Ballasore.

March 5.—I went to ye Bankshall to mark out and appoint a Plat of ground to build a Godown for ye Honble Company's Salt Petre, and having chosen the most convenient place, returned immediately to ye Factory.

March 7.—This afternoon about 4 o'clock I left Ballasore, and went down to ye Bankshall to embark on ye Sloop *Lilly* for Hugly.

March 8.—About 1 oclock this morning I went on board y^e^ *Lilly*, and sailed over ye Bar, where we had but 4½ foot water, a few inches more than our Vessel drew. Y^e^ wind being contrary we were forced to lie at an anchor all this day till 10 oclock at night, when we weighed and made sail with little wind.

March 9.—All ye last night and this day it continued calm till towards night, when we had a small breeze which brought us over ye first Sand or Brace, where we anchored all night.

March 11.—This morning before Sun rising we weighed anchor with a small breeze in our favour, and being got up with Kegaria,[2] we went on shore in our Boats, and landed at an old ruined Castle with mud walls and thatched. We saw one small Iron Gun mounted and an Iron Pateraro. Y^e^ Island

[1] Coss. [2] Kedgeree.

is exceeding pleasant and fruitfull, having great store of wild Hogs, Deer, wild Buffalos, and Tigers.

This afternoon we stood off towards Sagor, and anchored between Cock Island and ye Oyster River.

March 12.—We went in our Budgeros to see ye Pagodas at Sagor, and returned to ye Oyster River, where we got as many Oysters as we desired, and lay at ye mouth of ye River.

March 13.—We weighed and came to Jan Pardo.

March 14.—We weighed and got to Hugly by 7 oclock at night, all in good health, God be praised for it: This night we had an extraordinary great Storm: New moon to-morrow.

March 17.—Wrote ye Chief and Councell in Dacca in answer to theirs of the 2nd, 12th, and 22nd Ultimo. "That ye Nabob's goods were brought up and delivered to his correspondent, Ubbeeb Allah; and that they (being acquainted with ye customs of ye place) knew best what to do about trusting Mirza Maduffer"; so left it wholly to them.

March 18.—Ordered Matthias Harrison to deliver over ye charge of ye Sloop *Lilly* to Edward Tench. He and several others having petitioned ye same of me and ye Councell, to find out ye Channels, Sands, and dangerous places in this River.

March 19.—Dispatched said Sloop for ye purpose before mentioned.

March 20.—Received a Genll.[1] from Maulda advising, "That since they had sent all their goods for this year, a Merchant hath brought in 6 Bales [of] Silk [on] account [of] his last year's investment: who desires to know whether we will take it for the ensuing year, or return it him back again, and he will bring in his remains in White Cloath."

[1] A general service letter.

ATT A CONSULTATION.

March 21 (*Wednesday*).—Having received advice from Metchlep^m.[1] of ye arrivall of 3 Interlopers upon ye Coast, and suddenly designed for ye Bay, we took into serious consideration ye most speedy and effectuall way to frustrate their designs in these parts. Whereupon I produced a Paper where in all ye considerable Merchants of Ballasore have obliged themselves not to trade with Interlopers, under ye penalty of 1000 Rupees amerce, and told them that in a few dayes I did not doubt to procure ye like from the Merchants in Hugly. This being thought ye most effectuall way to prevent their trading in these parts, it was ordered, that advice be given to ye severall Chiefs in ye Bay, of ye said Interlopers designe hither; and that they endeavor to procure the like obligation of ye Merchants belonging to their Factories.

Boberay and Oberam, both M^r. Pitts's servants, and able men, desired to be entertained in ye Honble Comp^y's service, which was referred to a farther consideration.

Manuridas, sent by Bulchund as Droga of our Customes, complained for want of money for his expences, according to ye country custome. It was ordered he be given an allowance, and referred to me to agree with him ye cheapest way I can, and most for ye Honble Company's advantage.

20 chests of treasure having been sent up to ye Mint at Rajamaul to be coyned, it was ordered, "That out of ye Product thereof, 30,000 Rupees be sent to Dacca, 60,000 Rupees to Maulda, and ye remainder be sent down to Hugly, to forward ye next year's investment.

Ordered, 10,000 Rupees of ye 60,000 R^s. for Maulda, as a forestalment, be sent to M^r. Job Charnock, &c., to discharge a debt owing by Maulda Factory to Deepchund at Cassumbazar.

Ordered That some money (as little as may be) be given

[1] Metchlepatnam, *hodie* Masulipatam.

out to y^{e} Maulda Weavers, as y^{e} best expedient to recover in y^{e} old remains.

Having received advice from M$^{r.}$ Samuel Anthony, that one of their merchants had brought in 6 Bales of Tanna Silk on account of last years remains, and also another Merchant had brought in 140 Pieces of Cossaes; it was Ordered That y^{e} silk be taken at price current, and y^{e} 140 Pieces of Cossaes be bought, if cheap.

M$^{r.}$ Jonathan Prickman, 2nd of Maulda, being dead, it was Ordered, That M$^{r.}$ Samuel Anthony succeed as 2nd, and M$^{r.}$ Robert Hedges (who was appointed by y^{e} Honble Comp^{y} 3rd of Dacca, but that place being supplyed by M$^{r.}$ Crosse, before his arrival in y^{e} Country) be third; and M$^{r.}$ William Jolland to be there an assistant upon all occasions.

The Coynage at Rajamaul being at present in y^{e} charge of M$^{r.}$ Hill only, and that in case of mortallity it would be of Absolute Necessity to have one allways with him as an assistant, it was Ordered That James Smith be sent up thither accordingly.

Ordered 6 chests of Treasure be sent from hence to Ballasore to forward y^{e} next years investment; and that M$^{r.}$ J$^{n.}$ Byam be ordered to forward y^{e} building a Salt Petre Godown, at y^{e} Sandy Point near our Bankshall; and to provide Twenty Anchors and 6 cables.

M$^{rs.}$ Deborah Richards, y^{e} Relict of M$^{r.}$ John Richards, not getting y^{e} Stock she brought out with her, coyned, time enough, by reason of our troubles to return to England y^{e} last Shipping: did therefore make it her earnest request to be permitted to remain in y^{e} Honble Comp$^{y's}$ Factory at Ballasore till y^{e} next Shipping; intending then to return home, which was accordingly granted.

Wrote to Cassumbazar advising them that we had ordered M$^{r.}$ Hill to send them down 10,000 Rupees to discharge the debt owing to Deepchund, and ordered them to send M$^{r.}$ Hill their beam and scales, to supply his present occasions.

Wrote to Mr. Hill to deliver, out of ye product of ye 20 chests of Treasure sent him to be coyned, as followeth. 50,000 Rupees to Englesavad,[1] 10,000 Rupees to Mr. Charnóck, and 30,000 Rupees to Dacca, and to send ye remainder hither.

Wrote to Dacca advising that Mr. Hill was ordered to send them 30,000 Rupees towards ye years investment.

March 23.—Wrote to Maulda, advising that Mr. Hill had orders to send them 50,000 Rupees Siccas, and ordered them to give out money to their Weavers and Merchants for this years investment, and that we had ordered 10,000 rupees to be sent to Mr. Job Charnock, &c., to discharge their debt owing by their Factory to Deepchund at Cassumbazar. And we did farther enorder them, not to deliver out money to any person whatsoever till he has first obliged himselfe (under a Penalty) not to trade with any Interlopers.

March 24.—Dispeeded letters to Mr. Byam advising that in a few days we intended to send them 6 chests of treasure by the *Ganges*. We recommended to their care the speedy building of ye Godown for Salt Petre near ye Seaside, and ordered them to provide 20 anchors and 6 cables for ye Honble Compy's Sloops.

Received a Genll. from Patana dated ye 5th Instant, with their Diary for ye last month, advising "That they had endeavoured, by using all possible means, the getting out ye Nabob's & Duan's Phirwannas, retarded by ye Nabob's Officers, who made use of all wayes and means to draw money into their Master's Coffers; granting orders one day, and disannulling them the next.

Att a Consultation.

March 26.—Ordered yt Boberay, Mr. Pitt's Servant, be entertained in ye Honble Compy's Service at 15 Rupees per mensem, as an expedient to frustrate ye Interloper's designes in these parts.

[1] Angrezábád, the English factory at Malda.—[Y.]

Being informed that Manurudas, being Bolchund's servant, would not take a monthly allowance, I declared it before ye Councell; and it was agreed that he be given money as occasion should fall out, to supply his expences, and keep him from disturbing our affairs.

Information was this day brought in against Mr. Francis Ellis by most of ye Merchants in Hugly; that he, the said Ellis, had taken bribes to ye value of 4000 rupees or thereabouts, to pass ye Honble Comp^y's^ goods [in] ye Shipping. Part of which being positively proved against him, & 900 Rupees being confessed by him, it was there upon ordered that he be dismissed ye Honble Comp^y's^ Service, and that Mr. Joseph Dodd forthwith take ye charge of ye Warehouse upon him, & that the money which shall be proved to be taken by ye said Ellis to pass ye Honble Comp^y's^ goods, shall be endeavored to be secured for ye Honble Comp^y's^ use.

Post Meridiem.—Mr. Samuel Hervy, Chief of Maulda, (at present in Dacca) having been divers times ordered to repair to his Chief-ship, where there is great want of him, for ye better management ye Honble Comp^y's^ Affairs; and no signe yet appearing of his departure; It was agreed that orders should be drawn up, and sent to ye said Hervy, requiring him to repair to Maulda within 6 days after ye arrival of the letter with him at Dacca, and in default thereof to be forthwith dismissed ye Honble Comp^y's^ Service.

(Signed) W^M.^ HEDGES — W^M.^ JOHNSON
JOHN BEARD — RICH. FRENCHFEILD.
JOSEPH DODD

The Petition of Rogoodee, Weaver, to Wm. Hedges, Agent,

SHOWETH. That on ye Agent's going to Ballasore, ye said Agent gave orders to take Mulmulls[1] of ye Merchants on account of Agreement made for ye Company, upon which

[1] Mulmull (*malmal*) is muslin.—[Y.]

Mr. Ellis called your Petitioner and told him, that if he would give him any thing, he would take your Petitioner's Mulmulls; upon which your Petitioner promised him 100 Rupees, and brought Ramnarrain, one of ye Merchants, for his security. After which ye said Ellis told your Petitioner that he would not take 500 Pieces of your Petitioner's Mulmulls unless your Petitioner gave him 200 Rup., which your Petitioner (being Poor) could not doe. For which reason Mr. Ellis returned your Petitioner his Cloath again, though some of it was sorted by Mr. Ellis to be received: For Which your Petitioner desires you would be pleased to doe him justice.

The Petition of Wm. Hedges, Agent, from ye Hugly Merchants, viz.:—Muttrasaw, Rupsuliman, Rogoodee, Giachundsaw, Rogonaut, Horkissincotma, Ramchundparamanick, Ramnarrain, Mudducaun.

SHEWETH. That to have their goods taken for agreement made with ye Company, they have been forced to give Mr. Ellis, warehouse keeper, each of them, a Bribe, as per ye underwritten account, in mony and goods, appears: for which your Petitioners complain to you, desiring Justice:

Muttrasaw, 1,150 Rupees in mony and goods; Giachundsaw, 73 Rupees; Horkissincotma, 102 Rupees 8 Annas in mony and goods; Ramnarrain, for Mulmulls taken from him; Rupsuliman, Rogonaut, Ramchundparamanick, Mudducawn, Rogoodee, 4 Annas upon each piece, for 4,453 Pieces, amounts to 1,113 Rupees 4 Annas, for which he has taken out of one Chest of Dollars, delivered Rogonaut, 500 pieces of Eight on account.

Mr. Ellis acknowledged he was proffered ¼ Rupee per piece of cloth, and declared he was ready to take all ye money they would give him.

March 27.—Wrote Mr. Hervy at Dacca, advising him that we thought it good to give him a positive order to repair to his Chiefship at Maulda, within 6 days after ye receipt of ye letter at Dacca, to be on his way towards Maulda, clear of ye Factory and City of Dacca: and in default, to be forthwith dismissed ye Honble Company's Service.

Wrote to Mr. Pownsett, &ca., Ordering them to deliver Mr. Hervy his letter immediately upon receipt thereof, and to take notice of ye time when it comes to their hands.

ATT A CONSULTATION.

March 28.—Mr. Joseph Dodd being ordered up to this Place as one of ye Councell of Hugly, and there wanting one to supply his place as 2nd of Ballasore, It was thought fitt that M^r.^ Wm. Prickman be sent in his stead, and Mr. Robert Sherman be ordered thither to keep ye Honble Company's Books.

Ordered—15,000 Rupees to be sent to Cassumbazar from Rajamaul, to pay a debt owing to Deepchund, by ye Factory.

Ordered—6 chests of treasure to be sent to Ballasore, and that Mr. George Heron goe with them on y^e^ *Thomas*, and his charges up again overland be defrayed by ye Honble Company.

March 29.—Wrote to Pattana, advising them to be carefull of ye Quality, as well as ye Quantity, of goods en-ordered to provide against this year's shipping.

March 31.—We advised them at Ballasore of ye dismissing Mr. Francis Ellis ye Company's Service, and putting Mr. Joseph Dodd in his stead, and that M^r.^ Wm. Prickman is appointed to supply Mr. Dodd's place: and ordered Mr. Robert Sherman hither, to keep ye Hon. Comp. Books; and that instead of y^e^ *Ganges*, we had resolved on sending y^e^ *Thomas* with Six chests of Treasure.

April 1683.

ATT A CONSULTATION.

April 2.—Ordered y^t^ Muttrassaw be trusted with 6 chests of Treasure, and his Bills be taken on ye Merchants at Ballasore to ye value of 50,000 Rupees.

It being thought necessary for me to go to Cassumbazar, Mr. John Beard was appointed to act as Chief in my absence, and to follow such orders and directions as from time to time he shall receive from me and my Councell.

April 3.—Wrote to Balasore that we had sent them enclosed 2 bills of Exchange for 56,000 rupees: viz. One from Muttradas for 50,000 rupees, which is to be paid by severall Merchants of that place, who are to receive said money on goods to be provided this year: The other is on Kimchund for 6,000 Rupees, which is to be advanced, over and above, to ye aforesaid Merchants, a list of whose names, and what mony each of them was to receive, was likewise sent.

ATT A CONSULTATION.

April 4.—Mr. How being ordered to goe upon ye *Thomas* to Ballasore with Petre, to lye at ye Banksaul, declared he was not able to carry her over ye Barr, whereupon Mr. Scott was ordered to goe with him as his Pilott.

Having received 25,000 Rupees Siccas from Rajamaul, it was ordered that ye remainder of ye treasure in ye warehouse here, be sent up thither, in ye same Boates ye Rupees came downe in.

Wrote a dispatch for Mr. How and Mr. Scott, ordering them to depart hence with ye first opportunity.

ATT A CONSULTATION.

April 5.—Agreed with Chitturmullsaw and Muttradas, Merchants of this place, for 1,500 Bales of ye best Tissinda Sugar, each bale to weigh 2 Maunds 6½ Seers, Factory Weight, at 10 Rupees per Bale, and to be brought all in by ye 15th of 7ber next ensuing. Agreed likewise with ye afore said Chittermaul for 1,500 bales of Beerboa Sugar, each bale to contain 2 Maunds 6½ Seers, Factory weight, at 8 ru., per bale, to be brought all in, within ye above mentioned time.

This day M[r.] W[m.] Johnson and M[r.] W[m.] Rushworth departed hence towards Cassumbazar.

Wrote a Gen[ll.] to Ballasore, advising them we had sent 600 Baggs of Salt Petre to be ready against next shipping, and that they assist y[e] Master of y[e] Ship *Thomas* to turn said Ship into a Ketch: and that what mony shall be disbursed on that account they shall place to account current, Hugly.

Wrote a Gen[ll.] to y[e] President and Councell at Surratt.

ATT A CONSULTATION AT HUGLY.

April 7.—Having informed y[e] Councell that yesterday a certain number of Merchants came to me, and offered to undertake y[e] providing what goods we shall have occasion for this year, to be paid for when said goods were brought in, and at as cheap rates as if money were given out beforehand; It was resolved, "That the giving out of mony upon goods of any sort should be deferred at present, till my return from Cassumbazar, or farther consideration had upon y[e] same.

Y[e] Honorable Company having a Godown at y[e] water side, built of mud and straw, which hath been burnt several times, and one part of it or other always tumbling down in y[e] raine times, and y[e] repairing of y[e] same being a greater charge to y[e] Hon. Comp[y] than y[e] building a new one; It was Ordered (as well for y[e] security of y[e] Company's goods as y[e] saving of charges), That a new one be built of Brick.

Ordered—A Boat be built at Ballasore for y[e] Ketch *Arrival.*

April 10.—This afternoon, about 5 of y[e] clock, I went on board of y[e] Hon. Company's Budgero, for Cassumbazar, accompanied by M[r.] Joseph Dodd and M[r.] George Heron in another small Budgero of their owne, and 10 Ulocks[1]. for Souldiers, Cooks, Butlers, Servants, Peons, &c., and by 7 this evening we gott to ye English Garden together with M[r.] Beard and most of our Factory. Here I received letters

[1] *Ulák*, or *Holák*, vulgarly "*oolock*", a clumsy Ganges boat.—[Y.]

from Ballasore, advising that y[e] *W[m.] and Jn[o.]* [*William and John*], Capt. Read, Comãnder, an Interloper, had arrived in ye road bound for Hugly, they mett M[r.] Edw[d.] Littleton on ye coast, who dispatched them downe hither.

This night we gott up near Santapore.

April 11.—We lay at Bogatcher, a very pleasant and delightfull country: ye Gemidar [*i.e.*, the Zemindar] invited us ashore, and shewed us store of Deer, Peacocks, &c., but it was not our good fortune to get any of them.

April 12.—We got as high as Nuddia, in Cassumbazar River, by 8 o'clock in y[e] morning, and lay y[e] night at a place called Goalparra. The river from this place upwards towards Cassumbazar being full of shoals, our boatmen advised to lye still till morning: y[e] wind blowing hard at S.W.

April 13.— By 2 oclock in y[e] afternoon we got up to Ullumpore [Qu. Allumpore ?].

April 14.—By 1 oclock in y[e] afternoon we gott up to Maula, about 3 cosses short of Cassumbazar: from whence I went in a Palankeen by land, and arrived at y[e] Factory at Cassumbazar at 6 oclock in y[e] evening.

April 16 (*Naylor accused*).—I called a Consultation and accused M[r.] Naylour of trading with Interlopers, which being proved by three letters under his own hand, he was judged guilty by all present, his Person, Papers, and Goods ordered to be seized, to see whether we could find farther testimony against him, out of his owne books and writings.

April 17.—The Chief of y[e] Dutch and his wife, second, third, and fourth, gave me and my wife a Visitt, and according to y[e] usuall custome of these parts stayed and supped with us.

Upon search and examination of such Papers of Mr. Naylor's as we could find (the most material, together with his mony and goods, having been conveyed out of y[e] Factory (without M[r.] Charnock's knowledge, he pretends) some days before my arrival)—he had bought 6 Bales of Silk this year—I found that he, the said Mr. Naylor, had privately sent away from hence 4 Bales of Silk to Mr. Beard by Mr. Charnock's Dustick, for account of Mr. George Herron, Master of the Sloop *Goodhope* of which Mr. Beard never gave me the least intimation: nor did he acquaint me that Capt. Dorrell had informed him of Capt. Pitts's correspondence with Mr. Naylor, when I was at Dacca, till I showed him Mr. Naylor's letters; when Mr. Beard told me (in ye presence of Mr. Wm. Johnson) he was informed of Naylor's trading with Interlopers 3 months since, but never gave me ye least notice of it before.

Harding accused.—Upon information given me by most of ye Factory that James Harding, now entertained by Mr. Charnock as his Servant, had formerly been dismissed ye Hon. Compy's Service for Blasphemy and Athisticall tenetts, and that he was a person notoriously scandalous both in life and conversation (George Pitman, a Throwster, offering to depose that he saw Harding lye with Mr. Elliott's woman slave), I ordered him not to eat at ye Company's Table, and reproved Mr. Charnock for entertaining so vitious a person; to which he gave me ye hearing with little or no reply, resolving, I suppose, to satisfie me for ye present, and admit him again as soon as I leave ye Factory.

I was also informed of one Ununteram (ye same person who slippered ye Merchant who poisoned himselfe in ye time of Mr. Vincent, which cost ye Company a considerable amount of mony), being employed by Mr. Charnock in all ye Company's affaires; which, Mr. Charnock positively denying, I brought ye said Ununteram to confesse and affirme he had done all ye business of concernment in ye Factory ever since ye first month after Mr. Charnock's coming to be Chief. So little regard is to be given to what Mr. Charnock affirmes upon any occasion, as will more evidently appear in ye following relation.

Request being made on behalf of Mr. Naylor that he might

be admitted to walke and discourse with any in ye Factory, Mr. Heron obliging he should not goe without ye Gates, as soon as he had his liberty he went immediately to Mr. Charnock (then in ye Hall), desiring him earnestly to take notice of ye houre of his false imprisonment. I sent for Mr. Charnock to know whether Naylor had said any such words to him, which Mr. Charnock positively denied, with many asseverations, till I was forced to call Mr. Samuel Langley to affirme them to his face, and caused him to recollect his memory.

April 19.—Received letters from Dacca by way of Hugly, advising Mr. Hervy left Dacca ye 8th instant, and was upon his way towards Maulda.

This day Bolchund sent a kinsman of his to compliment me and bid me welcome to Cassumbazar, assuring me a kind reception if I thought good to come and see him.

April 20.—I called a Consultation to peruse Mr. Naylor's books and Papers. In his coppy book of letters began in January last, was found a letter to Mr. John Beard of ye 16th of January last, intimating he had written a Genll. to me, &ca., in Hugly, and enclosed divers letters which he, ye said Naylor, had received from Mr. Pitts, which made it appear he never traded with Interlopers; but Naylor being sent for and examined, he denied that ever he sent ye said letter, declaring he burnt it: nor did he ever send ye said letter to Mr. Beard, being purposely wrote to deceive and delude us.

Upon farther perusall of Mr. Naylor's books, we found he had lately bought several parcells of Silke of ye following dates:

1682.			RUP.	AN.
Xber 5th, paid Ramkissen Cupperay,		Acc'nt Silke	. 1326	5
8ber 11th, paid Kisnaram Perma	on	Acc'nt Silke	. 1212	5 . 5
Xber 15th, paid Cheramdut	on	Acc'nt Silke	. 1319	15
22nd, paid ditto	on	Acc'nt ditto	. 290	2
January 2, paid Kisnaram Perma	on	Acc'nt Silke	. 286	11½

Upon all which evidence John Naylor was dismissed ye Honble Company's Service, and Ordered, if he will not oblige to leave Cassumbazar and go to Hugly, and give security to goe into England by ye next shipping, all his goods and papers in our possession should be kept for ye Company's use and our indemnity.

This day was presented a Petition of Allen Catchpoole, John Threder, Samuel Langley, George Pitman, & George Stone, complaining of one James Harding, a most turbulent, violent-spirited fellow, in the following words, viz.:

SHEWETH. That in y^{e} Factory of Cassumbazar there is one James Harding, a person who was formerly dismist y^{e} Hon. Comp$^{y's}$ Service for Blasphemy and Athisticall tenetts, and since he hath been here, hath evidenced himself to be a person of a most unquiett turbulent spiritt, having all along been a great disturber of y^{e} Peace and Quiett of y^{e} Factory, and hath often bred differences amongst us: and for y^{e} future we can hope no better from a Person of his irreligious and scandalous principles; he having lately been taken in Fornication with a slave wench of John Elliott's, as is attested and ready to be deposed on oath by George Pittman, one of your petitioners, and divers other misdemeanors ye said James Harding hath committed. We do therefore humbly request your Wors^{pful}, &ca., to take ye Premises into consideration, and ease us of this inconveniency: and that this our Petition may be entered into your Dyary. And your Petition^{ers} shall pray, &ca.

ALLEN CATCHPOOLE GEORGE PITTMAN
JOHN THREDER GEORGE STONE.
SAM$^{L.}$ LANGLEY

April 21.—M$^{r.}$ Catchpoole's, &ca., Petition was taken into consideration, and after full examination, and hearing all parties, James Harding was found Guilty of all that was alledged in y^{e} Petition, and ordered forthwith to be Dismist ye Honble Company's Factory: but Intercession being made by Mr. Charnock for his continuance with him some time, to help him draw out and transcribe his account, liberty was given him, ye said Harding, to remain in ye Factory till ye 28th Instant.

April 22.—......Was Sunday.

April 23.—......I went to Muxadavad to visit Ray Bolchund, where I was received with all the respect that could possibly be shown me: and after awhile, taking me alone into a room, from Mr. Charnock and ye rest of ye company, Bolchund began to profess ye great respect and kindness he had allways for me; but that Mr. Charnock had been so unjust and so unworthy in all his dealings with ye people of ye country, that he had not forbore calling him to Justice, and giving him trouble, but for my sake; and in expectation that I would come and doe them Justice myselfe, declaring farther that till Mr. Charnock was turned out of ye Honble Company's Service their business would never be managed soe much to their advantage as otherwise it would: Assuring me that he knew Charnock to be a great Theife, not only to the Merchants and other natives of the country, but to his Masters also: his constant practice being to exact 2 Rupees on ye hundred from ye Weavers for pricing their Taffaties; and to sell ye Company's goods: and buy light money, 5, 6 and 7 per cent. worse than current, which these poor fellows, rather than lose their present employment and livelihood, are forced to accept; which at last must of necessity redound to ye Company's prejudice: and if for such faults as these, upon ye testimony of more than 100 Witnesses, I should not now dismiss him ye Compy's Service, I must leave their affaires here in a most distracted condition; and thank myselfe for all miscarriages that may chance to happen for ye future.

To all which I returned Ray Bolchund my humble thanks; letting him know Mr. Charnock was an old servant of ye

Company, who had hitherto served to their good content; and without clear proof of his wronging ye Company he could not be displaced; but if all he said appeared to be true, he should see I came hither to manifest my fidelity to my Honble. Masters in ye best manner I was able, without favour or affection to any man. With which he seemed satisfied: and so I took my leave and parted from him.

Returning home this evening to Cassumbazar, we were informed a great part of ye Towne was burnt, with divers houses in our Factory, which coming out of ye towne we found to be true: most of ye houses towards Muxadavad to our Factory were quite destroyed. In ye Factory were burnt all ye Stables, Kitchen, Buttery, Throwster's rooms, with 5 Mills, besides divers other little thatched houses; and had not great diligence been used by Mr. Samuel Langley, ye Silke and Taffaty warehouses had been burnt, ye Fire having twice caught hold of ye Window, which was happily quenched by him. What is burnt will be at least 2000 Rupees damage to ye Company.

April 24.—This afternoon an Inventory was ordered to be taken of all Mr. Naylor's goods, in his chamber, and in his chests; which upon examination were found to be only a little old trumpery, excepting one chest of Flint-Ware and another of China Ware: all he had of any value, together with his money, having been conveyed away 2 or 3 days before my arrivall at Cassumbazar. Mr. Charnock pretending 'twas all done without his knowledge, whereas ye least Bundle of another man's goods cannot be carried out of ye Factory without examination.

April 25.—We had a Consultation: Mr. Naylor entered into Bond of 1000 Rupees to depart ye Service of Cassumbazar in 6 dayes; to go to Hugly; there to reside, and not to return to Cassumbazar without licence first granted to him by ye Agent and Councell at Hugly.

Upon examination of ye Company's Books, and consideration of ye great remains standing out in ye Weavers' hands, it was Ordered—That no more Imprest money, or Dadney, should be given out to y^{e} Weavers; but y^{e} agreement should be made with a select number of y^{e} ablest merchants, to be bound for each other, in case of Mortallity, for all our Taffaties, &c., as y^{e} best expedient to prevent such bad debts in future.

This day I received letters from Englesavad advising me of M$^{r.}$ Samuel Anthony's death on y^{e} 23rd Instant, after 3 or 4 days sickness of a Feavour, occasioned by a Fistula in Ano. God Almighty prepare us all for our latter ends.

April 26.—In y^{e} morning I wrote letters to Hugly and Englesavad, and in y^{e} afternoon returned a visitt to y^{e} Chief of y^{e} Dutch Factory, who received and entertained us with great kindness and respect.

April 27.—This morning M$^{r.}$ William Prickman and his Wife arrived from Hugly. They came to carry away all their things, and to returne in a few dayes to Hugly, and thence to Ballasore, where he is ordered to be Second of a Factory.

April 28.—This day a great number of Silk Merchants and Weavers made their complaints against M$^{r.}$ Threder and M$^{r.}$ Barker; that they, the said Threder and Barker, tooke from them 4 or 5 tolas upon a Seer, over weight, on all their Silk brought into y^{e} Warehouse, besides one or two of y^{e} best Skeyns of Silk that was weighed, in every draught; which, amounting to a very considerable summe of Mony, they demanded satisfaction: Threder and Barker positively denying ye overweight, ye Merchants proved it by their books, but ye skeyne out of every draught was confest, and claimed as their due, having been always the custom. Proofs of overweight taken against them were as followeth:

		SEERS.	
Maniram Podar brought into ye Warehouse, viz. Maunds	29	23	
Product when weighed off . . .	27	9	
Lost	2	14	
Poncho Barrick brought into ye Warehouse in 9ber bund:[1] Maunds	88	11	
Produced	84	7	
Lost	4	4	
In March bund: brought in . . Maunds	98	9	5
Produced	91	27	
Lost	6	22	5
In April bund: brought in 2 Parcells of . Maunds	88	6	44
Produced	82	37	
Lost	5	9	44
	6	22	5
	4	4	
Lost in all by one man . Maunds	15	35	49

The like losses in proportion were proffered to be proved by Ramchurne Podar, Benderabun Podar,[2] and Chamoobishwas, who produced their severall books for evidence.

May 1683.

Att a Consultation.

May 4.—Mr. John Threder and Mr. Richard Barker being conscious to themselves (as I conceive) of their owne guilt, and fearing they should be dismist ye Honble Company's employment, before any business begun, desired to be removed from this to some other Factory, pretending they

[1] Obscure; but "November *bund*", "March *bund*", etc., probably means "according to abstract for November", etc.—Y.

[2] *Poddār* is a weighman, a cash-keeper.—Y.

could not live with any content where there were so many feuds and animosities, as at this place, amongst ye Honble Company's Servants; which request of theirs was taken into consideration, & Ordered, that they should be removed, according to their respective degrees and stations, as occasion offers.

Mr. Allen Catchpoole,[1] for ye reasons aforesaid, desired also to be removed, which was granted, and leave given him to goe with me to Maulda, and from thence to Hugly.

May 6.—The Cazze of Muxadavad and Cassumbazar sent a kinsman of his with a present of fruite.

This morning Mr. Naylor and Mr. Elliott went to Hugly. In ye afternoon there hap'ned another great fire, which destroyed a great number of houses at Cassumbazar.

I saw ye Taffaties and Atlasses[2] in ye warehouse, and gave directions concerning their severall colours and stripes, ordering Mr. Charnock to use his best endeavours to encrease their quantity; ye Honble Company writing very earnestly for y^m^ this year; which I fear he will not be able to perform, by reason of ye great prejudice ye Weavers generally have received against him by taking 2 per cent. of them to price their goods favorably; and paying of them with light money as aforesaid, since his being Chief of Cassumbazar; If these Weavers should prove obstinate and not work for him, nor any of ye able merchants deal with him, as they assured me they would not, ye Company will be exceedingly prejudiced by Mr. Charnock's ill management of their business this year.

In Mr. Charnock's Custody I saw divers paternes of good pieces of Prunella and other sorts of Silkes, as Black, Blew,

[1] Catchpoole, many years later, was President of the English Factory at Chusan, and, when that was broken up, Chief of a settlement established on the Island of Pulo Condore, where he was massacred, with other Englishmen, by their Macassar guard (1705).—Y.

[2] Satins.

Yellow, and Green Taffaties, most of them made by an English Weaver, who lived not to make a whole piece of Silke, but left ye evident testimony behind him that excellent good Silkes, and consequently as great quantities as can be desired, may be provided and sent home from this country: as well as of raw Silke, to what number of bales ye Hon. Comp^y^ shall think fit to order; if ye chief of this place will use his diligence. I conceive, if 3 or 4 Master Weavers, and as many able Dyers, were sent out with 5 or 6 Boyes apiece to be their Apprentices, ye trade of this place might be improved, to ye Company's great advantage; or at least if ye said Master Weavers and Dyers were but obliged for one or two years to instruct ye Natives.

May 9.—About 5 o'clock this afternoon I departed from Cassumbazar, with designe (God Willing) to visitt ye factory at Englesavad; and lay this night about halfe way to Muxadavad.

May 10.—This morning early we arrived in Muxadavad, and understanding that Ray Nundeloll was brought thither very sick, I gave him a Visitt; who exprest much joy to see me, and desiring me to give him something that I thought might be good for his distemper. I gave him a small Vyall of Balme of Gilead, for which he was exceedingly thankfull, and desiring James Price to take a dose of it, in ye Ganges water, which he did in his presence. The ceremony used by these Gentu's in their sicknesse is very strange; they bring ye sick person (as they did this Ray Nundeloll) to ye brinke of ye River Ganges, on a Cott, under a small Tent; 2 men were constantly employed in holding and moistening his hands with water, a 3rd man dropt water, and stroaked it on his breast; and a 4th did ye like on his belly. I left him in weake condition, spitting great gobbetts of bloud.

In ye afternoon I visited Bolchund, by whom I was courteously entertained.

This evening I left Muxadavad, and just as I passed by

Ray Nundeloll's Tent, I saw him lye halfe way in yᵉ Water, and that very moment he died. Order was immediately given to make preparation for his being burnt, and about 2 houres after we saw a great fire at Muxadavad, which we concluded to be his burning.

May 11.—We lay near yᵉ mouth of yᵉ Great River.

This night I despatched away James Price to Dacca, with divers Persian letters to yᵉ Nabob; to Abdell Suma, yᵉ Nabob's Duan; to Cassidas, Ray Nundeloll's "Peisdust";[1] to Emir Pussick, yᵉ Nabob's Master of yᵉ Ceremonies; to Boremull; to Codabux Chawn; to Mierza Mazuffer; to Gollobray;[2] & to Permanun, &c.

May 12.—About 6 in yᵉ morning we got into yᵉ great River, and by 9 we entered yᵉ River that leads to Maulda; and on yᵉ way discoursing with Mʳ· Catchpoole, he told me that once every 2 or 3 yeares Mʳ· Charnock was wont to pare away yᵉ inside of yᵉ Salt Petre Warehouse at Patana, and to Mʳ· Catchpoole's certain knowledge, one year Mʳ· Charnock sold 700 Maunds, which proved so good earth that it produced 500 maunds of Salt Petre.

This night we lay at Buglagotte, a place where Shaw Susa [*i.e.*, Shujā'] fought a great battle with his brother, yᵉ present Emperour Aureng Zeeb.[3]

May 13.—In yᵉ afternoon we arrived (God be Praised) in safety at yᵉ Hon. Comp. Factory at Englesavad.

May 14.—In yᵉ morning Mr. Hervy arrived at Englesavad.[4]

May 15.—We had a Consultation, wherein were read all yᵉ Hon. Comp. letters per yᵉ *Prudent Mary*, who arrived in

[1] *Pesh-dast* (Pers.), "an assistant"; properly, "surpassing, excelling".—Y.

[2] *I.e.*, Gúláb Ráí.

[3] Probably in 1659 (see *Elliot's Historians*, vii, 250). Aurangzīb was not present.—Y.

[4] See *note* at p. 71.

Ballasore y^{e} 20th ult^{mo}, and confirmed M$^{r.}$ Harvy in his Chiefship of Englesavad. Mr. Sam$^{l.}$ Anthony, 2nd of this Factory, being lately dead, my Nephew, Rob$^{t.}$ Hedges, was appointed 2nd in his place, and ordered to supply y^{e} place of 3rd also, till further directions from y^{e} Councell at Hugly.

This day I examined y^{e} remains in y^{e} Weavers' hands, which, when y^{e} *Society* went away, was 43,000 rup. and upwards; of which above 10,000 rup. are brought in, and [I] have hopes ye greatest part of ye debt will be recovered. However, for all good respects it was ordered that no more money for goods should be given out to any Weaver who had not paid for his "Remains"; and able Merchants taken in their places, who proffered themselves to deal with us for all our Investment: and their names were entered accordingly for that purpose.

May 16.—I went to see ye famous Ruins of a great Citty and Pallace of Gowre:[1] 'tis about 12 miles distant from ye English Factory towards Cassumbazar. We sett out at 5 oclock in ye morning, and gott to ye place by a quarter past 8. We spent 3½ hours in seeing ye ruines, especially of ye Pallace, which has been (as appears by ye gates of it yet standing), in my judgement, considerably bigger and more beautifull than the Grand Seignor's Seraglio at Constantinople, or any other Pallace that I have seen in Europe.

The Building was chiefly of Brick; the arches of the Gates and many other places were of black marble, and other black hard stones to supply ye want of it, which is exceeding rare and difficult to procure in this kingdome, there being not so much as one stone so big as a man's fist to be seen in this country nearer than Rajamaul. At 12 o'clock we repaired

[1] Gour. For its present state see *Gaur*, by J. H. Ravenshaw, B.C.S., 1878; and General Cunningham, in *Archæol. Survey*, vol. xv, pp. 39-76.—Y.

to a garden within a mile of the Ruins, where we reposed ourselves and Servants till 5 at night, and then returned to ye Factory, extremely well satisfied with our diversion. We were in all, besides myselfe and wife, Mr. Saml. Hervy, Mr. Joseph Dodd, Mr. Wm. Johnson, my Nephew, Robert Hedges, Mr. Wm. Rushworth, and Mr. Wm. Jolland.

May 17.—Between 9 and 10 oclock at night I left ye Factory of Englesavad, and proceeded towards Hugly, having been visited and accompanyed aboard ye Budgero by ye Dutch chief, his second, and another young man of their Factory at Maulda.

May 19.—We lay at Colcapore.

May 20.—It blew so very fresh at South that we were forced to track our boat till 4 in the Afternoon, when we saw a great black cloud arise out of ye North with much lightning and thunder, which made our Mangee or Steerman advise us to fasten our boat in some Creeke, which we did in ye next we came to, and no sooner fixed than a most violent gust of wind and rain mett us, which lasted but ¾ of an hour, and then ye wind came about at South. The night continuing very darke, we lay still till towards morning, and then made ye best of our way.

May 21.—We lay at a place called Revi, under Wooderay ye Gemidar.[1]

May 23.—At 7 this morning we gott to ye English Garden. About 8 Mr. Beard and ye greatest part of ye English mett us. At 11 we got to the Factory, all in good health, for which mercy ye Lord make us thankfull.

May 24.—Upon my return to Hugly, I was informed that Mr. Beard and Mr. William Prickman had each of them bought parts in a Ship and Cargoe with Mr. Douglas, and sent her to ye Maldivas for Cowries, which has much countenanced Interlopers. Besides, Mr. Beard knew of Mr. Dowglass's lading a parcell of Sapan wood out of a Ship of

[1] *I.e.*, Zemindar.—Y.

his that came from Syam, on board of ye Interloper *Pink*, one of Pitts Vessels (being told it by Capt. Raynes when I was at Ballasore), and took not ye least notice, nor informed me of it, till I was told it by Capt. Raynes in like manner. How this and such like actions will be resented in England, Time must discover.

Capt. Lake, of ye *Prudent Mary*, is an intimate friend of Mr. Beard, and by his example a great favourer of ye Interlopers; he has lately traded with Mr. Nedham for a considerable parcell of goods, which I am assured is true: ye mony being paid to him, for ye Captain, by Mr. Catchpoole, who told me of it. I am the rather induced to believe it true, in regard Mr. James Watson farther informed me that he heard Capt. Lake declare "if he did not like ye Company's employment this voyage he would turne Interloper ye next".

Att a Consultation.

After reading ye Honble Compys letters per ye *Prudent Mary*, all ye Treasure on said ship was ordered to be forthwith sent to ye Mint to be Coyned.

Ordered Mr. Lyttleton, Mr. Nedham, and Mr. Dowglass to be sent to meet at ye Councell Chamber at 4 in ye Afternoon.

Ordered that Mr. James Watson be sent to Cassumbazar according to ye Honorable Company's Orders.

Ordered Mr. Charles Cudworth, third of Maulda; Mr. Joseph Safford, assistant to Mr. Beard in ye accountants office; Mr. Charles Sydenham be sent to Cassumbazar, under Mr. Charnock; and that George Stone come from thence in his place; and like-wise that a message be sent to Mr. Francis Ellis to bid him depart ye Factory.

Mr. Ellis was this morning ordered to leave ye Factory; who about 4 in ye Afternoon sent a message to me and Councell to have an order under our hands for his departure, which was immediately granted in these following words:

Mr. Francis Ellis,

You having been dismist ye Honble Compy's Service for your Infidelity, you are therefore hereby required on Monday ye 28th Instant to take all your goods out, and leave their Factory, for better accommodation of your Successor.

WM. HEDGES	WM. JOHNSON
JOHN BEARD	RICHD. FRENCHFEILD.
JOSEPH DODD	

May 28.—About 9 this morning Mr. Littleton, Mr. Nedham, & Mr. Douglass came to ye factory, and being sent for, were asked "Whether they did now, or ever intended, directly or indirectly, to trade with any Interlopers that shall arrive in the Bay of Bengall?"

Mr. Littleton answered, that "he did not, nor ever intended to trade with any Interloper".

Mr. Nedham answered, "that at present he did not, but that he came out to gett money, and if any such offer should happen, he would not refuse it".

Mr. Douglas answered, he did not, nor ever intended to trade with them: but said "what Estate he should gett here he would not scruple to send it home upon any Interloper". And having given their respective answers they were dismist.

In ye Evening, Mr. Ellis, according to ye foregoing order, left the Factory.

May 29 (*Death of Mrs. Richards*).—Received a Genll. from Mr. Byam of 22nd Inst. advising ye death of Mrs. Richards on ye 20th ditto [see under page *March* 21].

About 4 in ye Evening Mr. Wm. Prickman, with his family, took their passage on ye Sloop *Lilly* for Ballasore; with whom Mr. John Naylor likewise proceeded, having promised not to trade with Interlopers.

Late at night came into y[e] Factory a Sergeant and 2 Souldiers, who came from Fort St. George on a small vessel of y[e] Hon[ble] Company's called y[e] *Conumeer*, who ran aground in the River Ganges. They advise that 3 of their Comrades went ashore for fresh water about Pipley, but came not off again, and are not yet heard of: y[e] rest of them intended to leave the Sloop, and come overland to Hugly.

May 30.—Ordered M[r.] Francis Davenport to goe and find out y[e] Sloop *Conumeer*, and Pilote her up to Hooghly.

June 1683.

June 4.—The Sloop *Conumeer*, on board of whom the Souldiers came from Madrass, being found out by M[r.] Davenport, her Pilote, arrived before y[e] factory.

June 5.—Received a Gen[ll.] from Ballasore dated y[e] 28th ult[o.] advising the three Souldiers reported to have gone ashore at Pipley for fresh Water, &c., were put ashore at Point Palmeras, and arrived in their Factory.

June 6.—Received a Gen[ll.] from Dacca of y[e] 30th past, advising that Gollob Ray, a merchant there, and our security to y[e] Nabob and King's Duan, on whome they had a Bill of Exchange for Rupees 10,000, refused payment, saying he was to demand more of us, Rupees 23,900.

Att a Consultation.

June 7.—Having received advices from our Vaqueel at Dacca that Gollob Ray had promised y[e] Nabob 30,000 rupees more than the former agreement, if a Phirmaund should be procured to excuse us from payment of Custome. In consideration that it is now done, and all y[e] Hon[ble] Comp[ys] concerns likely to returne to y[e] same or worser disorder and confusion than they were in y[e] last year, It was Ordered—That the promise of Gollob Rays be complied with; provided we may have a Phirmaund immediately to lett our business pass freely in all places, and that Mr. Pownsett become obliged for ye Payment of ye 30,000 Rup. upon delivery of ye Phirmaund.

ATT A CONSULTATION.

June 9.—Ordered Mr. Joseph Dod, Chief; Mr. Samuel Meverell, Second; and Mr. James Sowdon, Third of Pattana Factory; and that Mr. Dodd and Mr. Sowden proceed thither with all convenient speed.

ATT A CONSULTATION.

June 11.—Mr. John Threder and Mr. Richard Barker having formerly made an address to be removed from Cassumbazar Factory to some other, by reason of ye Contentions and Animosityes among them in that place, affirming that they believed they should live much quieter in some other Factory, their requests were this day confirmed, with a promise that they should be employed in ye first vacancy that happens in any other Factory, according to their respective degrees and standings; and it is ordered, that in place of Mr. Threder Mr. Wm. Rushworth succeed as Warehouse keeper, and that Mr. John Hains be assistant to Mr. Rushworth.

ATT A CONSULTATION.

June 14.—Mr. Byam having often desired in his letters that a Third might be ordered to Ballasore Factory: it was thought fitt that Mr. Henry Stanly be appointed Third, and that Mr. Leonard Bray be sent thither to assist in Copying.

Ordered Mr. Wm. Johnson, third of this Factory, and that he forthwith take ye charge of ye Warehouse of Mr. Dodd; and Nath. Letten to be Secretary in ye place of Mr. Rushworth.

Ordered—That ye Councell of Cassumbazar consist of Mr. Job Charnock, Chief; Mr. Jeremiah Peachie, Second; and

Mr. Willm. Rushworth, Third; and that no other act as of Councell there.

June 16.—In ye Evening, Mr. Perks, Supracargoe of ye *William & John;* Capt. Read, Commander; and ye Chyrurgion, Mr. Waldo, arrived in Hughly—Interlopers.

Att a Consultation.

June 20.—Muttradas, Roganaut, & Ramnarrain made complaint that Mr. Ellis had detained several sums of money and goods from them, which they pretended to have given him to pass their goods by this last shipping: and gave in ye particulars, viz.:

	RUPEES.	RES.
Muttradas paid him, in ready money	600	
do. In Romalls & Hummums, at severall times	700	
Together		1300
Rogonaut paid him in pieces, 8/8,[1] 500, valued at	1010	
10 Pieces of Mulmulls	92	
4 Pieces of Garrah	6	
2 Pieces of Mulmulls	26	
2 Pieces of Mulmulls	20	
1 Piece of Mulmull, 13	18	
1 Piece of Raiglins, 8	8	
		1175
Ramnarain, Jany. 15th, paid in cash	100	
do. 21st	800	
20 yards of Charkonnas	120	
1 Piece of Mulmull	13	
3 Pieces Dooreas	18	
2 Pieces Lunglia [*Lungi?*][2]	4	
		1055
		3530

Mr. Ellis appeared, and denyed ye greatest part of their demands, only confessing he had received ye 500 pieces of

[1] Pieces 8/8, *i.e.*, dollars.

[2] *Romals, Humhums, Mulmuls, Garrahs, Charconnas, Doreas, Loonghees,* all continued in the lists of Bengal piece-goods as long as the trade lasted. *Raiglins* is probably an error. *Raings*, a kind of muslin, are in Milburn's lists.—Y.

8/8, and some pieces of cloath, affirming likewise that he had paid Rogonaut Rupees 1000 in part of payment for y^{e} Dollers. At last, after a long debate, y^{e} Merchants agreed that, M$^{r.}$ Ellis swearing to every particular, what he denyed they would clear him of; which being declared to M$^{r.}$ Ellis, he desired time to consider of it—till ye next morning.

June 22.—We hear that y^{e} Governor hath invited y^{e} Interlopers up to this place, & for their better accommodation hath furnished them with an House near y^{e} Dutch Factory.

Having advice by a Dutch Sloop that arrived this morning from Ballasore, that 2 English Ships were arrived there, the Ketches were immediately dispatched to bring up what treasure they have on board.

June 23.—M$^{r.}$ W$^{m.}$ Rushworth, M$^{r.}$ James Watson, M$^{r.}$ Charles Cudworth, M$^{r.}$ John Haynes, & M$^{r.}$ Charles Sydenham departed hence to their places in y^{e} several Factories allotted them by consultation.

June 24.—By M$^{r.}$ Naylor, who arrived this morning from Ballasore upon a Dutch Sloop, I had information of y^{e} *Lilly's* being cast away on Ballasore Bar, as also that y^{e} 2 ships in Ballasore Road were Surrat Ships from y^{e} Maldivia Islands, with Cowries, &c.

Att a Consultation.

June 25.—Letters from M$^{r.}$ Charles Cross and James Price, our Vaqueel at Dacca, were read, advising of y^{e} Nabob's refusing to write to y^{e} King a second time in our behalfe, for a Phirmaund for non-payment of Custome, for reasons unknown to them. Whereupon it was ordered to be written by me in Persian to y^{e} Nabob.

Ordered M$^{r.}$ Francis Ellis be sent to, to meet at y^{e} Councell Chamber at 9 of y^{e} clock y^{e} next morning, to answer y^{e} demands made on him by y^{e} Merchants.

Att a Consultation.

June 26.—Mr. Ellis appearing before ye Councell, was informed that ye Merchants, upon taking his Oath of what money he saith he hath paid them, and what received of them, were contented to remit their demands, it being a business without which there can be no determination, there being only his Yea, and their Nay, Refused to take his Oath, unless there might be a recompence made him by ye Merchants for ye loss of his Employment, and ye Damage he has otherwise sustained; and it being farther desired that he show his books of account, where ye payments and receipts are written, he pretended that he could not come at them at that time.

A letter written by my Order in Persian to ye Nabob was read, approved of, and agreed to be sent.

July 1683.

July 1.—The Ship *Britania*, belonging to Mr. Dowglass, &ca., from ye Maldiva Islands, arrived before ye Factory, bringing advice of ye *Charles* (a Ship belonging to ye Honble Company) arrivall there: and that at their first going ashore, their first salutation from ye Natives was a shower of Stones and Arrows, whereby 6 of their Men were wounded, which made them immediately return on board, and by ye Mouths of their Guns forced them to a complyance, and permission to load what Cowries they would at Markett Price: so that in a few dayes time they sett sayle from thence for Surrat, with above 60 Tunn of Cowryes.

Att a Consultation.

July 2.—A particular letter from ye President of Surratt to myselfe was showed to ye Councell: wherein was intimated that one Thomas Haggerston, taken by ye said President into his Service, was run away with a considerable quantity of Gold and Pearle, to ye amount of above

50,000 Rupees, intrusted to him at Bussera and Cong,[1] to bring to Surrat, to save Freight and Custom. Desiring me, if he should chance to arrive at Bengala, to seize on his person and estate, and to send him to Surratt on ye first ship; the President being likely to come to trouble about him. And being informed that ye said Haggerston was arrived at Ballasore, in a ship belonging to one Mr. Burton, 'twas thought convenient that advice and order be immediately given to Mr. Byam, &ca., at Ballasore to seize upon him; and fearing that Burton may be in the Conspiracy, 'twas Ordered, "That an Eye be kept over him, that if he should absent himselfe he may be seized on likewise".

July 8.—Received a Gen^ll.^ from Ballasore advising ye death of Mr. John Byam, and ye arrivall of three English Ships in that Road ye 3rd Inst^nt.^, viz., y^e^ *Herbert*, y^e^ *Henry William*, and y^e^ *Hare*.

ATT A CONSULTATION.

July 9.—Copy of ye Comp^y's^ gen^ll.^ letter per y^e^ *Herbert* (received by y^e^ *Hare*), dated ye 15th November 1682, was read: which by a positive order has made Mr. Richard Barker, Second; Mr. Charles Cudworth, Third; and Mr. James Watson, Fourth of Councell in Cassumbazar; which was confirmed accordingly.

The Trust and business of the Mint being very great, and having advice of Mr. James Smith's death, it was taken into consideration to send a person to take charge of ye same, which Mr. Hill, and my Nephew Hedges, Second of Maulda, which is near Rajamaul, being a person very fitt for such an employment, was made Chief of that place, and ordered to continue his Secondship of Maulda, and repair thither when

[1] Cong, or Congo-bender (*Kunk-bandar*), formerly a flourishing port on the N. shore of the Persian Gulf, about 100 miles W. of Bandar-'Abbás. It was a mart for pearls (see *Fryer's Travels into Persia*, ch. x).—Y.

occasion permitts to look after ye Books, and to have one to assist him in keeping ye same.

Ordered likewise, That a writer be sent to copy out ye accounts of Rajamaul; and that conveniencies be hired for their habitation, or that they repair the house they now live in, fitt to accommodate ye Compys Servants; and keep ye Dust and Lead in ye Mintage.

July 11.—By order of Consultation, Permessuradass, our Chief Customer [Comptroller of Customs], was presented with Rup. 1500 Sicca, and to ye value of 500 r. more in Broad Cloath, and 300 Rs. more distributed among his officers, for his Civility in passing our Tallicas,[1] or Bills of Entry for Customes.

July 15.—Ye two Ships, ye *Henry and William* and ye *Hare*,—arrived before ye Factory.

Received a letter from Capt. Brenock, Commander of ye Ship *Kent*, dated ye 9th Inst., advising of said Ship's arrival in Balasore Road from Tywan and Batavia, and that they had severall goods on board, on account of ye Honble Compy, and fearing she may want repairs, having been 2 years out of England, and never out of ye Water, desires orders either for her coming up to this place, or going into Ballasore River, thinking it dangerous for her (being but a small Ship) to ride out ye Monsoon there.

July 16.—Wrote to Patana, ordering them to buy up all ye Salt Petre they can, to hinder ye Interlopers from having any and all other goods procureable at that place.

July 18.—Received letters from Dacca, of ye 7th and 11th Inst., advising that James Price (though with much difficulty) had at last prevailed with the Nabob to write to ye King's Vizer in our behalf, in favor of nonpayment of Custome (coppy of wh. letter is hereafter written), and that he hopes to procure Phirwannas to let our Goods pass on our Tallicas, as they did last year. Gollobray demands of us a large sum

[1] *Ta'líka* (Ar.), an inventory or invoice.—Y.

of mony to be deposited in his hands, to continue our security for this following Year, saying that he was our Security till ye time of 7 Months was expired (for which he had Rup. 20,000 in his hands); which time being long since at an end, and above 18,000 Rup. due upon our Tallicas, given till he had a greater sum in his hands, he could not procure us any Phirwanna. They also sent Coppy of ye Duan's Phirwanna to Bulchund, to demand Custome of us for all our last year's goods; and if we deny it, to send our Tallicas thither, where he will demand it of our Security. James Price desires that when they demand said Custome of us, we lett them send up our Tallicas; and when ye Duan demands it of our Security, he hopes, by ye Nabob's means, to get it delayed till ye King has returned his Answer to ye Nabob's letter.

Nabob Shauste Cawn's letter to ye Visier in our favour for procury of a Phirmaund[1] on our paying 3000 rup. yearly Piscash. In English, viz.:

"Your particular letter and Husbull Hookum[2] which you favored me with concerning ye business of ye English, I

[1] Phirmaund, Firmaun, etc., *i.e.* (Pers.) *farmán*, a mandate. Stewart, in the Appendix to his *History of Bengal* (4to., Lond., 1813), gives the following report from Surat to the East India Company at home, but not the text of the Firman:

Extract of a letter from WILLIAM METHWOLD, *Surat, dated February 21st*, 1633.

"The 2nd Present, we received from Agra the King's Firmand [Shah Jehan's], which gives liberty of trade unto us in his whole Country of Bengala, but restrains our Shipping only unto the Port of Piply: which Firmand was sent unto us by a servant of our own which was dispeeded unto Agra."

By the Neshaun [*Nishán*], or letters patent, of Sultan Shauh Shujaes [*i.e.*, Sháh Shujá' Nawáb of Bengal, second son of Sháh Jehán], dated A.H. 1066 (A.D. 1656), in the twenty-eighth year of Shah Jehan's reign, a notice is given to "All Governors, Farmers of Rents and of Customs, Captains, Watchmen, &c., that the English Company's Goods are, by the Great

[2] Properly (Ar.) *Hasb-ul-hukm*, 'according to order', the initial formula of a document issued on royal authority; thence the order itself.—Y.

received in good time: which, in complyance to yᵉ King's orders, was to this effect:

"'Understand what Custome yᵉ English paid formerly, and

Emperor's Letters, Custom Free over all his Empire"; and an order was issued "that the Factory of the English Company be no more troubled with demands of Custom for goods imported or exported"; that "They were not to be molested about anchorage dues; and that where ever they have order to build Factories or Warehouses, they be not hindered, but forwarded." In fact, if this Nishán is correctly translated, it granted the most perfect freedom of trade.

Again, in June 1672 (A.H. 1083), the Nawáb Shaista Khan of Bengal and Orissa confirmed these privileges, and granted distinct freedom to boats, ships, and goods from "Ballasore to Hughly, Cossimbazar, or Patana"—"Customs Free, without any demands whatsoever"—saltpetre included, which was then much in demand at home. The Emperor Aurungzebe had then been fourteen years on the throne. But the English complained that great exactions were, nevertheless, claimed from them, and that, instead of an annual present of 3000 rupees, they were "taxed like Hindoos".

In A.D. 1680 (A.H. 1091), a new Firmán came out: "In the name of GOD, Amen. To all present and future rulers in *Surat* that remain in hopes of the Emperor's favor:

"Be it known, that at this happy time it is agreed, of the English Nation, besides their usual custom of 2 per cent. for their goods, more 1½ Jezia, or poll money, shall be taken.

"Wherefore it is commanded, *That in the said place*, from the first day of Shuvaal, in the 23rd year of our reign, of the said People, 3 and a half per cent. of all their goods, on account of Custom and Poll-money, *be taken for the future. And at all other places*, upon this account, let no one molest them for custom, rawdarree, peashcus, phirmaish, and other matters by the Emperor's Court forbidden, nor make any demands in these particulars. Observe. Written on the 23rd day of the month Suffer, in the year 23."

Stewart gives (p. 540) various translations of the (Persian) Firmáns subsequently granted, and all of them apparently of a very liberal character; but regarding the last Firmán over leaf, about which many disputes took place at the sentence "And at all other places", I can hardly wonder at it being misread, if, as I understand, the flowing Persian of the period was written *without stops of any kind*, and if the "Armenian" or other foreign translators (none of the Company's servants at that time understanding Persian) inserted stops at their own discretion in the English.

Ex. Gr. The original Firmán may simply have *meant* that *at Surat*, compare ye difference between that and our last order for taking Custome, and Jidgea.[1] If they pay no more than they did formerly, they complain without occasion; if more, write what it is, and there shall be an abatement.

"In answer whereto I reply, formerly they paid only 3000 rup. yearly Piscash, in Hugly, and never any thing on account of Custome; and now, by what ye King orders and demands, 'twill amount to much more this season. They complain, and not without a cause; they having a Phirmaund, and Hodgee Sophee Caun's Perwannas thereon, in their hands, which cleared them thereof, and to pay Custome now they will not consent, but will rather withdraw their trading. Wherefore their desire is that for 3000 rup. Piscash (as they paid formerly in HUGLY), and 2000 r. more yearly on account of Jidgea, which they are willing to pay, they may on that condition have a grant to be Custome Free; goe on chearfully and quietly with their Merchandize, and warme their Heads with their Trade. For ye Commodities they buy in this Country and Export, the Custom is paid by ye Seller; for ye goods they Import, the Custom is paid by ye Buyer; and for ye Silver and Gold they bring out of their Country, they pay 3½ per cent. Coynage at ye Mint; soe that no Custom is lost to the King hereby. Pray acquaint ye King hereof, and according as he orders returne an answer."

July 20.—Sent letters to Dacca, ordering them that if James Price assures them he has made an agreement with ye

and at all other places, 3½ per cent. was to be charged for customs and poll money for the future, and nothing more.

But if the translator put a full stop, *improperly*, after the words "be taken for the future", and made the next sentence a fresh one, "And at all other places, upon this account", he misled the Company to believe that the 3½ per cent. gross was to be charged *only at Surat*, and that merchandize was to be *free* "at *all other places*" in the Emperor's dominions—a widely different matter.—R. F. B.

Mr. Hedges came out to take office in Bengal just when the difficulty appears to have become troublesome.

[1] (Ar.) *Jizya;* the poll-tax which Moslem law imposes on the non-Moslem.—Y.

Nabob for his writing a second time in our favor to ye King, to give him 5000 rupees in his hand for himself and his officers. and to pay y^{e} said sum to whomsoever James Price shall direct. And also that they become obliged to Gollobray or any other person for payment of 25,000 rup. more, upon receipt of a Phirmand from y^{e} King to excuse us from Custome.

I had some discourse with M$^{r.}$ James Harding, who being in hopes of admission[1] into y^{e} Company's Service, confessed to me very freely that all y^{e} accusations laid against M$^{r.}$ Thredder, concerning y^{e} great gains and advantage he makes by overweight of Silke, was certainly true, and often complained of by y^{e} Merchants to M$^{r.}$ Charnock, who alwayes past it by, and took no notice of it.

M$^{r.}$ Harding farther informed him, that y^{e} relation given me at Cassumbazar of y^{e} 5 bales of silke proffered to be sould to y^{e} Company (which was produced, of over weight of silke gained from y^{e} Merchants) was certainly true, and complained of to M$^{r.}$ Charnock, who at first seemed concerned, but soon passed it over. That he was not so confident or well assured of M$^{r.}$ Barker's infidelity as he was of M$^{r.}$ Threder's, but this much he knew, that all the business of the Warehouse was done and performed by M$^{r.}$ Barker, and that he had heard there was a certain agreement between Threder and Barker, the latter being to receive a certaine sum in lieu of all profits; and was confident that Barker was no such fool as to hold his tongue without a considerable advantage.

Continuing my discourse with y^{e} said M$^{r.}$ Harding, I desired to know y^{e} reason why M$^{r.}$ Charnock was so cross to me, & thwarting every thing I proposed or did for y^{e} Honble Comp$^{y's}$ service? who replyed, "M$^{r.}$ Charnock had no other reason for his soe doing, but that he looked upon himself as disobliged by you at your first arrivall, for not turning out M$^{r.}$ Catchpoole at his request, and was thereupon resolved to blast and frustrate all your actions & proceedings as much as

[1] Re-admission (see April 21st).

he could, and never to councell or assist you more as long as he lived."

July 25.—Received letters from Dacca, viz., one from y[e] Nabob, advising that he had wrote to y[e] King a second time in our behalfe about our Customes, and hoped to recieve an answer according to our desires.

Another from y[e] Chief and Councell, advising that y[e] King's Duan could not be brought to lett our Tallicas pass—till y[e] King's answer to y[e] Nabob's letter be received—without payment of y[e] last year's custome.

And another from Gollobray, intimating that he had not received y[e] 5000 rup. ordered to be paid him by M[r.] Pownsett; nor y[e] obligation for y[e] 25,000 rup. more, on receipt of a Phirmaund Custome free.

July 26.—Dispeeded letters for Dacca, ordering them that if they had not paid y[e] 5000 ru. promised y[e] Nabob, upon his writing a second letter to y[e] King, and obliged themselves for payment of 25,000 ru. more, upon receipt of a Phirmaund to pass our goods custome free, they should forbear doing either of them, having agreed with Gollobray to pay y[e] 5000 ru. here, and that I would become obliged for y[e] payment of y[e] other 25,000 ru. more, upon receipt of y[e] Phirmaund. And desired them to use their utmost endeavors to persuade y[e] King's Duan not to demand Custome of us till y[e] King returns his answer to y[e] Nabob's letter.

July 27.—Received advices from Dacca, dated y[e] 19th inst., that y[e] King's Duan had demanded of them 8000 Rupees on account of remains of last year's Tallicas (Bulchund having formerly received 10,000), ordering his Peasdast to see it suddenly paid in to y[e] King's Cuzzanna:[1] where upon y[e] Chief went to ye Duan's (to see if the presence of an Englishman would availe any thing), intending to desire him to stay till they had answere from hence (whither they had written) about this business; or to prevaile with him not to force it

[1] *Peshdast*, see *note*, p. 87; "Cuzzanna" for *khazána*, 'treasury'.

from us *there*, but to send our Tallicas to Bulchund, that he might demand it of us *here*, where ye said Tallica was taken. But when he came to ye Duan's, and had sent to let him know that he was there to waite on him, answer was returned him that if he came about the above mentioned Business, "he might goe from whence he came": & could by no means get admittance, so was forced to returne home with his business uneffected.

July 28.—This day my Servant, Samuel Pressey, departed this life, after 6 or 7 days continued Flux and Fever: and this day it pleased God to visit me with a Fever.

July 29.—Received Advices from Fort St. George, dated 30th ult., of y^e *New London's* arrivall there, with 3 Interlopers, viz., Alley in y^e *Lumbly Castle*, Smith in y^e *Constantinople Merchant*, and Aubany in y^e [ ], which last passed by towards ye Northward. All of them designe to doe what they can upon ye Coast, and afterwards come downe hither.

August 1683.

August 1.—Letters from Cassumbazar advise ye death of M^r. William Rushworth on ye 28th unt^o.. after 6 dayes sickness, of a continuall fever.

August 7.—This day it pleased God to free me of my fever, which has continued on me these 10 days.

August 8.—Received a Gen^ll. from Dacca of 25th ult^o. advising that notwithstanding their great care and pains about a Phirmaund to clear our business at Rajamaul Mint, ye King's Duan remains obstinate, saying he will not alter what was done by his Predecessor; which they understand was to pay 4 per cent. Also that James Price had told them, that for all his owne pleadings with ye King's Duan, and divers others who spoke in our behalfe (nay, ye very Nabob himselfe), he could not prevail with him to stay for Custome, till answer to what ye Nabob wrote concerning us to ye King was received; but has sent his Phirwanna to Bulchund, to demand it of us here.

August 22.—Mr. Richard More, one that came out a Writer on ye *Herbert*, left this world for a better. Ye Lord prepare us all to follow him! Received a letter from my Nephew, Robert Hedges, at Rajamaul, dated 10th inst., advising his arrivall there, and entering upon his charge.

August 24.—Wrote to Cassumbazar, ordering them to take up what money they can procure at Interest, till such time as they can be supplyed from ye Mint: that they may be going on with their Investment, and that they be sending downe their goods as fast as they can get them ready.

August 25.—Wrote to Fort St. George, giving them a full account of affaires here, and desiring them to build us 2 Sloops of about 25 Ton apiece, with Smack Sailes.

August 26.—Received a letter from my Nephew, Robt. Hedges, dated 19th Instant, desiring ye Second's place of Englesavad might be disposed of to some other Person, the place wherein he is requiring more than ordinary diligence; and advising of Mr. Thomas Hills being desperately sick and past recovery.

ATT A CONSULTATION.

August 27.—My Nephew's letter was read, and his request granted. Mr. Jeremiah Peachie was made 2nd of Englesavad, and Mr. Nicholas Davenant, Third of that Factory, instead of Mr. Charles Cudworth, who by ye Honble Company is ordered to Cassumbazar.

Mr. Charnock, in his Diary in June last, makes a note of ye 5th of that month, that news was brought him that Bulchund's Servant had stopped 3 boats of Treasure with my Dustick or pass, the seals not being legible. Mr. Charnock certifies this dustick was mine; and the Treasure belonged to the Company. However, Bulchund sent him word, that for the future he would let no boates whatsoever belonging to the English pass his Chouky or Watch house at Muxadavad without the chief Dustick of Cassumbazar. I consider M$^{r.}$ Charnock did this on purpose to lessen my esteeme at home with y^{e} Company (he knows he cannot doe it here), to show that the Chief of Cassumbazar's Dustuck is in greater esteeme with y^{e} Government (though inveterate enemies) than mine.

This caused me to write to Bulchund, to know the truth of the Diary note, who returned answer he was not soe Ignorant in the affaires of the world but that he very well knew I was ye Chiefe in Bengall; assured me my Dustick had, and should always, pass with greater respect and freedom than any other person's whatsoever, and to that purpose had given orders to all his Choukies to observe it accordingly.

ATT A CONSULTATION.

August 31.—Ordered that the Copper that came by the *Kent* from Batavia be delivered to ye Merchants on account of Dadny at r. 12 ann. per Maund, it being more by 3 per cent. that can be sold for ready money.

Ordered that 5000 rupees be paid to Gollobray's Gomasta for his master's account, so much being paid by him to ye Nabob and Officers on his writing to ye King in our behalfe for a Phirmaund, and that the Agent give his obligation for 25,000 ru. more, to pay to Gollobray on the receipt of the King's Phirmaund, custom free.

September 1683.

September 2.—Captain Udall told me Mr. Ellis, at their being together at Cassumbazar, advised him to come out ye next Voyage as Interloper, and to let him be concerned with him. Farther, y^{e} said Capt. informed me, goeing into y^{e} Silke Warehouse at Cassimbazar, he saw them weighing Silke and take a Skeyne out of every draught; and espying a bag with Silke, into which they put the said Skeyne, demanded whether that was the sweeping of the Warehouse?—to which he was answered by M$^{r.}$ Threder and Watson, "They are small perquisites and profitt belonging to y^{e} Warehouse Keeper."

Being exceedingly troubled that the Company's Servants in y^e^ severall Factories in the Bay were all in generall soe unkind and disrespectful to me, more than to Agent MASTER,[1] who was nothing near so respectfull and civill to them, and desiring of an old Standard what might be the reason of it? [he] readily replied, "We were all affraid of Agent Master. He had power to turne any of us out of our place. You have not. We are now all placed by the Company, as well as yourselfe, otherwise Mr. Master would have found lesse respect amongst us than you have done." Which I am sure is soe little that till it be otherwise, the Company's Concerns will never be managed to their best advantage. Mr. Cudworth and Mr. Watson can now brag and give out that their Friends are so powerfull at home, they are confident no man dare doe them any prejudice.

June 7 Mr. Pownsett was ordered to become oblidged to Goolobray for the payment of Ru. 30,000 upon delivery of a Phirmaund, but refused to doe it, or so much as to speak or intercede for us to ye King's Duan at Decca, saying he was afraid he should be imprisoned for the money.

Said Mr. Pownsett stuffed his Diarys with false Stories, & said he presented Rupees 9 and 1 gold Mohure to the Fousdar of Hugly, and 10 Ru. to his Servant—when ye said Fousdar never takes a present of any man,—and presents wine to those that never drinke any.

Mr. Ellis bragged to Capt. Minching, telling him "You shall see what a man I shall be in 9 months time, I shall be above them all"—speaking of me. Mr. Beard and Mr. Evans (the minister) keep an intimate and great correspondence with Mr. Naylor, & soe they doe with most of the Interlopers' Party.

[1] Streynsham Master, Governor of Madras, 1677-1681. "MASTER.—Dec. 31, 1878, at the Rectory, Chorley, Lancashire, the Rev. James Streynsham Master, M.A., Rector of Chorley, and Hon. Canon of Manchester, aged 80 years." It is curious to find the old family name so many years after.

September 5.—Received advices from Rajamaul, dated 31st ult., advising of Mr. Thomas Hill's departure out of this world, about 10 of the clock the same morning; and that the next day they would send me about 25,000 Ru. per boate.

Received the following letter from Mr. Samuel Langley:

"Cassumbuzar, 3rd 7ber 1683.

"Sr.—The contents of the following lines are only a short declaration of the many abuses received from Mr. Watson, and to justify my selfe how little I have deserved any from him.

"On the 28th Ultimo Mr. Watson, in the Taffaty Warehouse, without any provocation, called me Pittyfull Prodigall Scrivan, and told me my hatt stood too high upon my head, as Capt. Raynes can manifest, and at the same time he challenged me to fight, with domineering Language; and that too often repeated by him: which was sufficient cause and provocation enough to answer him in the same kind; but upon consideration that he was my superior, and of Councell too, I thought it more prudent to lett it fall at ye time, and not returne two to his two-hundred words. But his incivility ceased not for all this my Submission to him, but so soon as I came out of the Warehouse, he abused me againe, and said, 'Come, Lett us goe on t'other side of the River, and there try ye businesse'; and in these words said, 'Capt. Raynes! Will you be his Second?' which, whether or no were civill to challenge, especially a stranger, I leave to your breast to decide. Mr. Haynes severall times, as well as Mr. Sydenham and Mr. Seere, has heard him say to me these Words, 'If you will not goe out of your Chamber (which I had per a Genll. letter), I will turn you out, and make you know my power', which whether it were soe great as to doe that, I leave others to Judge: but this was unkindly and imprudently done of him, by reason they were not to be his; and I never denying the resignation of them to Mr. Threder, as he will speake (though I might till he had them per same power), as he was my Superior, and soe of consequence his due; and being unwilling to raise a dispute, though I often told Mr. Watson, in hearing of Mr. Haynes, that so soon as the other Chambers were ready I would remove that very minute, but he was too severe, and would make me remove before the floor of the first room was laid, all ye workmen being then at work upon it; and how, both at the open table and in Mr. Charnock's room, he abused Capt. Raynes, and how sharply he severall times took Capt. Udall up, I refer you to him for a relation of ye same.

"He, in the Room, called me Sirrah, and said, 'If you speak another word, I'll hitt you a Slap of the Face'; and at the same time told Capt. Raynes 'he was more a Merchant than he a sailor', as Capt. Udall,

Mr. Haynes, and selfe can testify; and how Mr. Barker, in rude language, gave Capt. Udall ye Lye in Mr. Charnock's room, with other affrontes.

"The foul play Capt. Raynes has received from Mr. Watson, especial Threder, I am ashamed to write, nay to think of. Mr. Watson has taken all the workemen off Mr. Haynes' Chambers, soe that they now lye unfinished; and one day when I was at Breakfast in Mr. Haynes' Chamber (which was ye next morning after Capt. Udall left this place), he went into my room and clapt crossbars upon my Window next the Street, as thick sett and as like any prison I ever saw, as Capt. Michin will inform you; and he left this word with my men, 'If your Master asks Who did this? say I did it': but I only mention this as a designed, premeditated malice of his, for else soe many barres could not be fixed in soe little time, they being, as above hinted, put up the morning after Capt. Udall departed hence, Mr. Haynes, Mr. Seere, and selfe goeing some part of the way with Capt. Udall, leaving Mr. Sydenham by himself at Supper. In our absence how he was abused and scolded at by Mr. Ellis, Threder, Barker, Watson, and Elliott, I refer you to Capt. Minchin, and his own letter sent herewith, but to Capt. Udall for a full account of all grievances, which are dayly great and are likely to be greater, unless speedily remedied, for none that is your friend can live at quiet here; but Threder is worse than the worst of my enemies.

"I am, Sir,

"Your faithfull Servant,

"SAMUEL LANGLEY."

ATT A CONSULTATION.

September 6.—The letter yesterday received from Mr. Langley being read, concerning ye abuses he had received from Mr. Watson, &c., 'twas thought convenient to send for Capt. Udall, Capt. Minchin, & Capt. Raynes, to examine them about it, they being lately arrived from Cassumbuzar, and had been present at ye greatest part of ye abuse—who gave in their testimony, viz.:

Capt. Raynes affirmes that Mr. Watson challenged Mr. Langley, and asked *him* whether he would be *his* Second.

The other particulars, as Mr. Watson's abusing Capt. Raynes at ye Publique Table, and in Mr. Charnock's Room; his quick reply to Capt. Udall; his calling Mr. Langley Sirrah, and threatening him with a Slap of the Face if he spake another worde; Mr. Barker giving Capt. Udall the Lye, &ca., were affirmed by all of them to be true.

And Capt. Minchin, remaining there a day after the others came away, affirms that, talking with Mr. Watson about his abusive Language and quarrels, and telling him he might chance to be sent for by the Agent and Councell, to Hugly, to answer what he had done, he presently replyed, "That if he were sent for, he questioned whether he should come downe or not, for he had no dependance upon them, he being placed there by the Company, as much as the Agent and Councell in Hugly, and soe not in their power to remove him", and much more to ye same purpose.

After examination of the Witnesses, the evill consequences that might accrew from such quarrells and contempt of our Authority and Government in this place, if not speedily remedied, being taken into consideration, 'twas thought good Mr. Watson be sent for to this place, to answer to what was certified against him, and to receive such punishment as the meritt of his offence shall deserve.

Having received advice from Mr. Robert Hedges at Rajamaul of ye death of Mr. Thomas Hill, and there being a former order in Consultation that there should always be three persons at ye Mint, in case of Mortality (that being a place of trust and necessity requiring a person that speaketh the Language), 'twas thought fitt to send Mr. Samuel Pine, to be a further Assistant to him at that place.

Dispeeded letters from Cassumbazar, ordering them to dismiss Mr. Ellis their Factory, whom we understand they entertain and carress; and that they send Mr. James Watson to this place within 3 dayes at farthest after the receipt hereof, to answer such wordes and misdemeanours as are laid to his charge; and ordered Mr. Langley to this place.

September 15.—Mr. James Watson arrived at Cassumbazar, and brought the following Genll. Letter:

"Cassumbazar, 12th September 1683.

"Right Worshipfull & ye Councell,—We have received yours of the 29th past and 6th current, which are soe far from procuring any money at Interest here, that ye Merchants, to whom we are already indebted, have severall times called on us for payment; and that we have little hope of being supplyed from ye Mint, having received but Rupees 20,000 in a long time; and we have present occasion for 2 Lacks more to pay for ye 1000 Bales of July bundl Silke lately contracted for. However, we desist not from endeavoring mony at Interest.

"We are packing and chesting what Silkes are now in the House ready, & they shall be sent to you with all speed possible. You should have had some afore, had not the continual Raines hindered us.

"Wee never gave any Invitation to Mr. Ellis, or John Elliot, to come up hither, nor to any person that came in their Company, & know no reason as they might not be as civilly entertained as any of the rest; but we are so far from harbouring or Caressing any that have been unfaithfull to the Honble Company, that we should upon all occasions use our utmost endeavour to hinder them, as there [are] some circumstances already doth sufficiently demonstrate. John Elliot departed in the Company he came up with. Mr. Ellis is providing himself elsewhere, tho' we would presume to acquaint you that we never hitherto had been informed what his Crimes of Infidelity were for which he was dismist the Hon. Compa employ, more than by his own relation, who utterly denies the least unfaithfulness to his Masters, and declares he hath been unjustly dealt by, and far from their Orders, and more particularly in ye 23rd Paragrau of their Genll. letter by the *Prudent Mary*, which includes 'that ye Councell of the *Bay* may, upon due proof, remove any Chiefe or other of their Servants that are unfaithful, they not being of the Councell of *Hugly*' (of whom he is one). All things of this nature, or any else of great import, being to be seriously considered and discussed by a general *Councell* of the *Bay*, which ought to be annually called, as hath been the Custom of former Chiefs till now of late, which consists of all Chiefs of the Subordinate Factories, or as many of them as can be spared, and this used to be in the most commodious Season, which is just after departure of the Shipping.

"We would not be thought to be more in fault for giving Mr. Ellis and his Lady a little lodging and diet (he accounting himselfe still the Honble Company's Servant, & this being a place where there is no accommodation of any other English or Christian Inhabitants), than other Factories have been, for entertaining those against whom have been evident proofs of great Infidelity to ye Honble Company, particularly Mr. Catchpoole, who hath had the accommodation of the 3rd Lodgings in Hugly Factory, and, if we are not falsely informed, hath been suffered to sett in Councell, when it never belonged to him. This was after he intended for England; besides which, he is still encouraged and entertained in a very high degree.

"In persuance of your Orders, Mr. Watson comes herewith, tho' we cannot imagine what great offence he hath committed to be called from the Honorable Company's business here, in this juncture of time, when a great deal more help is required. If every Malicious, Idle Report must take place, and thereon the Honble Company's Servants be called from their employ, the Businesse must of necessity lye still, as we humbly conceive will bee found in this businesse of his, as it will be made apparent under some person's hands: if it be that of Mr. Raynes (who is not in ye Honble Compn Service), who tooke him from table after Supper, and drew him out of the Factory, and then assaulted him (a couple of Swords having been privately sent out afore); and if it concerns Mr. Haines and Mr. Langley's lodgings, it was by the Chief's Order.

"At finishing hereof, in cometh Nansook, a Merchant, sent by Bulchund, to tell us that our last year's Custome hath been satisfied at Dacca by one Golobray, a Merchant there, and that he will write to ye Right Worshipfull the Agent, to know whether he is content to give in the Tallica of goods for ye present year to Permessaradas or himselfe, and desires us to write also to him. We, never yet having had the least intimation of what was ever transacted at Dacca, could give no other answer than a promise to advise you of what he saith. As to sending Copies of the Genll. Accounts, they have been balanced but a small time, and at present Mr. Sydenham and Mr. Seare are both very sick of Fever.

"We remaine,

"Right Worshipfull att your Command,

"JOB CHARNOCK. "JAMES WATSON.
"RICHD. BARKER. "JOHN THREDER.
"CHARLES CUDWORTH.

"Mr. Longley shall be forthwith coming towards you. Your Jylibdar,[1] after he had received his letter, would not stay for the Genll., but stood upon departure."

September 16.—Mr. Samuel Langley arrived in HUGLY.

ATT A CONSULTATION.

September 17.—Mr. James Watson and Mr. Samuel Langley were summoned to appear before us, to be examined about their quarrel in Cassambazar, concerning which both of them brought several attestations of words that passed between them, of soe little import that we thought it a business not

[1] Pers., *Jalábdár*, or *jaláodár*, lit. 'a bridle-holder', a servant in charge of pack-horses or mules, etc. The word occurs repeatedly in this diary, but is now obsolete in India.—Y.

worth our Cognizance, and only Insisted on Mr. Watson's questioning our Authority: for the purpose whereof we sent for Capt. Minchin, who testified to his face these following words spoken by him: "That he questioned (if he were sent for by the Agent and Councell to Hugly) whether he should come downe or not, for he had no dependance upon them, he being placed by the Company in Cassumbazar, as much as the Agent and Councell at Hugly, and soe not in power to remove him." Where upon there arose so great a debate amongst the Councell that it was thought convenient to referr the determination of it till the next consultation.

Wm. Hedges   Wm. Johnson
John Beard   Richd. Frenchfield.

September 22.—The underwritten is Coppy of Capt. Minchin's affirmation against Mr. Watson, to the truth of which he was this day sworn before the Agent.

"Hugly, 20th Sept. 1683.

"I, William Minchin, doe affirme that, talking to Mr. Watson about his abusive language and quarrells, and telling him he might chance to be sent for by the Agent and Councell to Hugly, to answer for what he had done, he, the said Watson, presently replyed, 'That if he were sent for he questioned whether he should come downe or not, for he had noe dependance upon them, he being placed there by the Company as much as ye Agent & Councell in Hugly, and soe not in their power to remove him'; and much more to the same purpose, the truth whereof am ready to depose on oath, if hereunto required.

"To the truth of this I subscribe,

"Wm. Minchin.

"Sworne the 22nd 7ber 1683, before me,

"William Hedges.

"Witnesse "William Johnson.
"Allen Catchpoole.
"Nath. Letter."

Mr. Eyre told me Mr. Hervy's Servant sett ye Factory afire, on purpose to gain a poore Woman (his wench) a piece of ground: and that at Maulda he has made a Budgero worth 1000 Rupees.

ATT A CONSULTATION.

September 24.—Upon discourse concerning what manner of punishment should be inflicted on M$^{r.}$ Watson for y^{e} words spoken by him, mentioned in Consultation of 17th Instant, which were produced against him by Capt. Minchin—finding ourselves divided, we gave in our opinions as followeth, and left the determination thereof to our Honorable Masters.

"I, William Hedges, am of opinion that M$^{r.}$ Watson ought to be suspended y^{e} Honble Company's Service till such time as answer be sent out of England, and their Honours' pleasure be further known; whose positive orders in their letter of the 20 7^{ber} 1682, are: That they will have entire and absolute Obedience paid to y^{e} Agent and his Councell—and M$^{r.}$ Watson 'questioning whether he should come downe or not'—(if sent for) 'having no dependance (as he pretended) upon us'—'being placed in Cassumbuzar by the Company, as well as the Agent and Councell in Hugly, and consequently not in their power to remove him'—is soe great a contempt of y^{e} Honble Company's Authority, and their Commission given to ye Agent and Councell here, and may probably be of such ill consequence—by encouraging others (if he goe unpunished) to do the like—that I conceive this y^{e} most favorable sentence that be pronounced against him, but humbly submitt this my opinion to y^{e} Honble Company's great Wisdome, and better Determination.

"W$^{M.}$ HEDGES."

"Having well considered the words said to bee spoken by M$^{r.}$ James Watson, Fourth of Councell in Cassumbuzar, in the company of Capt. Minchin, M$^{r.}$ Cudworth, and others, in relation to their nature and demerit, and with all due Honour, reverence, and respect to our Honble Masters, their Authority and Commands, and to the Authority and Commands derived from them to their Agent and Councell here, [I] doe humbly crave leave to dissent from the opinion of the Right Wors^{pful} Agent, which is to this purpose: 'That the said M$^{r.}$ Watson, for those words spoken, ought to be suspended the Hon. Comp^{a} Service till their pleasure therein be known', and doe hereby declare my dissent. And that for y^{e} reasons following:

"I find by our Honble Master's letter, dated 20th 7^{ber} 1682, in ye 23rd and 24th Paragraph, Power derived from them to y^{e} *Agent and Coun$^{cl.}$ in the Bay* expressly (which Councell is elsewhere stated), That in case of Unfaithfulness, want of Dilligence, and Obstinacy, to suspend, &ca., any Chiefe or any other of their Servants that shall be found Guilty of those Crimes. And the *Councell of the Bay* is as expressly distinguished from the *Councell of Hugly*, over which they have noe such power.

"Now I humbly conceive this crime charged upon Mr. Watson is noe such crime as is there mentioned; but if it were, it ought to come before ye Councell of ye Bay, and not be determined by ye Councell of Hugly only, much less by Three, there being no more at present in actual exercise of that trust, viz., The Right Worshipfull Agent, myselfe, and Mr Johnson. And I also find that in case of Negligence and Obstinacy there ought to be admonition given by which Obstinacy and Disobedience, &ca., may be discovered and discerned, as reference being had to ye said Letter will appear.

"2ndly. The offence with which Mr. Watson is charged being Words spoke in a familiar discourse between ye persons before named, which Words Capt. Minchin, his accuser, doth not say were spoke in ye forme in ye Diary exprest, but words to that purpose, which words Mr. Watson denies to have been spoken by him, but acknowledges they were spoken by some person then in Company, which words (supposing he did speak them), as they were not either of the Crimes in ye Honble Compys Letter mentioned, soe it is also evident he did not intend to doe as he said, for no sooner did an order come to him to come downe, but he yielded obedience without any delay.

"3rd. The Punishment in ye Right Worshipfull Agent's opinion to be inflicted bears no proportion to, but vastly exceeds, the offence, committed; which punishment is like to be his ruin, at least it will incapacitate him to doe the Honble Compy that service that otherwise he might be able to doe, should ye Honble Company restore him. Therefore,

"4th. There being ye Ruin of ye said Watson in danger for an offence in words only, nothing of Unfaithfulnes, Negligence, Obstinacy, or Disobedience being charged upon him, neither Sloath nor Luxury imputed to him, I dare not but dissent. And for the same reason for which I dissent, I give my opinion—

"That the said Mr. James Watson ought to be admonished, and sent to ye place of Fourth of Cassumbuzar, where our Honble Masters ordered him by their letter of the 15th 9ber 1682, Paragraph 22nd.

"Humbly submitting my dissent from the Right Worshipful Agent, and the reasons upon which I have soe done, as also my opinion, to the Wisdom of our Honorable Masters.

"JOHN BEARD."

"It is my opinion that he who shall question the Agent's and Councell's power by saying 'they had nothing to doe with him', and 'he was put into his place by ye Honble Company, therefore not in *their* power to remove him', are words of soe ill a consequence, that in obedience to ye Honble Compys letter by the *Prudent Mary*, we can doe no lesse than suspend him his employ till our Honble Masters' pleasure be further knowne concerning such refractory persons. And as they were pleased to degrade Mr. Catchpoole and Mr. Threder for disrespect to Mr. Charnock, their Chief, wee doubt not but they will (as they mention in said Letter) have all entire obedience and respect paid to their Agent and Councel. In all which I submitt to their most serious Judgement.

"WILLIAM JOHNSON."

The Suspension of M[r.] Watson being carried in the affirmative, M[r.] Watson was sent for, and the Agent told him his business was thoroughly weighed and considered by the Councell, & he was to declare him, the said Watson, suspended the Hon. Comp. Service, and that he might reside in Hugly till y[e] Hon[ble] Comp.'s pleasure be farther made known to the Councell.

And that the Hon. Comp[ys] Business may not lye still at Cassumbuzar for want of M[r] Watson, we immediately ordered M[r.] Nicholas Davenant to be Fourth of Councell at Cassumbuzar, and to assist M[r.] Charnock in the Taffety Warehouse; and that letters be wrote to stop him, being on his way to Maulda, whither he was, on a former Consultation, ordered Third.

WILLIAM HEDGES.
JOHN BEARD.
W[M.] JOHNSON.

Minute by Mr. Beard:—

"I humbly pray that my assent to M[r.] Davenant being placed in y[e] room of M[r.] James Watson at Cassumbuzar may not be interpreted that I should dare to have any hand in putting any person in the said Watson's room, who was placed there by the Hon[ble] Comp[ys] Orders, he having not, in my opinion, committed any offence worthy suspension. But he being suspended by y[e] vote and opinion of the Right Worshipfull Agent & M[r.] Johnson, I think it needful there be one in that place, that the Hon[ble] Comp[ys] affairs may not suffer, and that M[r.] Davenant is the fittest person for that place in the Country, being bred a Mercer, and an ingenious, sober man.

"JOHN BEARD."

September 25.—Received advice from Ballasore of the 19th current, of the arrival of Four Shippes in that Road, viz., the *Welfare*, Capt. Wildey, from Persia; a Free Ship from Vizagapat[m.], and two Interlopers, Alley and Smith.

September 26.—Mr. Beard declares 'tis his opinion that Mr. Ellis is, and ought still to be, admitted of this Councell by Virtue of the Company's last letter, notwithstanding his Infidelity: because Mr. Charnock is of that opinion.

This day Mr. Richard Mohun, in the *Recovery*, arrived from Achin and Malacca: advises he met with two of the Company's Ships in the Streights, one Smith the commander of one of them, and Cole commander of the other. They told him they were bound for China, to seeke out and settle a Trade there where they could find admittance. That the Company had sent out 6 Ships of them this year. One of those had £30,000 Stock on board, besides a good quantity of cloth. That the Merchants who had orders to dispose of this Stock and Cargo were all aboard another Shipp. That aboard of one of said Shipps was one Mr. Thomas, who was distracted.

Mr. Mohun farther declared that the Governor of Malacca told him they expected orders out of Holland, ye next Shipping, to forbid and stop all Xtian Shipps whatsoever from going through either of the two Streights of Sunda or Malacca. That if the businesse of Bantam had not luckily fallen into their hands, they had resolved to have demanded satisfaction of the Nabob of Dacca, and fallen out with him for ye sundry affronts and injuries received from him; and that they might not be prejudiced themselves for want of Rice to store their South Sea Factories and Garrisons in the mean time, they had prudently settled a Factory to furnish them in a plentiful manner with Rice at Arracan. And when they made peace and settled themselves in a fortification in some most commodious part of the River's Mouth, they would either oblige ye Natives and Government of Bengal to interdict and forbid their trade with all manner of European Christians, or else were resolved to run ye hazard of doing it themselves. And then Adieu to ye Bay of Bengall (ye best Flower in ye Company's Garden), and all India besides, if they please to command it. And if it does not please God to putt it into ye Company's hearts to doe something to prevent this evil the next year, by settling and making a Fort in one of the Islands, I fear they will be excluded for ever hereafter.

This is also, in my judgement, the only remedy to prevent the Interlopers infesting of us.

This day likewise arrived news of the two Interlopers, Alley, of the *Lumley Castle*, and Smith, of the *Constantinople Merchant*, arrival in Ballasore Road: at ye same time came in Capt. Wildy in the *Welfare*, from Gombroon and Fort St. George. Capt. Alley came up to Hugly in his Barge, rowed with English Mariners in coats with Badges, and 4 Musicians. [He] applyed himselfe first to Dr. Douglass and then to Mr. Littleton, for advice and directions in all his concerns; put himselfe into a great Equipage with Flags, like an Agent, and tooke about 70 or 80 Peons to wait on him.

Capt. Alley, for ye better conveniency of private discourse, and notice not to be taken of them, went to our Garden this Afternoon to meet Mr. Evans, our Minister, and his Brother in Law, Mr. Frenchfeild: what the design should be I cannot imagine. Mr. Beard's encouragement & partnership in trade with Mr. Dowglass has made divers persons extremely regardless of the Company's strict orders in their dealings and commerce with Interlopers.

Answered Mr. Charnock's general Letter of ye 13th Instant as followeth:

"Hugly, 26th Septembr 1683.

"Mr. Job Charnock, &ca, Councell,

"Sirs,—Wee have yours, 13th Current, and are sorry you are not able to procure money at Interest. We hope you will be speedily supplyed from the Mint.

"Your Bales of Silke and Chests of Taffaty. will be welcome—resolving to ship them as soon as they arrive in.

"What Invitation you gave Mr. Ellis we know not, but thought it improper yt one dismissed ye Company's Service and this Factory should be received and entertained by you.

"We cannot but resent your writing on his behalf, and thinke your reflections on this Councill very unworthy, assuming (on his bare assertion) we have dismist him wrongfully, without serious consideration.

"If you have not been acquainted with his crime, 'tis possible we did not finde nor thinke ourselves obliged soe to doe. We shall be accountable for that to our Masters, as also whether he be of this Councill, or Legally discarded, notwithstanding the Paragraph cited by you in ye Hon. Compa. letter.

"You say it has been ye Custome of former Chiefs (till now of late) to Call a Genll. Councill of the Bay annually, which you positively affirme consists of all the Chiefs of Subordinate Factories, or as many of them as can be spared, and that this used to be in ye most commodious season, after ye departure of ye Shipping. You had done well to have quoted some precedent of this kind, being wholly ignorant of such a Custome, and [we] are credibly informed by divers persons that for these 10 years last past Mr. Charnock was either not thought fitt to be summoned, or never had the Honor to sitt in such a General Councill. You had been no less kind if you had told us how you came by that knowledge, that the Chiefship of every Subordinate Factory denominated or entitled him to be one of the Genll Councill of the Bay, which we expect your next should inform us, being clearly of a contrary opinion; and desire likewise to know who shall be Judge; how many of those Chiefes can be conveniently spared.

"As to our entertainment of Mr. Catchpoole in ye 3rd Lodgings, we presume neither ye 3rd or 4th of this place ever made any complaint to you of the Injury done them, though you have impertinently taken upon you to reprove us for it.

"You did well to submitt to our orders in sending of Mr. Watson: it was thought fitt, upon serious consideration (without giving you any further account of it), to suspend ye said Mr. Watson ye Hon. Comp. Service, and to order his residence at this Factory till their pleasure be further known.

"And that our Masters' concerns may not suffer by his absence or removal, we have thought fitt to appoint, and doe hereby order, Mr. Nicholas Davenant to be in his place, assistant to Mr. Charnock in ye Taffity warehouse, and Fourth of Councill.

"We shall not trouble ourselves to convince you of your mistake in saying you never yet had ye least intimation of what was ever transacted at Decca, having proofe sufficient under your own hand to ye contrary.

"Mr. Langley will speedily return to you to assist you in writing. The Gyllibdar staid two dayes sollicting in your Factory for your Genll. Letter, after Mr. Langley had dispatched him, by the testimony of Mr. Watson.

"We admire what made you send peons to force our Gyllibdar back to your Factory, after he had gone 12 Cosses on his way, and dismisse him againe without any reason for it.

"We are,

"Sr Yor Affectionate Friends,

"Wm. Hedges.

"Jn. Beard.

"Wm Johnson."

Received the following letter from Mr. Ellis.

"Cassumbo, 28th 7ber 1683.

"Right Worspll, &c., Councell,

"Srs,—Your persecutions have been soe many and great since your Agent's arrivall, that they are intollerable when I consider upon what grounds you dismist me the service, which was irregularly done, because without ye Councell of ye Bay. Besides, ye power ye Honble Compy gave never reached to further than suspension, untill ye Genll. Letter per ye *Prudent Mary* came, where ye Councell of Hugly is excepted, whereof I am one. Here follows the Rules you were to walke by, in our Honble. Masters' own words, viz.: 'And therefore we doe hereby enlarge that Power we formerly gave, of suspending from our Service any in their judgement that shall not behave themselves Faithfully and Diligently as they ought to doe'. But you have not suspended, but turned me out, without any regard to those orders given, pretending you have done me ye greatest justice in ye world. But I hope in God to meet with much better in Father-Land for ye inexpressable damage done me, & doubt not but 'twill require greater satisfaction than you at present are aware of. Now your pretence for turning me out was for participating with Muttradas in his roguery. If so ('tis very strange to me, and will be much more to my Honble. Masters, when they come to understand ye truth hereof) why was not ye said Muttradas turned out likewise? he being ye Chief Instrument and occasion of that great Infidelity you taxe me with. Alsoe his Guilt last year in that unpardonable offence of Lading the Interlopers and, as I am credibly informed, goeing on in that track, he or his Brother Bollubdas for him.

"Then there's ye loss of our Hon. Employers' priviledges, a Crime in ye highest nature; and he, one of the Chiefest Actors therein, by sending his Goods to all places upon our Dusticks, thereby cheating the King of his Customes; otherwise our Phirmaund had never been called in question.

"Another materiall thing I must insert before I come to conclusion, that is, to give you Gentlemen of the Councill to understand, and to put the Agent in minde of, a letter he showed me from Sir Josiah Child upon his arrivall, wherein he is positively forbid to have any dealings with Muttradas and 3 or 4 Merchants more (I think Jeychund saw, Ramnarrain, Rogoonautt, and Ramchund), yett, notwithstanding these afore-goeing circumstances that these persons, especially Muttradas, should not only be carressed and countenanced in ye Honble Comp^ys^ Factory of Hugly, but traded withal for large summes of money, consulted with about their affaires, and taken abroad where ye Agent goes to contrive and forge Falsitys against honest men, is a riddle to me; but I question not but it will be unfolded to my Honble Masters in good time, to somebody's great shame and remorse of conscience for their unjust actions.

"I am, S^rs.^

"Yours att Command,

"FRANCIS ELLIS.

"I desire this may be entered and sent home, that it may come to the Honble Comp^ys^ perusall. F. E."

October 1683.

October 1.—Mr. Daniel Joachim Schlu, one of the Danes Merchants that were turned out of Bantam, now living here in the Dutch quarters, gave me a Visit, and amongst other discourse told me, "When he was at Batavia some months since, Gen^ll.^ Spelman told him so soone as he had possessed himselfe of Bantam and ended ye War, his next designe was to call ye Nabob of Decca to an account for ye severall affronts and abuses received from the Natives of Bengall; and to make ye most advantageous conditions with them that they could," with much more to this purpose; the said Mr. Schlu apprehending by ye General's discourse, he intended to block up the River with Fortifications, and make himselfe Master of the Bay, as he had done of divers other Countries.

October 2.—Chittermull and Deepchund, two Cassumbuzar Merchants, this day assured me Mr. Charnock gives out all his new Sicca Rupees for Dadny[1] at 2 per Cent., and never gives the Company credit for more than 1¼ rupee, by which he gains and putts in his owne pocket Rupees ¾ per Cent. of all the money he pays, which amounts to a great Summe in ye Yeare, at least £1000 Sterling.

One Edward Barlow, late mate of the *Delight*, Capt. Smith, Commander, being turned ashore by his Commander at Achin,

[1] *Dādnī;* money advanced to weavers, and the like, by those whom he is to supply with goods.—Y.

came passenger on Mr. Hohun's Shippe from thence, tells me he came out of ye Downes with ye Mexico Merchant, Capt. Packston, which latter going into Plymouth, they have not since seen him. They were both ordered to go to Achin. The *Delight* had been there near 7 Weeks, but Packston arrived not in all that time, so believe he went through ye Streights of Sunda. Says he left Gravesend the 4th January last. One Capt. Harding, in the *Carolina,* & Capt. Cole in the *Smirnaote,* sailed out of England some months before them for ye South Seas.

I was this day advised that Mr. Charnock putt off Mr. Ellis's Cowries at 34 pund to ye Rupee, in payment to all ye Peons and Servants of the Factory, whereas 38 Punds are really bought by them for a rupee.[1] For which reason also Mr. Beard sent up his Cowries, which he received from ye Mauldivas, to be put off and passed by Mr. Charnock at Cassumbazar.

Received a Genll. from Cassumbazar, dated the 29th Ulto. advising ye Death of Mr. Chas. Sydenham the 18th, and Mr. John Sears ye 29th do.

Att a Consultation.

Mr. James Harding having severall times petitioned that he might again be entertained in the Honble Compys Service, according to their Orders in their Genll. Letter the 27th of October 1682, wherein they say, "If he be found diligent, able, and faithful, he may have such preferment as we think he may deserve", 'twas this day taken into consideration; and I having declared that the said Mr. Harding had told me at Calcapore, on his way to Dacca, that Mr. Threder had much wronged the Company in his charge of Warehouse keeper at Cassumbuzar, and afterwards refused to testifie ye same when demanded of him at Cassumbuzar, and [in] ye Businesse of Mr. Threder, upon examination; the question being put

[1] A 'Pun' (*pana*) is a certain number of Cowries, generally 80.—Y.

whether y[e] said M[r] Harding should be readmitted into the Comp[s] Service? 'twas carried in the Negative.

The Agent's Account Cash to the end of Last Month was received and passed.

W[M.] HEDGES. WILLIAM JOHNSON.
JOHN BEARD. RICH[D.] FRENCHFEILD.

October 8.—This day Capt. Alley went to visit the Fousdar: he was unwilling to goe alone, and gott Permesurados (his Protector), our Chiefe Customer, to goe to y[e] Fousdar's, and be there at his arrivall. As soon as they were seated, the Fousdar demanded of him "Wherefore he came not to visit him before he was sent for", answered "He understood that the Fousdar was a great friend of the Agents, and consequently feared he should not be well treated."

The Fousdar demanded upon what account he came hither? Alley replyed, "As an Englishman, and upon the same Service as y[e] Company traded here." The Fousdar told him y[e] English Agent had divers Phirmauns from y[e] King, and Perwannas from the Nabob and the King's Duan, which he had not. Permesuradas answered for him, and said all should be well to the Fousdar's satisfaction, meaning he should have a good Present sent him.

Alley went in a splendid Equipage, habitted in Scarlet richly laced. Ten Englishmen in Blew Capps and Coats edged with Red, all armed with Blunderbusses, went before his pallankeen, 80 Peons before them, and 4 Musicians playing on the Weights, with 2 Flaggs before him, like an Agent. A gawdy shew and great noise adds much to a Public Person's credit in this Country. As for Soldjers, they are of absolute necessity here in divers respects, and especially whilst we are thus infested with Interlopers, to keepe us from publick affronts, as well as overawe our owne people and mariners, who are now very numerous and insolent amongst us, & (by reason of Punch) every day give disturbance.

October 10.—The inconvenience of the Hon[ble] Comp[ys] exempting the Council of Hugly for being questioned for their actions, or possibility of being displaced, was seen this day. A Councill being called, one of them went out upon his occasions, not regarding the notice given to him, and another time would not come when he was called, pretending business.

The Dutch Director refused to admit of the Interlopers in his Quarters. M[r.] Naylor trades with them for considerable profits, and sells Taffaties cheaper than bought by M[r.] Charnock at Cassumbuzar.

I was this day informed that last Saturday, in the afternoon, being the 6th Instant, when I went to the English Garden, M[r.] Beard took occasion to meet Capt. Alley and M[r.] Davis, the Interloper, at M[r.] Littleton's house. Whilst M[r.] Beard continues thus to countenance and keep a familiar private correspondence with disaffected persons and Interlopers, there is little hope of doing them any prejudice in this place.

October 12.—I received a Gen[ll.] from Ballasore dated y[e] 6th Inst., advising y[e] Interlopers find soe little encouragement in that place, that Capt. Smith, in the *Constantinople Merchant*, intends to sail for Hugly.

M[r.] Charnock's reply to my Gen[ll.] of the 26 Ultimo received this day.

"Cassumb[r], the 6th October 1683.

"Right Worshipfull, &[ca], Councill,

"Wee have received yours of the 26th past. Since our Last wee have procured with much difficulty Rupees 15,000, att Interest, at Rup. 1 2 an. per Cent. per m[m]. Our Silk Taffaties are now going to be laden and sent towards you as fast as the small assistance we have will admit of.

"We doe confirme what [we] wrote you in our last about M[r.] Ellis, that according to the Hon. Comp[ys] Letter by the *Prudent Mary*, he, being one of Huglie Councell, could not be *dismissed* their employ, and afore y[e] letter came, there was only power of *suspension*, soe that he accounts himselfe still of Councell.

"You will find Gen[ll.] Councells to have been called in former Chiefs' times, and by the Agent Mathews, and Major Puckle, when they were here in the Bay, if you please to peruse the diaries left by M^r. Vincent. They did not consult only with one or two, but called all, or as many as could be spared, of the Chiefs of the Subordinate Factories to the Consultation, when Messrs. Hall and Smith were suspended, and settlements made, amongst whom M^r. Charnock was then thought fitt to have the honor to be summoned to said Councell, but it was the shipping time, & he could not come down to attend: and who ever he was which advised you that for ten years past 'he was not thought Fitt', or 'Never had the honour to be summoned', was under a great mistake. However, for better Confirmation, the Honble Comp^y have thought him, not only worthy to be Second in the Bay, but to succeed in the Agency. But, put the case, there had not for several years past been any General Consultations, doth that argue there must never be any? Our Honble Masters, to avoide that dispute, have fixed a Councell, making a distinction from the Bay and Huglie, who have wholly power to examine, suspend, or dismiss from their Imploy any that are guilty of breach of their expressed orders; and that is not confined to one or two of them at most.

"Your vigorous withstanding calling Generall Councills of the Bay, and at last telling us you will be accountable only to our Honble Masters, is no ways consonant to their Orders, who (in our Opinion) will receive little satisfaction thereby, it being soe much in Diameter[1] to their Interests.

"We did not reprove, but looked on it as our duty to minde you of the unreasonableness of M^r. Catchpoole Lying in the 3rd Lodgings at Huglie: he that was Third there, and looked on himselfe wronged by not being preferred to a higher employ, did make known his grievances, and the Honble Comp^y placing M^r. Charnock 2nd of Council, hee thought he could do no lesse; and the other hath no right, by their expresse commands, which say, If he accepted not of the 6 in Councell of this Factory (for M^r. Threder is nominated afore him) he should not be in any employ in their Service.

"Your suspending M^r. Watson is altogether opposite to the Honble Company's orders, there being neither Unfaithfulness, Negligence, Luxury, nor Disobedience proved against him; the most was but matter of Words, and therefore we hoped admonition had been sufficient for the first time, which we desire you to consider of. And the Wittness at first declared afore the Councell he could not be positive who spake them; and whatever he did afterwards should have been [stated] afore said Councell likewise, that M^r. Watson might have made his defence. (The Law condemning no man without having his accusers face to face, and not Sworne privately.) Besides, there was not above half of the Councell, one of whom dissented.

[1] Opposition.

"If it were for Action, the Hon. Comp. will ill resent any person to come into any of their Factories (not being in their Service) to raise discussion and challenge any of their Servants, and much more to send forth Swords clandestinly afore hand, which must be referred with every other circumstance to them. His absence from here is detrimental to their affaires, and the more [so], two Writers being lately dead, and another besides him called downe in the very height of business, so that if any thing in writing, or what else, bee neglected, Wee must quitt our selves thereof. We request he may be sent up immediately, to adjust his accounts.

"Concerning ye Decca affaires of Custome, it will appear how much wee have been acquainted therewith. If ever we were informed of such a person as Golobray, or his being security for the Right Worshipfull Agent (a thing altogether unpracticable), or his satisfying the Customes of last year, or sending up James Price, this, or his Commission, then we are to blame in writing the contrary. The proof you mention to have under our owne hands specifies nothing of the above mentioned. But all your general letters from Decca to us were only to accompany severall perwannas, and their Copies (excepting the case of Mr. Prickman & a Perwanna for the Mint), of the Nabob and Duan to Bulchund, to release the goods upon Tallicas, and to turne out Permesuradas, and to recover the money he had unjustly extorted from us. In order to which, the Nabob's Assole was sent downe therewith to see it put in execution.

"But to this day we know Permessuradas is not displaced, and much feare none of the money is yet retrieved. But by accident, lately came to our view a Coppie of the King's Duan's, Meer Amud's, Perwanna to Bulchund, expressing that your Security, Golobray, had given an account of the Tallica for last year's goods, amounting to Rupees 3,97,627, which at Rup. 3½ per Cent. Custome amounts to Rup. 13,917; and that the said Golobray, being security, had already paid into ye King's Cajanna[1] Rupees 900. This the Duan hath ordered Bulchund, by said Perwanna, to receive of us now; and for the future saith he will receive ye Customes yearly at Decca, of said Golobray, which will prove not only a great detriment to ye Comp^y.^ but a disgrace to the whole Nation; and, without doubt, had timely care and the right way been used, as was advised, it had never come to this height.

"As for ye Jyllibdar, we conceive he is to attend *our* Answer to your Generall, and not Mr. Langley's particular. The reason for our calling him back was to have sent said Generall by him; but afore his returne Mr. Watson was going, by whom we thought fitt to send it, for its speedy conveyance.

"Wee stand in great need of Rarities for presents, and factors' provisions, and Beames and Scales.

[1] See *Note*, p. 103.

"Wee have not an ounce of Copperas by us, nor is there any procurable but the Country Copperas, which wee have tried, and will not doe; soe that no more Black can be dyed unless some be speedily be sent.

"Wee Remaine,

"Att yr Commands,

"Job Charnock.

"Richd. Barker.

"Charles Cudworth.

"John Threder."

I received the foregoing factious, disrespectfull letter from Mr. Charnock and Council, declaring Mr. Ellis still of Council here, not being in our power to turne him out, though Infidelity was confest by himselfe, and manifestly proved against him.

Mr. Charnock resolves the question that every Chief of a Factory (being one of Council of the Bay) may come or stay away when summoned to Council, as he thinks convenient, by saying "as many as could be spared", of which they themselves were to be judges, and that it was then Shipping time when Mr. Charnock was summoned and could not be spared; stuffing his Letter with diuers false storys and impertinencies, which require great time and leisure to answer. Insomuch that if ye Hon. Compy. doe not thinke fitt to rectifie this disorder, their businesse will soon run to confusion. The countenancing and writing to Mr. Charnock, Mr. Beard, Mr. Hervey, and Mr. Pownsett, having made them in their owne Conceite more than soe many Agents, saying as Mr. Watson did, "they are Chiefs, and put in by the Company as well as himselfe", and will send their Goods and answer our Letters when they please. Mr. Hervey has not wrott one Genll. Letter to us since his first arrivall at Maulda, now 5 months since, nor sent us his Diarys. The Company must be necessitated to follow the Dutch rule, and command absolute and entire Obedience to be given to their Agent, or their affaires in this Country will run into great disorder and suddaine distruction. I can but discharge my duty, and God's Will be done for ye rest. If my Second had been true to me, all these euills had been preuented.

October 15.—I received a Gen[ll.] Letter from M[r.] Hervey, &ca., Council at Maulda, complaining of the Government for protecting the Company's Merchants and D[rs.] [debtors] from paying their just demands, and desiring a Perwanna may be procured from Decca, complaining of one Jamshier Beigh for demanding and exacting large annual Presents, vexing and ruining some of our Servants, and that if such a Perwanna, with an Assol or Messenger, cannot be procured, he shall not be able to send some $\frac{1}{10}$ part of this year's Investment, and that will come 25 per cent. or more above its due value; and presses to have the perwanna, though it cost Rup. 5000.

The truth of all this is, M[r.] Hervey was forced, when he left Decca, to give M[r.] Pounsett for security, to pay what sums soever he should be condemned to pay the Weavers and Brokers there (with whom he had a great Suit at Law for 6 months' continuance). The said Weavers and Brokers recovered 3,300 rup. of M[r.] Pownsett. M[r.] Hervey now contrives the procuring this Perwanna, that M[r.] Pownsett may satisfie himselfe out of y[e] Price which y[e] Company must pay for it, though 'tis not worth a straw to the Company; and besides, 'tis to be feared y[e] Company will be strangely overrated for all their Goods that come this yeare from Maulda. I would not be bound to secure them for 30 per cent. At this rate the Company will soon be ruined in Bengall. This is the effect of making every Chiefe one of the Councill of the Bay, & independent of that of Hugly, & the Company's writting to them of their business, which has made every one of them slight and disregard the Agent and Councill's orders to them.

October 16.—M[r.] Elliott, the Interloper, is gone up to Cassumbuzar with Captain Lake, to assist him in buying goods, &ca.

October 17.—Sent Coppy of Maulda Generall to Dacca,

ordering them to procure a Perwanna according to their desire.

Wrote to Cassumbazar, pressing them to hasten down their goods, as fast as they come, that the Shipps now in Port lose not their passage about the Cape,—which was all the answer I thought convenient to give their Generall Letter of 6th Instant, to avoid running into long disputes.

October 18.—Mr. Pownsett brags of his private instructions from ye Compy. & some great men of the Committee, that he regards nothing that's wrott him from Hugly.

October 21.—Received a General from my Nephew, Robert Hedges, at Rajamaul, advising that he had received an imperfect Perwanna from those at Decca, which ordered the Droga of the Mint to employ all the men at once, and not let them rest at times; and to deliver each man his due proportion of money every day, according to what [is] delivered in: Which is of no import, the Droga having formerly promised him a greater share in what mony [may be] delivered out than is really his due: but having heard of this Perwanna, is so enraged against him for complaining, that he is resolved to be revenged, and delays our business as much as possibly he can.

October 22.—A Peon, returned from Maulda, told me, whilst he was there, a Peon brought Mr. Hervey a Letter from Capt. Alley. Mr. Hervey gave answer to said Letter by a Peon of his own: who for 2 or 3 dayes, that he staid here for an answer, was kept privately in Capt. Alley's house, for feare any of my Peons or Servants should see him: this Peon of Mr. Hervey's was mett by the same Peon of mine, about halfe way on his returne to Malda.

I know Mr. Hervy has a parcell of 20 chests of very fine Mulmulls & Cossais, which he pickt up at Decca, and has a mind to send them home: 't is to be feared he will doe it by Capt. Alley.

The Dutch Company in Holland have sent out this yeare

a Shipp directly for this place, with absolute power given the Supracargo, independent of the Directore: save that yᵉ said Directore and Councill are ordered to furnish him with what money he shall desire, and be aiding and assisting him upon all occasions with their authority. The Sopracargo is called Sigr. Lints; his businesse is to Spie into & make discovery of our Trade,—to buy Silke and Silkes as we doe,—and to see whether they may not trade directly out and home, without goeing to Batavia: which they find a tedious way, and not so beneficial to them as ours. In short, I doubt the coming out of this Ship will be of greater detriment and worse consequence than is generally apprehended by our people here. The Dutch, finding the shortness of this way, will hereafter in all probability be competitors with us in our sorts of Silke, and all other commodities which we usually trade in.

October 23.—Received advice from Ballasore of the *George* & *Golden Fleece's* arrivall in that Roade the 12th Instant.

October 26.—Capt. Alley went this day in great state to visit Bulchund, with 3 Persons with him; beside 10 Englishmen with Blunderbusses, and about 80 Peons. He has agreed to pay 3½ per Cent. Custom on all goods imported and exported: upon which they parted good friends. Capt. Alley, Capt. Smith, and that Gang are frequently visited, to our shame and the Company's discredit, by every considerable person in this Factory, except my selfe, who never yett saw one of them. They and our Captains caresse one another dayly. I heare they send adventures home by them.

October 27.—The last night, Mr. James Watson desired a Dustick of me for a Budgera with some Persian Fruit to Cassumbazar. When yᵉ Boat was putting off, Mr. Watson ordered the Chiefe Boatman or Manjee to take in Mr. Harding, and carry him to Cassumbazar. The mangee refusing to doe it without my orders, Mr. Watson struck him twice, and forced him to take him in. Thus, by the countenance and similar practices of Mr. Beard, is the Company's Honor and my Authority slighted and contemned: otherwise they would as soone eat fire as attempt to doe it, would he stand by me, and not argue and dispute my authority, and as much as in him lyes render it contemptible. This scandalous, unfaithful person, Harding, is now sent up to serve Mr. Charnock in dispight of me; though, God be praised, I live in honor and esteem, whilst Charnock, Hervy, and Beard are the most despicable persons to the Government and Native Merchants that ever lived in the country.

October 28 (*Sunday*).—This day I received a letter from Mr. Crosse of Decca, dated ye 21st Instant, enclosing a Perwanna which James Price has procured from the Nabob to our Fousdar, ordering him immediately to seize and send up to Decca the 3 Interloping Captains. I durst not give notice of this to Mr. Beard, having sufficiently experienced his prejudice and dislike of every thing I doe, and knowing his intimacy with Mr. Littleton, and meeting Capt. Alley, and sometimes at said Littleton's house—but dispatched away Mahmoot Herreef, another trusty Vekeel, to ye Fousdar, promising him a large gratuity if he got this business effected, and ye Captains seized and sent away to Dacca: of which I expect a good account this Afternoon. What might not be done if we were unanimous amongst ourselves, as they would and must be if [I] had authority to turne them out when they did not doe their duty!

This afternoon my Vekeel brought me word ye Captains excused not waiting on ye Fousdar—being Sunday.

ATT A CONSULTATION.

October 29.—The *Prudent Mary* and the *Herbert*, being positively ordered by the Honble Compy to be the 2 First Ships despatched from this place, we thought it convenient to send ye *Welfare* & ye *Kent* directly to Fort St. George, with their full Lading of Saltpetre, that they may be dispatched early from thence, and not endanger their passage about the Cape: having been a long time out of England, and not in a capacity to beat it out in bad weather. The *George* was likewise ordered to follow them with her Kintledge of Saltpetre, and to touch at all the Lower Factories to take in what goods [may be] provided at those places; and the *Golden Fleece* ordered to continue here to carry away what goods we shall have remaining after the *Prudent Mary's* and the *Herbert's* despatch.

The Fousdar sent 10 Portuguese Firelocks, 10 Peons, and 2 Horsemen to bring Capt. Alley and the rest before him.

This morning they excused going, with many frivolous excuses, writing and sending to Bulchund to intercede for them, and to enquire into ye cause of their being sent for. In the evening the Fousdar's Soldjers (not to return empty handed to their Master) brought with them Mr. Davis, belonging to Capt. Smith, and Mr. Smith, Chief Merchant of the *William and John*. The Fousdar demanded their Captaine, and told them they should be his Prisoners till their Captains made their appearance.

October 30.—This morning Bulchund came to give me a visit. After some previous discourse, I told him the last time he was here (about 14 months since) I promised him a Persian Horse; I had now one at his Service, which he accepted with some ceremony. Entering into farther discourse, he shewed me severall letters and Perwannas he had received from the King's Duan of Dacca, en-ordering him to demand and receive Custome of us. I replyed we had lived here about 50 years without payment of Custome; the Nabob had wrott a letter to the King in our Favour; we expected their answer, and made no doubt but it would be to clear us of Custome. Bulchund told me we had waited above a year for such an answer, but assured me it would never come without his advice and assistance; and now required me to give my positive answer to one of these two questions :

"Whether I would consent to the payment of 3½ per cent. Custome upon our own Tallicas or entries : Or, lett him take custom of his own subjects for all the goods they sold to us." For which he gave us time till this afternoon to consider of it.

Amidst our discourse, Bulchund told me he had some proposals made him by Mr. Charnock concerning payment of custome. Bulchund had replied, "What have you to doe with such proposals? You are under the Agent's direction, & I am going to him, and he and I will agree upon it."

October 31.—This morning the Interlopers made their addresses, by advice & assistance of Mr. Edward Littleton, to Bulchund, to gett Mr. Parkes and Mr. Davis out of the Fousdar's Custody, with promise of great reward. In the afternoon Bulchund sends a note to the Fousdar, telling him he would be security for the 2 Merchants in his custody, and answerable to the Nabob for all demands and pretences he would make upon them. Whereupon the Fousdar sent them to Bulchund with a guard of Soldiers, and Bulchund immediately dismist them, and bid them go to their houses: Soe insolent and proud is this Bulchund growne with his vast state, as not to regard any Perwanna that comes from the old doting Nabob of Decca.[1] The Company's affairs will never be better, but always grow worse and worse with continuall patching, till they resolve to quarrel with these people, and build a Fort on ye Island Sagar at the mouth

[1] Shaista Khan, the Nawab of Dacca, held the government from 1663 to 1689, except during part of 1677 and 1678, when Fedai Khan, the Emperor Aurunzebe's foster-brother, held the government. Shaista Khan was son of Vizier Asuf Jah, and nephew of the Empress Noor Jehan.—*Stewart*, p. 296.

In the diary of Dec. 2, 1683, the Nawab is stated by Mr. Hedges to be then 82.

of this river, and run the hazard of losing one yeare's trade in the Bay, in ¼ of which time there 's noe feare of bringing these people to our conditions. If this be not speedily taken in hand by us, there 's no doubt to be made but 't will soon be done by the Dutch, who talke of it freely, as often as we meet with them: and then we must expect to be soone turned out of this country.

November 1683.

November 5.—Bulchund, after much entreaty and fair promises, went to returne Capt. Alley's visit, but sent me word by a Merchant that he designed only to pick his pockett of Rup. 4000, which Capt. Alley was to give for the Honour done him.

This afternoon a Perwanna came to Bulchund from the Nabob of Decca, commanding Permesuradas (that great Villaine) to be turned out of his Service. Whereupon Bulchund caused it to be proclaimed by beat of Drum, that all men who had any complaint against Permesuradas should come and make their appearance and demands before him. In a few hours' time more that 3000 poor men gathered together, complaining with full mouths of his exaction and injustice towards them: some demanding Rupees 10, others Rupees 20, per man, which Bulchund very generously paid them in the Cazee's presence, to the amount of about Rupees 2000. This, it is feared, will be all ye satisfaction that will be given for about 5 Lack of Rupees which Permesuradas has forced from ye Merchants and poore Inhabitants, and Bulchund puts all the rest into his own Pockett, with ye Name and great applause of doing great and exemplary justice. 'T is happy for us that we are rid of soe great a Villaine upon any score whatsoever.

November 6.—This day Capt. Wildey made complaint to me that Capt. Hayward had not justice done him, for that Hayward was an antient Commander, and had been Commissioned by the King; and ought to weare the Flag, and not Capt. Lake, as was formerly ordered in my absence at Cassumbazar by Mr. Beard: whereupon I sent an order to Capt. Hayward in these following words:

"Whereas Capt. Charles Hayward, Commander of the *Henry and William*, has formerly been a Captain in His Majtie's Service, and is the oldest Commander now in this place, I doe desire and en-order him, the said Charles Hayward, to wear a Flagg as Admirall.

"Witness my hand. In Hugly, this 6 November 1683."

The like order, *mutatis mutandis*, I sent to Capt. Lake, to take downe his Flag-staffe and Pendent.

This Capt. Lake, being a great dissenter, & an inseparable companion of Mr. Beard's, has taken divers occasions to affront and speak ill of me behind my back, saying that nothing is done as it should be, and that he will putt the Company in a way when he goes home: and, I am told, in common discourse speaks as near Treason as he can, not to be taken hold of by the hearers. He 's a base, unworthy fellow, & I hope 't will lye in their power to lett him know it.

This night I received letters from Decca. On the way they were intercepted and broke open by Mr. Charnock, which he presumes to doe, being Second of Councell in the Bay. These two Councills, of Hugly and of the Bay, cause such disorder and confusion, that I fear ye Councill of [the] Bay will drive that of Hugly out of doors, and the Company's business too, in a little time, if speedy relief doe not come to prevent it.

November 7.—This day Bulchund sent for all those yt. made yr. complaints against Permesuradas yesterday and had mony given them; and put them in Prison, forcing them to refund all they had received, and much more, to be released: and compelled all men in general yt. had ever been wronged by ye Wicked Villaine to give discharges under their hands, sealed with y^{e} Cazee's Seals, y$^{t.}$ they received their money back again. It is y^{e} most cursed proceeding of cruell Tyranny y$^{t.}$ ever I heard of in my life. I am told Bulchund has given Permesuradas a Serpaue,[1] and restored him into favour again.

I 'm certainly informed M$^{r.}$ Beard has bought a third part of y^{e} Shipp *Brittania*, in Company with two Interlopers, M$^{r.}$ Nedham & M$^{r.}$ Dowglass, and sends her to Achin, which causes his great friendship with all that party.

November 8.—The Fousdar received another Perwanna, directed to him by the Nabob of Decca, procured by James Price, forbidding any Merchant whatsoever trading with any Interlopers: & confirming his former Perwanna to send the 3 Captains to Decca. Bulchund and he had a private conversation about it—to what purpose I did not understand. I doubt, *not* to our advantage: Bulchund having granted Capt. Alley free liberty of trade, & to pass all his goods with his owne Dustick. I am told Alley has bought Bulchund's new house, below the Dutch Factory, for Rupees 10,000 ready money.

November 9.—The Fousdar summoned all the Merchants to appear before him, and told them he had received a Perwanna, forbidding all men to trade with Interlopers, and required every one of them to oblige under his hand not to buy nor sell with them; and if anyone had received Dadney, or Impost mony, on account of goods, if ever it be known and not discovered to him, they must expect to be answerable for it to ye King, and make satisfaction as far as the Sale of their persons, wives, and children. I resolved, God willing, to prosecute this business to the utmost of my power, and hope to bring it to a good issue.

November 10.—Permesuradas went to sett in y^{e} towne belonging to y^{e} Dutch. Calling all men before him, he demanded 3 yeares' Gigeea,[2] or head money, w$^{h.}$ he pretended

[1] *Sirpão*, properly *sar-o-pā*, "head and foot," a complete dress of honour.—Y.

[2] *Jizya*, see p. 101.

they are in arreares to him, and forced it from them with all the Barbarous Rigour imaginable.

November 12.—Bulchund sent me a message that he had given order to all his Officers to stop all our trade unless I would agree to the following proposall.

"That since we had now been full 12 months, and had not yett obtained the King's Phirmaun to free us from payment of Custome, he was contented to allow us yett two months' time more from this day, provided we would then be obliged to pay him all the last and this yeare's Custome, according to our Entrys, or else we must be content not to receive or lade a parcel of goods more this Shipping."

Whereupon I called a Consultation, and thought good in such an emergency to send for all the Commanders of the Company's Shipps, & take their opinions; who unanimously concluded there was an absolute necessity to refer it to me to agree with Bulchund on these or better termes, if I could by any means procure them of him; the Government being so corrupt at present that this man does all he pleases without regard to the King or Nabob.

In the afternoon I visited Bulchund, when, after divers arguments *pro* and *con*, we came to this conclusion: That we should have free liberty to receive and lade all our goods this Monsoone or Shipping; and if before that time we could not produce the King's Phirmaun or Husbull Huckum[1] to the contrary, we would pay our Custom for this and the last year past to *him* in Hugly: upon which agreement y[e] Old Fox treated me with all possible respect and kindness; and as a farther testimony, one Peter Torris, a Dutch Foreman, being imprisoned by him, besought me to procure his releasement: which I did, and 't was as readily granted by Bulchund, though he had great demands on him. To-morrow they must be compounded the best I can.

November 13.—This day Capt. Alley dyned aboard Capt. Lake of y[e] *Prudent Mary*, with M[rs.][2] Honor, Clerke, and divers

[1] See note, p. 99.

[2] Presumably for "Messrs."

Interlopers, making great mirth and jollity by firing guns all the afternoone.

November 16.—Bulchund sent me word he was proffered by Capt. Alley & Co. Rupees 10,000 for himselfe, and Rup. 1000 for his Bramanin, to have liberty of free trade; and if I would promise to give him the like sum, he would engage to send Capt. Alley, Capt. Smith, and Capt. Read all Prisoners to Dacca, and to forbid ye Merchants trading with them: to which I agreed, and expect Bulchund's performance of his promise.

November 17.—Mr. Derick Johnson, a Dutchman, told me ye present Directore assured him 16 Saile of Shipps and 2000 men were ready to come & brake with this Government, when the differences happened between ye Old and Young Kings of Bantam: and this year he is confident a sufficient strength will be sent him to require satisfaction of these people for all the affronts and indignities they have putt upon them.

This Evening Bulchund sends me word he has refused to accept of Capt. Alley's proffer of Rup. 10,000 & Rup. 1000 to his Fockeer, but will accept of mine, and send the 3 Captains to Decca: not expecting to be given the money till they are on their way past Cassumbuzar.

From Cassimbuzar I am certainly informed Mr. Naylor is there with a great sum of money, buying up all the Taffaty and other Silks he can, for the Interlopers, who imploy him as their Factor, and declare to Bulchund *he* will pay *his* Custome for it. Y^e^ said Naylor has dayly corresponded with Mr. Charnock, having been always his intimate friend; and without question either provides him goods out of the Hon. Comp.'s Warehouse, or connives at the Weavers and Piccars[1] doing of it. Mr. Charnock is the more to be suspected, not having given the least notice of this Villainy of Mr. Naylor's in any of his Gen^ll.^ Letters, which he is wont to doe upon

[1] *Paikār*, a broker, an intermediate dealer or agent.—Y.

other slight and frivolous occasions. I am advised from Cassumbuzar he has paid more than Rup. 2700 for Custome at 3¾ per Cent., by which I conclude he has Mustered at least Rup. 20,000. Mr. Charnock must be assistant to him under hand, or 't were impossible for him to lay out soe much mony. The best of the Company's Servants (at least those that are soe esteemed) being thus subject to corruption, they can never be well served till they take the Dutch Course and Method of impowering their Agent to turne out those that offend in this nature, and yt. keepe Company and Feast dayly with ye Interlopers, as ye most precise of us doe here frequently, and take parts of Shipps and trade with them. If this grievance cannot be soon redressed, as discovery is made of it, ye Company's trade can never be carryed on to their most advantage.

Three things must be done to make ye Honble Compy's trade prosperous in this Country.

1st. The Interlopers must be supprest in England. 'T is impossible to be done here. I see they will dayly grow upon us without effort.

2nd. Custome must not be paid. If we pay 3½ per Cent. one yeare, we shall pay 5 the next, to excuse opening, pricing, weighing, and measuring our goods: and by degrees these people's exactions will grow to be insufferable. Ye duty of Custome (computing the trade which will and may easily be carryed on yearly in Bengall), I conclude, will be taken on £600,000 Stock. The Custome of that money, inwards, at 3½ per Cent., and Custome on its returnes home at 3½ per Cent. more, is 7 per Cent., which will amount to £42,000 per annum: for ye one halfe of which charge I will venture my life and fortune to take off the payment of Custome for ever, and to agree with this King upon such capitulations as shall be not only a vast advantage, but a perpetuall honour to our English Nation.

3rd. A General Regulation in ye Factorys, for which

there 's a necessity, of Investing greater and more absolute power in ye Agent: though he prove never soe great a Villaine, he must be intrusted (as the Directore is) for ye present, and then a better sent in his place. He must be feared, or ye Company's business cannot be done to advantage.

November 23.—This morning I went to visit the Fousdar, being this afternoone to sett out in his tents, in order to his going to Ballasore. He expressed great kindness, and gave me a Serepaw.[1] In the Afternoon the *Kent* was dispatched for Fort St. George with her lading of Saltpetre.

November 26.—I am advised from Cassumbuzar that M^r. Naylor bought up great store of Taffatys and all other Silks, to soe great a sum as to have paid 2100 rupees for Custome, at the rate of 3¾ per Cent. Computing which rate, he must have bought for more than the value of 70,000 rupees.

November 30.—Capt. Alley was most kindly and respectfully entertained by the Fousdar abroad, in his tents, and had a Serpaw presented to him. The Fousdar summoned all our Merchants to come before him, and forced them to take up money of Capt. Alley, commanding to provide him goods with all speed, that he may be despatched in 15 days at farthest. Soe deceitful and base are all the Magistrates in this country, that, as I have said before, 't is impossible to suppresse the Interlopers in this country. This day dispatched y^e *Hare*, Capt. Poston, for Persia, Laden with Sugar.

December 1683.

December 2.—This morning early, news was brought me our grand enemie (that corrupt Villain), Bulchund, was Dead. He fell sick in his tyrannicall progresse in these parts; forcing money from all persons; and continued sick till he came to his owne house at Muxoodavad, where he dyed on ye 29th Ultimo. Permesuradas is kept under cus-

[1] See p. 136.

tody of the Fousdar's Officers till orders come from Decca and the Nabob's pleasure be known who he will please to put in Bulchund's place. Whosoever comes in his place, 't is to be feared, will stop our goods, and force us to begin again and bribe anew: and soe it will be when ye Nabob dyes, who, being 82 years old and very feeble, cannot live long.[1]

December 4.—Mr. Johnson informed me that Capt. Minchin should say, in ye hearing of Capt. Udall, Capt. Cooke, & Mr. Catchpoole, after his returne from Cassimbuzar, "it lay in his power to ruine two of that Factory, viz., Mr. Barker & Mr. Threder, but that he was under an oath not to discover it." To explain this Riddle, Capt. Udall left two Servants of his behind him at Cassimbuzar, who came downe with Capt. Minchin in that Boat. They affirme Mr. Barker and Threder delivered divers bales of Silkes to the said Capt. Minchin, as they passed down the river a little below that Factory. Thus it 's plaine Mr. Charnock's favorites may doe anything, whilst Mr. Langley must not buy a few pieces of Baftaes, but they must be seized and taken from him.

December 6.—'Tis advised by Mr. Charnock at Cassumbazar that Mr. Naylor gives 15 and 20 per Cent. dearer for his Taffaties and all sorts of Silkes that he buys for the Company. When Naylor was here in Hugly, he sold those Silkes he had by him much cheaper than those bought by Mr. Charnock, as formerly noted in this Diary.

December 7.—This Evening I received advice from Mr. Crosse at Decca, that the Fousdar's Letter of this place was read to the Nabob in open Durbar on ye 26th Ult^o.^, in these following words:

"That he had received the Nabob's Perwanna, and in complyance therewith had sent for the Commanders of the

[1] According to Stewart (*Hist. of Bengal*, p. 323), Shaista Khan resigned charge *circa* 1689, and not before. He then retired to Agra, where he died Anno Hej. 1105, or A.D. 1693; so he survived Mr. Hedges' remark nine years at least.—R. F. B.

Interlopers' Shipps, who refused to come: whereupon he sent Peons, &c., to seize on them, but [they] were afterwards sett at liberty by Bulchund, who said he would be responsible for them to the Nabob, & that none would be their security for fear of the Old English Traders (meaning the Company's Servants). Which last sentence has done us much harm; for ye Duan (our implacable enemy) rose up immediately and said, "These are the tricks and devices they use to let no others trade besides themselves, that then they may sell their goods at what rate they please, and be subject to no orders: whereas this New Company (as he termed them) are willing to pay 5 per Cent. Custome, which we deny; that they were merchants as well as wee; and to hinder their trade would be ye King's damage." Here upon the old doting Nabob (being ruled since the death of Ray Nundelol by what he hears any one say) replyed, "They should trade freely." Soe that now the Business being thus determined by the Nabob, there 's no possibility of rooting out or doing any prejudice to Interlopers: they are more kindly treated upon all occasions than we are: and 'twill be as impossible for us to hold out long without payment of Custome, as well as they, if we doe not resolve to fall out with these people very speedily.

December 11.—A boat stopt at the Custome house; her chief Boatman declares he tooke in his lading at the English Factory at Maulda, and came with Captn. Alley's Dustick, who received all his boat's lading. I'm credibly informed there 's a clause in Alley's Charter-Party, giving liberty to Mr. Hervy to lade such a quantity of goods as therein provided. 'T is possible this boat's lading is in part of it. Mr. Hervy has resigned up the management of his Factory to Mr. Peachey, being troubled with the Gout. He may doe what he pleases, he is under no control. If I should offer to put another in his place, he would be well enough again immediately to doe the Company's business himselfe. He regards nothing but to enjoy his little Seraglio of 6 Strumpets, and live at ease upon the Company's Expence.

An account depending between a Gomasta, or Factor, of one of our Merchants here, and Mr. Hervy, for Rup. 105, we were requested to take the said Merchant's security till the Month of January next (the said Factor being employed at present in providing goods for this Factory), and ordered Mr. Hervy and Councill in our Genll. letter not to give the said Gomasta disturbance till ye time aforesaid. Mr. Hervy, notwithstanding, imprisoned the Gomasta, telling him, "the Agent and Council had nothing to doe with his management of Affaires in this Factory; nor were otherwise concerned than to remitt them money to buy the Company's cloth." This affront is insufferable; but I must have patience.

December 15.—Received answer to a Generall from Cassumbuzar, wherein Mr. Charnock tells us plainly, in these following words:

"Whereas you order us to restore the Peon to George Pitman which he had formerly, and did more business for him than for ye Honble Compy., it is to be supposed (our Honble Masters having thought fit to trust such a concerne as the charge of this Factory to our management) that we are best able to appoint whatever peons are most fitting for to watch the throwing shopp."

To this may be replyed, in his own words,—that the Compy. having thought fit to intrust the Agent and Councill of Hugly with ye management of their affairs in ye Bay, they may be as well able to judge of such a matter as Mr. Charnock. This, with his refusing to turne out John Griffin, though twice ordered to doe it, is such an affront to the Company's authority invested in me, as can be no longer endured than till the next letters out of England, without utter ruin and destruction to the Honble East India Company's affaires here in Bengall.

December 20.—Mr. Crosse advises that the Nabob hopes to

receive a Husbull Hookhum from ye Vizier for our enjoyment of a Free Trade without payment of Custome.

December 21.—The *Prudent Mary* received her despatches for England.

December 27.—Received a letter from Mr. Crosse, advising the Fousdar of this place had wrott in ye Interlopers' favour to the Nabob for his Phirwanna and protection of them, for which they would give him an annual present. The Nabob was ready to grant a Perwanna, had not James Price (being present) put it into the Nabob's head to send for them up thither to make the Agreement himselfe, to which end a Perwanna is dispeeded hither, and $M^{r.}$ Davis will be sent of that errant, where James Price will not fail to doe him all y^e prejudice and Mischief he is able.

The Shawbunder of Ballasore wrott to the Nabob also in their Favour, and that if we left the Country, the New Company's Trade would be much the greater, and their paying Custome bring great profitt to the King, &c. The Nabob replyed he believed this was wrott out of spight, revenge, & malice; to satisfie which he would not make us leave the country, who would returne againe and take y^e Port townes, hinder and take their Ships, and afterwards force a trade as we pleased ourselves.

The place of Customer, as well as Collector of the King's Rents, and Government of this place, is given to Aziz-beig, a person $y^{t.}$ speaks Turkish and showed himself my great friend at Dacca. The said Asiz-beig departed Decca for this place y^e 19th Instant.

December 31.—I am informed $M^{r.}$ Naylor has this day sent down 35 bales of Silke to Capt. Alley, which he buys up at Cassumbazar, not without great probability that he is assisted by Mr. Charnock: y^e Merchants $y^{t.}$ usually traded with our Factory having at present an unhappy dispute and quarrel with $M^{r.}$ Charnock, as if it were on purpose to make them carry their Silk to y^e Interlopers. To confirm the truth of this information, Mr. Naylor has certainly drawn a bill for Rupees 16,000 on Capt. Alley, which he has satisfied.

[*End of* 1683. *Though this date is continued, as was then the custom, till March* 25, 1684.]

January 1684.

January 2.—Letters from Muxadavad advise that ye New Governor sent by the Nabob to seize Bulchund's Estate has given his Sonn 2 of his Father's Horses, and Rup. 1000 in his purse (the young man having been entered one of the King's Soldjers in his infancy), and commanded him to goe to his quarters under his Superior; and so turned him out of his house, and tooke all his Mother's Jewells from her.

They have, by information of the Servants, dug in severall places of the house, where they have found great summes of money. Under his bed were found Lacks 4½; in the House of Office, two Lacks. They [have] in all found Ten Lacks already, and make no doubt but to find more, besides vast summes let out to severall Merchants at interest, and conveyed away to other parts of the Empire, and Nine Lacks formerly owned and sent to the Nabob as soone as Bulchund dyed.

January 3.—I went this morning to visit and welcome Aziz-beig, our new Goverr. and Collector of the Customes here. He is a Persian born, and received me with great kindness and respect; assuring me of his favour upon all occasions. He speaks Turkish currently, and seems much delighted that I understand that Language. I make no question but in his time ye Company's businesse will passe ye better for it.

From Cassumbr. I am advised Mr. Charnock has taken ye freedome to put me into his Diary of November last, informing "that he caused Peons to follow a Boat with English

Colours and my Dustick, whose goods were seen to be conveyed to Mr. Dowglass his house": matter of fact is true, without ye least circumstance or appearance of evill, as Mr. Charnock would insinuate from it.

One Sigr. Francessci D'Acha, a Portuguese, formerly a Soldjer at ye Fort in the time of Sir Jeremy Sambrooke, having by his industry and fairdealing gotten to be master of a small Shipp, for his own and ye English Merchants' account at Syam, usually consigned himself to Captn. Vincent; finding him gone for England, would have recommended himselfe to me. I being opprest with more business and trouble than I was well able to manage, desired him to make choice of some other person: he chose Mr. Douglasse. About 2 months since, Mr. Duglasse came to me for a Dustuck to pass his goods, first obliging [himself], if we paid Custome, to pay in like manner for all he received. This by the Councill and all mankind was judged better to doe than lett them pay Custome till ye Company's business was settled, to avoyd an ill example. Charnock, out of malice, says (or at least suspects) these were Interlopers' Goods. I call Mr. Dowglasse before Mr. Beard and ye Councill to declare the truth: he affirmes the goods were for account of D'Acha and his owners, except 200 pieces of Dutch Taffaties sent to Achin, and 10 Pieces for his owne account: and that he never had ye confidence to aske me for a Dustick to passe unlawful goods, nor did I ever give him any.

Such groundlesse assertions as these are insufferable; I can no more bear them than an honest, virtuous Woman can be questioned for her Chastity. It 's absolutely necessary that one of us two be displaced. He brags never no chief was yett able to contend with him and Hervey, & makes no doubt but to give me my Mittimus this next shipping. Ye Company best know their own concerns and advantages, and I must acquiesce in their determination, whatever it be.

January 5.—Mr. John Haynes, from Cassumbuzar, advises at large, Mr. Charnock having engaged Mr. Hervey and Mr. Pownsett to meet at a General Consulltation whether I will or no: and declares they will doe such ridiculous things, that I am ashamed to discover their folly soe much as to write or take notice of them.

January 10.—Letters from Pattana advise Mr. Beard's Brother-in-Law, James Lowdon, railes at me and abuses me insufferably; saying I did ye Compy. no service at Decca; that he could have done much more; and doubts not but to see me turned out with disgrace as Vincent was, by the next letters out of England: with much more to ye like purpose. These contempts I am forced to endure at present, not to bring ye Company's concerns into confusion.

January 12.—From Cassumbuzar 't is advised ye Merchants and Picars appeal again to ye Cazee for Justice against Mr. Charnock. Ye Cazee cites Mr. Charnock to appear; he not appearing, the Merchants take a testimonyall from the Cazee, appoint a Vekeel or two for them, and pretend they will goe and complaine to ye Nabob at Decca. In the mean time goods come slowly from that Factory: 't is probable they will not send returns of half the goods they have agreed for. I am credibly informed the persons Mr. Charnock deals with are soe poore they will not be able to answer their debts by above a lack of Rupees of what 's given out this yeare only, besides ye remaines standing out of ye last.

This Diary was thus far sent home to my Brother Sambrooke & other friends in England by ye *Herbert*, Capt. Henry Udall, Commandr., to satisfie them and justifie me in all my transactions for ye Honble. East India Company, which (God knows) have been allways performed with greatest dilligence & Integrity, to ye best of my Judgement, notwithstanding the false reports and aspersions of my declared enemies in Bengall, and ye Prejudice that some of ye Company have unjustly conceived against me.

I omitted entring my dayly transactions in this Booke, as I ought to have done, in expectation to have gott them transcribed for me out of my Diary kept for ye Comp^y. But that favour would not afterwards be granted to me when I was dismist their Service.

July 1684.

July 2.—Falling this day into discourse with M^r. Daniel Joachim Schlu, a Dane (formerly belonging to their Factory in Bantam), amongst other things he told me that M^r. Richard Frenchfeild was, underhand, a great favorer of ye Interlopers; particularly when M^r. Thomas Davies was at Decca. The better to conceal his goods, ye said Frenchfield sent down his cousin Pointall to M^r. Cooke's Shippe, then riding at anchor at Kedgeria, and, under pretence of bringing up goods of his owne and his said cousin's, brought up also 20 Maunds of Opium for account of M^r. Cooke,—as he, ye said Cooke, told M^r. Schlu, in the presence of George Herron.

The said M^r. Schlu farther told me, for an instance of M^r. Frenchfeild's dealing with Interlopers, that he had bought all ye said Cooke's Copper and Tutenag at his first arrivall, and had now about ye value of Rup. 3 or 400 of Cooke's in his possession, and assisted Cooke upon all occasions; notwithstanding all which kindness ye said Cooke was so unworthy as to call M^r. Evans (ye Minister) and him two great knaves: saying they cheated him of halfe a rupee per maund in all the Copper and Tutenag which he sold them. Where, by y^e by, I cannot but acknowledge M^r. Evans busies himselfe too much in trade and merchandize, for a man of his Coat: being certainly one of ye greatest traders in Hugly.

July 7.—Received a Generall from M^r. Pownsett and

Councill of Decca, accompanying their Diary for ye month of May last. On the 5th of which Month (without any former advice given, or liberty desired, of this Councill, as alwayes customary) Charges Rup. 305 : 10 to Account, for a Beetle Box, Plate, Arrack Bowl, Spitting Cupp, and Silver handle for a Fan: all of Silver; besides Rup. 50 for Cloth of Gold Pillows, and other furniture.

If this freedom be allowed to every Factory to build (as Mr. Charnock does at Cassumbazar), and to buy and provide what Plate & Furniture they please for their Chambers (as Mr. Pownsett does at Dacca), under pretence of entertaining Strangers, without notice given and liberty granted by this Agency (which is not only irregular and disrespectfull to ye character conferred on me by ye Honble. Compy., but tends like wise much to their prejudice), all things will then run into disorder and confusion.

This day at a Consultation held concerning ye repair of Mr. Moseley's house, which ye Governor. would not suffer him to mend, having a desire to it himself, Mr. Beard tooke occasion, on behalf of Mr. Thomas Ley, to affront & abuse me in a most rude & unhandsome manner; growing pale with passion, shooke his head, & made such a filthy noise with his mouth as cannot be expressed. This prejudice conceived against me (I judge, upon account of opinion in Religion, he being a most rigid Presbyterian) is so great, and ye dayly disrespects & affronts cast upon me so insufferable (having private information given him by Sir Josiah Child that he should be Agent), that no Public Business can be freely and calmly argued in Consultation without ending in a quarrel; which I find so exceeding detrimental to ye Company's concernes, that I choose to bear any thing rather than their affairs under my management shall suffer by it.

Mr. Ley, on ye other hand (being one of ye same profession in Religion, and judging themselves persecuted in England), holds and combines with Mr. Beard in every thing, right or wrong, just or unjust, out of Malice to me.

Mr. Ley of himself knows nothing of ye Country affaires, or of ye Company's business, nor has he the least insight or knowledge of merchandize in general, not being skilled in the common rudements of Arithmatick, nor able to cast up any account, nor divide with 4 figures.

Mr. Pownsett, in all his Diary of May last, gives no particular account of what he had done or acted for Mr. Charnock, more than that he had sent a Genll. to Cassumbr. "concerning their businesse",—as if I and this Councill of Hugly were such traytors to ye Company, as not fitt to know what was transacted betwixt them in that grand affair of ye Company's consernes; Mr. Pownsett being otherwise very full and particular in all other business and advices what soever.

In like manner Mr. Pownsett gives no account of what is wrott him from Cassumbzr. more than "Recd. a Generall from Cassumbr. concerning their troubles": the said Pownsett, or Charnock, neither of them giving ye least notice to what those Troubles are, that we might endeavour to gett them removed; which I could very easily have done at a small expence (considering ye greatness of ye affaire), not exceeding Rup. 2 in 3000, the Native Merchants having wrott a Genll. letter to me, advising they were ready and willing to stand to my award and determination of ye differences betwixt them and Mr. Charnock: which he out of meer pride and malice would not consent unto (pretending ye inconvenience of his coming to Hugly), that I might not have ye credit of composing their differencies.

Mr. Pownsett, in his May Diary, gives order likewise for making a Budgero without leave from this Factory; & indeed, does what he pleases, as if altogether independant of us, and a distinct Agency: following ye practice of his admired Patrons, Mr. Hervy and Mr. Charnock.

I am also this day informed Mr. Charnock has ended his differences with ye Picars and Merchants by arbitration of certain Moor Merchants, who had adjudged Mr. Charnock to pay for all ye Silke he sent home ye last yeare Ru. 5 : 12an. per Seer, which is halfe a rupee more than it 's worth : and, together with charges, will prejudice ye Company above a lack of rupees.

I received a letter lately from Mr. Crosse of Decca, advising me (amongst other things) in ye following words, viz. :

"At present I have not any thing of moment to advise, but that Mr. Pownsett, having wrott so often to ye Worshipfull & to Cassumbr. that no Perwanna could be procured for redresse of their grievances without a present to the Nabob, which now being ordered, and he not knowing how to goe to worke to effect it, fearing ye disgrace that may fall on him should he after all not obtaine one,—hath gott Golobray to stir in ye business, by putting Rupees 2000 into his hands, and giving a writing, that if he gets a Perwanna he is to have ye said 2000 rup. for charges and his paines, and not to give any other account thereof."

In another letter of ye 30th June, Mr. Crosse advises me farther, viz. :

"As to what Mr. Charnock writes agnst. James Price, he will be shortly with ye Worshipfull to vindicate himselfe. And for Golobray (though he be a base fellow), I believe he hath not had any hand in hindering a Perwanna for Cassimbazar troubles ; for if he hath, certainly Mr. Pownsett (from whom, I suppose, Mr. Charnock must have that advice) would never have entrusted him with ye procuring of said Perwanna. But the business is this: Mr. Pownsett does despaire of getting one, and to hide his owne Ignorance from Mr. Charnock, writes that Golobray and James are ye occasion, when they have both been assisting to him ;—thereby thinking to make ye world believe you to be their abettor in a businesse detrimental to ye Hon. Company."

By these two letters from Mr. Charles Crosse, it 's very apparent how industrious Mr. Pownsett has been to cast ye odium of Mr. Charnock's and his owne miscarryages upon me.

July 17.—I was advised by Mr. How, Commander of ye Company's little Shipp *Thomas* (newly returned from Fort St. George) that I was Dismist the Company's Service; Mr. Beard made Agent in my place; & Agent Gyfford made President of ye Coast of Cormandell & Bay of Bengal.

July 25.—This day Five Dellolls, or Brokers, of Decca, after they had been with me, went to Mr. Beard's Chamber to pay their respects to him; taking with them James Price, ye Vekeel. Mr. Beard demanded, "Who they were?" James answered, "The Dellolls of Decca." Mr. Beard replyed, "I know their business very well; I know what they come for." Mr. Frenchfeild coming into Mr. Beard's Chamber yt. very instant, said, "I am sorry these men have found ye way to Hugly: this will spoil the Company's business"; and soe ye men were dismist.

Their designe in coming to Hugly was to prove to me before Mr. Pownsett's face (if thereto required) that he, ye said Mr. Pownsett, bought cloth of Severall sorts at Rupees 6, 7, & 8, which he charged to ye Company at Ru. 10, 11, & 12, and some at Ru. 13 per piece; but finding Mr. Beard and Mr. Frenchfeild prejudiced against ye discoverers, and unwilling to detect Pownsett's villany, and I being dismist ye Company's service, concerned myself no farther in ye businesse (despairing to doe any good where I met with such opposition), but advised ye Dellolls to returne to Decca. The like cheat was clearly proved to me against Mr. Samuel Hervy, deceased, who otherwise, by fair dealing, could never have gott Rupees 220,000, as he has done in a few years out of nothing: his first setting up being with Rup. 1500 he won, or rather cheated, at play, of a Purser of a Shippe at Ballasore, soone after his first arrivall in the Bay of Bengal.

James Price assured me $y^{t.}$ $M^{r.}$ Pownsett, appearing in Publick Durbar at Decca in y^{e} business of $M^{r.}$ Charnock, the Nabob commanded him "to be gone out of his sight"; saying, "y^{e} English were a company of base, quarrelling people, and foul dealers."

July 29.—$M^{r.}$ Charnock, in his letter of this date, says the Chief of Decca had procured y^{e} Nabob's Perwanna to have their differences arbitrated by Merchants, whereas this Perwanna was procured by Arz-dast,[1]—else why was it not procured by $M^{r.}$ Charnock's letter, which y^{e} Nabob rejected, refusing to answer it?

In truth, $M^{r.}$ Pownsett was proffered this Perwanna long since, when James Price was there, if he would have given for it Rup. 600; since which time $M^{r.}$ Pownsett has agreed to give Goolobray R. 2000 to procure him this Perwanna, upon condition that he is to give no account of its expence: which, with y^{e} help of my Arz-dast, he procured accordingly.

August 1684.

August 16.—We had news brought us that 4 Dutch Shipps were arrived in y^{e} Ganges as high as Barnagur from Batavia. They report $Gen^{l.}$ Spilman & his Second of Councill are both dead; that y^{e} 3rd of Council, one Camploys by name, is made General; and that $M^{r.}$ English had been there, from y^{e} $Comp^{y.}$, in a Shippe of 60 Guns. At his arrival they told him y^{e} King of Bantam would not suffer him to goe into y^{e} Road of Bantam, but that (if he pleased) he might goe to Batavia and buy refreshments: of which proffer he accepted, and was afterwards dismist, not being suffered to lade a penny worth of goods. The Duch men could not inform us whether $M^{r.}$ English returned for England or went to Suratt.

[1] '*Arẓ-dāsht*, practically the same as *arẓī* (vulg. *urzee*), "a petition".—Y.

On these Shipps came one Soleman, an inhabitant and freeman for several years in Batavia, now made Comissarie Gen^ll. of all India, which gives him precedency of y^e Govr. Gen^ll. himselfe, and impowers him to call all persons whatsoever to account for all their actions. He has condemned the late Gen^ll. Spilman's estate (after his death) to pay rup. 90,000 to ye Company; and displaced ye Secretary Gen^ll. (though his own brother-in-law), fining him ye sum of P.[1] 60,000, of all which sums ye said Comissarie is to have ⅓ part. He is to goe to all Factories in India, and to command what Shippes he pleases to wait on him; to examine all bookes; inspect and enquire into all their affaires; & to regulate all their concernes as he thinks convenient, and judges may tend to their most advantage. He brings with him a Fiscall and a Secretary, Divers Servants, 24 soldiers in Red Coats, with a Sergeant, Corporall, Drummer, & 4 Trumpeters.

It 's likewise reported by those that come in these Shipps that the Dutch, hearing of our preparations and designe in England to send out 18 Shipps to restore the King of Bantam, the Hollanders had fitted out and manned 14 men of War from 54 to 75 great Guns apiece, ye least of which had 250 White men in them besides Natives, with 4 Fire Shipps, to fight us and endeavor to frustrate our designe.

August 19.—M^r. W^m. How, Comand^r. of ye Company's Shippe *Thomas*, gave me a Visit after dinner in my Chamber, & desiring to speake with me in private, I tooke him into my Counting House, where, after a respectfull preamble, begging excuse for ye freedom he tooke with me, told me he observed in general discourse with divers persons belonging to the Factory (whose names he would not discover) that there was a conspiracy and combination against me to doe me all ye prejudice they could; and, First, they

[1] The symbol is doubtful; probably it should be *Rupees* as before.—Y.

intended to call me to an account for several things I had acted in ye Company's service, the particulars he knew not, and could not learne.

Secondly, That all endeavors would be used to prevent my going home the way I intended, by Persia, and so overland.

I demanded for what reasons these persons intended to deal so unkindly with me: whether he knew any order ye Company had made formerly, or lately sent out, to ye contrary? Mr. How replyed, "he knew of no reason nor order, but was confident endeavors would be used to stop me if they could." I then told him, "after this role they might as well rob or plunder me of all I had, bind and send me home in Chaines, as exercise such arbitrary power." He had nothing more to say to that; but advised me to beware of what he had told me, and prevent it if possible: telling me farther my adversaries would pretend this way of going home would be prejudicial to ye Company, & an occasion for all men to take ye same course. I thought all men had ye Freedom to goe home which way they pleased, till ye Company forbade it, & that divers persons had both gone & come this way before me.

Mr. How informed me farther, 't was reported I had conveyed away my Estate out of ye Factory, & had putt it into ye hands of ye Company's Chief Banian. I assured him the contrary: that I had all my present Cash in the house, & intended to keepe it there till ye President's arrival, not doubting that I should find him a person that feared God, and soe far respected ye law as to doe no unjust action: with other words to ye same purpose. I gave him my hearty thanks for his kind information, and so we parted.

August 21.—The Dutch Director sent to know whether he and his Lady might give me a visit some time the next weeke. I sent him word he should be kindly welcome whenever he pleased.

The said Messenger told me they had 13 Ships sent them out this yeare from Holland to Batavia.

August 27.—I received a letter from Mr. Stables (Secretary of ye Fort), dated yesterday, from aboard ye Sloope *Arrivall*, 4 miles below Jan Pardo, advising President Gyfford was arrived there (but had not ye manners to write me himselfe), and ordered 4 Budgeros and 10 or 12 great boates with provisions to be sent down to him with all expedition. Whereupon I immediately dispeeded Mr. Frenchfeild, Mr. Johnson, & Mr. Ley to his Honor, with 2 Budgeros, boates, and provisions.

August 28.—I borrowed the late Duch Fiscall's Budgero, and went in Company with Mr. Beard, Mr. Littleton, Mr. Dowglasse, Mr. Innes, Capt. Browne, Capt. Hayward, Capt. Pyne, Capt. Norgrave, Capt. Banes, & Dr. Harwar, as far as ye Devill's Reach, where I caused ye tents to be pitched, in expectation of ye President's arrival, and lay here all night.

Our boats lay in a very fine Eddy, capacious enough to receive 100 Ships, where they may ride free from ye danger of ye Freshes: this being, in divers men's opinions, the most convenient place in all the River to build a Factory.

August 29.—The President not appearing, we took up our tents & fell downe to Tittaghur, where we dyned. Soone after I was advised of ye President's being come from Barnagur, from whence he arrived a little before sunset, with all his company, which, together with the Soldiers, were numerous. We lay here till after Midnight; and for better conveniency I left ye company of Mr. Beard, &c., in the Duch Budgero, and lodged with Mr. Dowglasse, whose Budgero being heavy, & 2 or 3 of his boatmen running away from him, we were not able, at a certain point, to stem ye Freshes, which ran so violently that we were forced to lye by till the morning, when, with much labour and difficulty, we tracked our boat ahead; but making slow advance, M$^{r.}$ Dowglasse, M$^{r.}$ Innes, & I went aboard of Capt. Browne's Pinnace, which came rowing by us. Crossing over y^{e} River to avoid y^{e} violence of y^{e} Current, we were forced by y^{e} stream to y^{e} other side, the water carrying us with that strength that our men could not prevent the boat's head running and striking against ye bank, which caused a great lump of earth to fall into our boat; with which, ye boat turning her side to ye Banke, another vast quantity of earth, containing divers tons, fell downe; but it pleased God that only a little part fell into our boat: had we been halfe a foote nearer ye bank we had all been drowned,—the best swimmer (so I am informed) not being able to save himselfe in ye midst of so many violent Eddys or Whirle Pooles: for which great deliverance I beseech ye Lord to make me truly thankfull. After this escape I went about a mile by land in ye raine and dirt, but spying a boat coming towards us with some of ye President's Soldiers, we prayed them to take us in; one of them, knowing me, did it very readily. In y^{e} boat was Captain Richardson, commander of y^{e} Soldiers, who treated me with the greatest respect and civility. With this boat I got near y^{e} Dutch Garden, where y^{e} President and all his retinue had been some time arrived; and seeing I came not, M$^{r.}$ E$^{d.}$ Littleton sent his Palankeen & Peons to meet me, who carryed me with all speed to the Garden, where I was no sooner arrived, but I immediately embarked with y^{e} President and M$^{r.}$ Beard in y^{e} Company's great Budgero, and arrived in Hughly about 4 o'clock in y^{e} afternoone.

August 30.—A Dutch Shippe riding over against this Factory saluted us with 11 guns as we passed by her. Coming near our Factory, the Shippe *Ann*, Capt. Browne, began to fire guns, in one of which (by ye Gunner's neglect) was a Shott. No sooner was ye President gott ashore, but Aziz Beigh, ye Governour, complained of it, pretending the Shott had killed a man, hoping to have gott some money to accommodate the matter; but failing of their designe, let fall ye pretence.

About halfe an hour after ye President's arrival in Hugly Factory, he called me, Mr. Beard, Mr. Francis Ellis, Mr. Richd. Frenchfeild, Mr. Thomas Ley, and Mr. Richard Gough, into the Counting House, to hear his Comission read; which being done by John Stables,[1] his Secretary, I wished his Honor much joy, with ye rest of ye Company, assuring them I did readily and willingly submit to ye Company's pleasure: to which the President made no other reply but "'t was very well". The Secretary showed me the seal to the Commission, telling me "'t was the Company's". I replyed, "I made no doubt of it."

September 1684.

September 1.—President Gyfford[2] called a Consultation; being sett, he sent for me, desiring me to produce my Cash Booke, and deliver up ye Company's Cash: which I did immediately, & tooke Mr. John Beard's receipt for its ballance.

He then demanded "Whether I had opened and stopt Mr. Beard's Letter, which he would have sent home per y^e^ *Defence* to Sir Josia Child?" and read Capt. Heath's certificate of that business, with some other discourse to ye same purpose.

Having heard what ye President said, I desired ye favour to aske ye President and Council a question or two before I returned them an answer, which being granted,

First, I desired to know "Whether I was dismist the Company's Service or not?"

[1] Mr. John Stables, afterwards chief at Vizagapatam, and killed, with four other factors, in 1689, when the Mogul decided upon expelling the English.—Bruce, *Annals*, vol. ii, 650.

[2] President Gyfford was "dismissed" in 1687, and succeeded by Mr. Yale.—Bruce, *Annals*, vol. ii, 571. Date of letter not given.

They tolld me "They were of opinion I was dismist their Service."

Then I desired to know by what Authority or direction they asked me this question.

The President tolld me they had no other authority for it but ye Company's Letter. The Paragraph being read relating to that businesse,'t was said they should make enquiry to know whether I had stopt Mr. Beard's letter or not? I bade them enquire where they pleased, & then they would know the Relation that was given them was notoriously False. However, I thought my selfe no-ways obliged to stand two tryalls for one and ye same offence; adding that when I was next tryed for this fault it should be before impartiall Judges and an equall Jury, who, I hoped, would give me good satisfaction for ye great damage and prejudice I had received, if they did not find me guilty. Besides, I tolld them I thought it a great dishonor to ye Company to make any question of ye truth of that for which they had not only judged and condemned, but punished me also for, by dismissing me their Service, without suffering me to speake for my selfe: that this manner of proceeding was like those that hanged a man first, and examined ye business afterwards.

Upon this answer the President tolld me, "They had no more to say to me at present": whereupon I tooke my leave and retired to my Chamber.

September 3.—The River of Ganges is risen so high as it has not been known in ye memory of man—the water being 3 or 4 foot high in ye Bazaar. It is reported more than 1000 houses are fallen down in ye Dutch Quarters, and boats may row round their Factory in Hugly.

September 4.—I received Letters from Decca of ye 14th Ult^o.^, advising the Waters were risen so high that men waded to their middle in most of the Streets.

At Pattana they say the whole country is over flowne; that

they fear this flood will make rice dear, and cause a great scarcity of all provisions.

September 16.—About 1 o'clock this morning there arose a suddaine and violent Storm of wind, lightning, and thunder, accompanyed with fierce showers of raine, which continued all this day.

September 17 & 18.—The Storm continued: the Wind variable between the N.E. and S.E., the Moon two days after Full. The wind, after this storm, springing up at North, 't is generally concluded the monsoon is broken up for this year.

We hear it blew hard those three days, viz., ye 16, 17, & 18 instant, at Ballasore; and if it should prove [the end, yet] ye monsoon has [been] very favourable in respect of other years.

September 23.—President Gyfford and most of ye Councell, especially Mr. Beard, carrying themselves very unkindly and disrespectfully towards me, I was no longer able to endure their insolent behaviour; and being resolved (as soon as I could gett a convenient house) to leave ye Factory, I removed this afternoon to a house in ye Duch quarters, where Mr. Vincent lived 2 years since, being ye best house procureable in all ye towne, for which I was beholding to ye present Duch Directore, Sig^r.^ Martinus Huysman, who ordered the proprietor of it to lett me have it upon the first intimation of my desire to hire it.

September 26.—I went to visit the Duch Directore and give him thankes for his kindness in so readily ordering a house for me in his quarters. He obliged me to stay Supper with him, treating me with great civility and respect.

September 29.—Mr. Jonah Willshaw gave me a visit. In discourse he told me he had lately been with Mr. Beard, who spoke many detracting and reproachful words of me, declaring, amongst other things (after his canting manner), it grieved his Spirit exceedingly, and troubled him to y^{e} heart, to see every body continue to show me such great respect, and wondered why, and for what cause, they did it.

October 1684.

October 3.—President Gyfford set out for Cassumbazar, no Merchant with him but M$^{r.}$ Richard Gough; all y^{e} rest were his own attendants, who came with him from ye Fort (*i.e.*, Fort St. George).

November 1684.

November 6.—The Dutch Director sent to desire he might be permitted to give me a visit this afternoon.

I sent him word he should be heartily welcome whensoever he thought fit to doe me the Honour; so he came accordingly, bringing with him his Lady and his Daughter, M$^{r.}$ Mesdock, y^{e} Fiscall, and another of the Councill, together with M$^{r.}$ Hendrick Ben, their Chaplain, or Domine, as they call him.

November 10.—I went to meet President Gyfford at y^{e} English Garden, on his returne from Cassumbuzar, where he arrived y^{e} last night, but thought good to continue and repose himselfe there till y^{e} nation [?] could come and waite upon him, and conduct him to ye Factory. We dyned here all together, and at 3 in ye afternoon embarked on ye Budgero, and in lesse than an houre's time arrived in ye Factory at Hugly. On ye way I heard ye President declare he was now very well assured y^{e} trade of this place could never be carryed on, and managed to y^{e} Company's advantage, till they fell out with the Government, and could oblige them to grant us better termes: which he thought very feasible. And this is no more than I advised y^{e} Hon$^{ble.}$ Company and all my friends in England two years since, and foresaw a necessity of taking such a course, in a few months after my arrival in these parts.

November 11.—This Afternoon, between 2 and 3 o'clock, Mr. Francis Ellis sent me a letter by a Peon (Capt. Charles Haywood, Commander of ye *Henry & William*, and my cousin, Nathanael Letten, standing by me when I received it). I found it to be a most scurrilous, base, railing letter from Thomas Haggerston, with an adjoyned Account Current to it, wherein he makes me his debtor no lesse than Rup. 197,998 : 8.

It seems ye letter was sealed up and directed to me from Balasore by ye said Haggerston; but Mr. Ellis tooke ye freedom to breake it open and detayne it to show President Gyfford, when he returned from Cassumbazar, and then sealed it up and sent it to me: Captain Hayward telling me, so soon as he saw the letter, he believed it was the same letter which Mr. Ellis shewed him and Capt. Browne this morning together; so that ye opening and detaining a letter of mine is no crime in them, though it be judged so in me.

November 13.—Bullubdas, one of ye Company's Merchants, gave me a visit this day, telling me, amongst other relations concerning ye Company's affairs, that Mr. Edward Littleton was desired by President Gyfford to goe up to Cassumbuzar to buy him some silke, where ye said Littleton has agreed for 200 bales for account of the President, who, by ye Company's orders, is not permitted to trade in that commodity. If this relation should prove a mistake, [still] I am certaine the President kept a most intimate and friendly correspondence with Mr. Littleton all ye time he was at Hughly, and invited himself to supper at Mr. Littleton's house, and carried Mr. Charnock with him, who was Littleton's mortall and inveterate Enemie. I never durst take upon me to visit Mr. Littleton, or show him, or any other person, such respect, whom the Company declared an Interloper. But it seems the proverb is verified, that, One man may better steal a horse than another man looke over ye hedge.

'Tis well known how kind ye President has been to a Gentlewoman at Madras, who came passenger upon Capt. Alley to Porto Novo; that Agent Beard, Mr. Evans (the Minister), & Mr. Frenchfeild were often in company with ye Interlopers, especially ye two latter, who are seldom out of their Company.

This Afternoon Mr. Richard Gough told me that Mr. Richd. Frenchfeild had signed two certificates against me, of which one, subscribed by himselfe alone, that he is informed I tooke 8000 Rupees of ye Merchants at Ballasore for a Bribe; the other Certificate he signed in company with Mr. Roger Braddyl, declaring that he, ye said Richard Frenchfeild, had complained to me of Mr. William Johnson's ill sorting the Company's goods, to their great prejudice. To which I made Answere, "I had no friend in ye Country but Mr. Johnson, and that if he sorted ye cloth otherwise than it ought to be, either he or his Father in England must be answerable for it, and make the damage good to the Company."

Mr. Braddyll declares I said, "If I should looke into, & make strict enquiry & examination of every little complaint, the Company's business would be delayed, & returns not made them in time for ye Shipps to save their passage, which latter (of two evils) would be the greatest." These are ye words, or to this purpose (as near as I can remember), that Mr. Gough told me. More than that, he assured me in general ye President and Council (to his knowledge) were resolved to use all possible means and endeavours to disturb and ruin me, if they can, before I leave Bengal; and particularly, he told me, they intended, by some means or other, to hinder my Voyage to Persia, and "probably (said Mr. Gough) this is the course they have thought good to pitch upon for that purpose". I pray God of his infinite mercy to defend and preserve me from all their malicious contrivancies.

November 14.—Discoursing with Mr. Robert Dowglasse, he told me, 'twas reported amongst ye adverse party, that now there was a contrivance found out (most likely to be that of Haggerston's going to Decca) to stop my voyage to Persia; but he was not willing to tell me ye person's name who said it.

I was this morning informed by Mahmood Herreef, ye Comp.'s Vekeel, that Meleck Burcoordar, ye King's Fousdar, pretended he would heare & judge of a complaint made to him by Thomas Haggerston, "that I had seized & taken from him to ye value of near two lacks of Rupees, and particularly in ready money R. 6664 : 10," for which sum ye said Fouzdar demanded my receipt. Whereupon I went immediately to Agent Beard, declaring to him my innocency in this businesse, desiring him to take care I might not suffer by such unjust proceedings; to which he made me this cold reply, "He would doe what he could for me"; by which I easily perceived, if any misfortune happened, I must bear the brunt of it myselfe.

Bullubdas assures me President Gyfford brought downe 60 Bales of Silke from Cassumbuzar for his own Account.

November 17.—Mr. Derrick Johnson, a Duch man, formerly employed as Skipper for ye English in severall voyages, tolld me that all ye Tissinda Sugar Boats belonging to ye Dutch were arrived at Hugly, and our Sugar Boats stopt at Meerdaudpoor: that ye. Directore was long since advised their Petre Boats were discharged from Pattana & on their way to Hugly,—ye Great Mogul having ordered Shaste Chan, Nabob of Decca, not to permit any Stop to be put upon the Hollanders' negociations, nor prejudice to be done them, for that they were very potent at Sea, and might be provoked to stop their Pilgrims or Haggis going to Mecca, who he desired might goe and returne with greatest freedom.

If the Company thought fit to bestir themselves in this

manner, it would questionless produce like effect; and till they quarrel with this Government (as I have often said, and advised my friends) it can never be expected that their Trade should prosper in India, especially in these parts.

November 21.—Mr. John Pownsett arrived from Decca. 'Tis reported his chief errand is to complaine of me and James Price, accusing us to ye President and Councill. The particulars I cannot yet be informed. I can clearly prove him a false person, and unworthy their service as any one that they ever employed.

November 22.—Mr. Richard Gough came this day to my house, desiring to reside with me, assuring me that he was now resolved to adventure his life and fortune, and goe overland with me into England, by way of Persia and Aleppo. He gave me to understand, though not in direct plaine terms, that ye Company had given ye President & Council orders, in case they saw it for their interest, to quarrell and break friendship with the Government; to which ye President and Mr. Charnock readily assented, and gave their opinions that no good was to be done with these people without compulsion. But Mr. Beard, Mr. Ellis, Mr. Frenchfeild, & Mr. Ley, for their owne private interest and regard; to carry on their little trade in ye Country, being persuaded to this opinion by Mr. Evans, the Minister, declared themselves of a contrary judgement, and would not consent to it.

November 23.—It rained and blew very hard all this day: ye Wind began at S.E. in ye morning, and thence veered to ye North and N.W., where it blew hardest. We were in good hopes all the stormy and bad weather had been past for this season. The Moon was in ye last quarter, about 25 dayes old.

November 25.—Dr. Harwar tolld me that Mr. Frenchfeild and two more of ye Council accompanyed Mr. Pownsett on Saturday night, the 22nd instant, to visit Mr. Thomas Davies, ye Interloper,—a notorious shame, yt. ye Company's Servants should hold so friendly and intimate a correspondence with their greatest enemies.

November 26.—This day, between 5 and 6 o'clock in ye Afternoon, Capt. Richardson and his Sergeant came to my house in ye Chinchera, and brought me this following message from ye President and Councill, viz.:

That Mr. Gough being one of ye Company's Servants, ye President and Councill desire me not to entertaine him in my house, nor suffer him to goe with me in the Shippe I intend to goe in to Persia.

To which Message (in presence of Mr. Gough) I returned this following answer, or words to the same effect:

"That I intended no disrespect to ye President and Councill, nor to entertaine any one that is in ye Company's Service. That Mr. Gough told me, when he came first to my house, he was dismist ye Company's Service; and for their better assurance and satisfaction, I asked Mr. Gough the question before them, 'Whether he was ye Company's Servant or not?' who readily replyed, 'I am not'; and that ye said President and Council had given him leave to returne home for England, and y^t.^ he was ready to depose he lay under no promise or obligation to them not to goe home by way of Persia; and being a free born Subject of England, and knowing no order of ye Company's forbidding his goeing home by way of Persia, thought it very lawfull of him soe to doe. And if he did any thing contrary to ye obligation he lyes under to ye Company, he and his security are ready to answer it in England."

As to ye latter part of Capt. Richardson's message, "Not to suffer Mr. Gough to goe with me in ye Shippe I intend to goe in to Persia", I returned this Answer: "That Mr. Gough was not yet fully resolved whether he would go with me or not. When I knew his mind more fully I would give them notice. In the mean while desired time to consider of it."

To the truth of which we have here unto subscribed our hands the day and yeare above written.

W^{M.} HEDGES. RICHARD GOUGH.

November 27.—Captain W$^{m.}$ Hilder, commander of the *Quedah Merchant,* confirmed y^{e} same news tolld me y^{e} 25th instant by D$^{r.}$ Harwar, that M$^{r.}$ Frenchfeild, M$^{r.}$ Ley, & M$^{r.}$ Pownsett went on Saturday night last (being y^{e} 22nd Current) in y^{e} afternoon to visit M$^{r.}$ Davies, y^{e} Interloper, and staid with him till 11 at night.

President Gyfford and Councill sent me a letter by Capt. Richardson and Sergeant Tidford in these following words.

"Hugly, 28th Nov. 1684.

"To William Hedges, Esqre.

"Sir,—Whereas we sent to you on y^{e} 26th Instant Lieutenant Richardson and Sergeant Tidford with a message, 'That M$^{r.}$ Richard Gough, being one of y^{e} honorable Company's Servants, we desired you not to entertaine him in your house, nor suffer him to goe with you in the Shippe you intend to goe in to Persia'; to which you were pleased to returne the following answer by the same persons, viz.:

"'That you have no disrespect to us, nor doe entertain any of the Company's Servants. That M$^{r.}$ Gough tolld you he was clear of the Company's Service. When he came to your house he desired a lodging, and soe being destitute (you understanding him to be a Civill Gent$^{n.}$) you gave him a lodging. And as to his going with you into Persia, he is wavering and unsettled in his mind; but when you knew the certainty of his mind, then you would return an answer to us.'

"Therefore this is to acquaint you that (whatsoever M$^{r.}$ Gough hath said, or pretends he will sware) we declare that we have not dismist him y^{e} Hon. Comp.'s Service, or given him any further liberty than to go home upon one of the Hon. Company's Shipps, which was all he desired: so that we expect your complyance with y^{e} first message we sent you. This is all at present from

"Your Friends and Servants,

"WILLIAM GYFFORD.
"JOHN BEARD.
"FRANCIS ELLIS.
"RICH$^{D.}$ FRENCHFEILD.
"THOMAS LEY.
"EDW$^{D.}$ OXBOROUGH."

To which preceding letter I returned ye this following Answer.

"To ye Honble Wm Gyfford,
"President—& Councill. "Chinchera, 28th Nov. 1684.

"Hond Sirs,—I confesse ye report given ye Honr & Councill by Capt. Richardson and Sergeant Tidford is very agreeable to what I tolld them; I am most heartily sorry for the occasion of it, and beseech your pardon for not returning my positive answer to your letter now sent me till to-morrow morning, when I will not fail to wait upon your Honr & Councill, and hope to give you good satisfaction in what [is] required of

"Your Honrs most humble Servant."

November 29.—This morning, according to my promise, I waited upon ye President and Council. I used all the Arguments I could to persuade them not to use any violence or rigour towards Mr Gough, desiring them to peruse their own consultation Booke, particularly that of ye 26 of September last, or thereabouts, where they declare they could not dismiss Mr Gough ye Compy's Service, not having done or committed any act to deserve it; but they further declare the Company would not compel any man to serve them against their will, and upon yt score gave him liberty to goe home, advising him only not to goe with me by way of Persia.

I took further occasion to informe ye President and Councill that I conceived this last letter of theirs (where in they acknowledge they had given him liberty to goe home on one of ye Company's Shipps), and Mr Gough not consenting or covenanting to any such proviso (as he proffered to depose), the worst that could be said of it was, That he, the said Mr Gough, and his Security were bound to answer the damage that should arise to the Company by his going home this way, more than if he went home upon one of their Ships. To which little of moment was replyed, more than, That they who gave him liberty to goe home understood it to be with such a covenant and restriction, and were resolved (as President Gyfford very gravely tolld me when he was non-plus't) not to be baffled in the business.

Agent Beard asked me, Wherefore I appeared for Mr. Gough, and espoused his quarrel. I answered, my appearance was only to make good my promise yesterday to them, and not espouse any one's quarrel. Mr. Gough & I were both here in their power, and they might doe what they pleased with us. Whereupon they ordered Mr. Gough to attend the result of their consultation, and permitted me to take my leave of them.

I was no sooner gott to my house, but News was brought me that Mr. Gough was seized and secured in a violent manner by the Sentinel, and confined to a Chamber by ye President: the truth of which was confirmed to me by a note from Mr. Gough himselfe, who desired I would come and speake with him this Afternoon; which I did, and found him in a Chamber of the President's Lodgings. At my departure, Mr. Gough accompanyed me down the Stayers to my Palankeen, where, meeting with Captain Richardson, Mr. Gough asked him whether he was his prisoner or not? Capt. Richardson told him he was. Mr. Gough demanding, "By whose Order?" Capt. Richardson replyed, "By Order of ye President and Councill." The Corporal, at my coming into ye Factory, told me likewise that Mr. Gough was under restraint, but I might freely speak with him.

December 1684.

December 6.—This Afternoon President Gyfford and Councill sent to speak with me. When I was with them, they discoursed and examined me about several transactions. First, concerning Mr. Thomas Hill's estate, who dyed at Rajmahal. I told them I had never any of it in my possession; that my Nephew Hedges had about 5000 Rupees of his which he would not suffer Mr. Catchpoole (who was his Executor) to carry away with him; and for ye same my Nephew would be accountable to them. Next they discoursed me about Goolobray, and the sending James Price to Decca; about Mr. Johnson's ill-sorting of Goods, when Agent Beard told me he had ordered Mr. Braddyll to put out of ye way one Bale of every sort of Goods, and protested he knew not what was become of them.

'Tis observable, by ye way, that Mr. Beard confesses here, before ye President and Councill, in a boasting way, that he had ordered Mr. Braddyll to tell a notorious Lye; whereas he always pretends to be more righteous than any other person, and that he would not willingly commit ye least sinne for ye greatest good in ye World.

President Gifford and Councill discoursed me likewise concerning Mr. Gough and my going home by way of Persia. The President took great paines, with most impertinent, rediculous arguments, to dis-swade me from going that way; but could not tell me the least appearance of Prejudice, or make out any damage that would come to ye Company by it: and whereas he pretended the Company might have a great desire to speak with me (which argument he most enforced), I told him he had no reason to insist upon that, in regard the Company had permitted me to stay here, or at Fort St. George, another yeare if I pleased,—which stopt his mouth. After an houre & halfe or two hours' frivolous, impertinent tattle, I tooke my leave of them.

This night, about 6 o'clock, ye President left ye Factory at Hugly, and lay at ye Dutch Gardens, about 3 miles down ye River.

December 7.—This being Sunday, the President diverted himselfe (as he told me the next day) with shooting and walking abroad in ye fields.

December 8.—I went to visit President Gyfford at ye Dutch Garden, & take my leave of him. After dinner, Capt. Richardson, Commandant of the Soldiers, told us that, passing by the Duch Shipps, they hailed ye Boates, asking them "Whether they were going to Bantam with their Soldiers";

which so much enraged the President yt. he vowed all manner of revenge that lay in his power when it should please God to bring him to ye Fort, especially in regard ye Duch had so much slighted and disrespected him at Hugly as not to take ye least notice of him since his arrival in these parts, and had always shewne themselves exceeding kind and respectfull to me.

About 5 in ye Afternoon, finding my selfe somewhat indisposed, I tooke my leave of ye President, wishing him a good voyage, and a safe returne to ye Fort.

I must needs say, for all the good he has done here, it had been greatly for ye Company's Interest that he had never come to ye Bay, not having done the least single action to compose and settle, but rather to disjoynt and embroyle, all their affaires, which will now very hardly be brought to run in their wonted channels for many yeares: which course was inconsiderately and imprudently taken on purpose to undoe all that I had done, and enter upon new measures, thereby (if possible) to putt a Slur upon my conduct; whereas it was absolutely necessary for ye present state of ye Company's affaires to remaine in yt. posture, and to be carryed on with the same method as begun—unless they had resolved to quarrel with ye Government.

December 14.—Mr. Haynes, coming from Cassimbr., gave me a visit, and told me another fresh Perwanna was come from ye Nabob, commanding ye Fousdar of that place to send Mr. Charnock to Decca, or force him to pay ye Merchants R. 45,000, for Ballance of all accounts due to them; whereas Mr. Charnock pretends ye said Merchants are Debtors to ye Company the Sum of R. 150,000: soe that by this account the Company will be prejudiced near two Lacks of Rupees. Besides, Mr. Haynes tells me (to his knowledge) Mr. Charnock has never adjusted accounts with ye Merchants since Mr. Littleton's time, but has always continued to give out new Dadny without clearing of old accounts.

December 15.—James Price assured me that about 40 years since, when ye Island called Gonga Sagur was inhabited, ye Raja of y^t. Island gathered yearly Rent out of it to the amount of 26 Lack of Rupees; and that ye same Raja had a Country belonging to his Government extending from ye River of Rangopula to the great River that comes from Rajamaul, which brought him in yearly 45 Lacks of Rupees. This country affords great Store of large Timber to build Shipps.

December 17.—Sig^r. Nicolo Pareres, a Portugall Merchant, assured me their whole community had wrott ye Vice King of Goa, and besought him earnestly to send them 2 or 3 Frigates, with aid and assistance of Soldiers, to possess themselves of ye Islands of Kegeria and Ingellee, for which purpose they had sent him draughts and large descriptions of ye said Islands.

December 23.—James Price tolld me he had advice from ye King's Court, that his hopes of getting a Phirmaun not to pay Custome is now frustrate, M^r. John Pownsett having given under his hand at Decca (and thereby become obliged) to pay Custome of 3½ per cent.; whereas in all my time ye Duan was afraid to receive money under ye title of Custome, for fear it should be pretended by us hereafter that he forced it from us.

This afternoon I visited the Duch Director, & desired the favour of him to lett me have a Pilot to carry my Shippe through the new found Deepe by ye Island of Gonga Sagur: which he faithfully promised, with many expressions of kindness and respect to me.

December 25.—This evening information was given me that Haggerston had advised ye Fouzdar, from Decca, that he had visited Mirza Muzzufer and ye King's Duan, who were both very kind to him; that they had brought him to speak with ye Nabob, who had assured him of his Perwanna to bring me or Agent Beard before him, and would doe him justice.

If it came to this issue, I knew very well upon whome the Storm would fall, and therefore took a resolution to goe aboard Shippe the next morning as far as Barnagur, 20 miles below Hooghly, being well assured this wicked designe of stopping of me proceeded from our own Nation, who should have protected me with all their power,—the seizing of Haggerston's estate, which he ran away with all from Surat, being done meerly at ye request of ye two Presidents of Surat and Fort St. George, for ye Nation's Honour & Service of ye Comp^y.^; ye present Agent Beard, Mr. Johnson, and M^r.^ Wm. Frenchfeild having signed to every paper, and acted with me joyntly in this affaire. Yett so barbarously malicious have they shewne themselves, as not only to use their utmost endeavors to stopp my Shippe and Goods, thereby frustrating my designe of going home by way of Persia, but doe what in them lyes also to expose my person to ye cruel tyranny of ye Mogulls, who are very ready to embrace all such opportunitys of getting money upon any account whatsoever: our people little considering that by these indirect, inhumane courses they make an example for themselves to be served hereafter, when occasion presents, & so by degrees bring all ye disputes and controversies arising betwixt ourselves to be determined by the Moor's Justice, or Who bids most? which will prove soone a severe Rodd to whipp our owne Briches.

December 26.—This morning early I sent for Mr. Hendrick Ben, ye Duch Domine, who had always profest himself my great friend, desiring him to present my Service to ye Directore, and tell him ye reason of my suddain Departure, to pray him to lett me wear his Flag in my Budgero downe the River, and to assure him, though I had not time to take my leave of Agent Beard (not thinking it safe), yett his house being in my way, I resolved to waite upon him.

Here ye Duch Boor showed himselfe in his naturall colours. (I believe it impossible to know a Hollander's temper and naturall hatred to an English man so well in any other part of ye world as in India.) So soone as he heard I was in danger of falling into trouble, he sends me worde by ye same Messenger, "He durst not lend me a Flagg, nor assist me in anything whatsoever; and as for my Visit, if I pleased, he accepted of ye will for ye deed." This I looked upon as so ungentile & clownish a message, that I neither tooke my leave of him nor applied my selfe to him any more for a Pilott, hearing he had publickly declared I could not, nor should not, goe out of Bengall without his assistance.

About 10 o'clock this morning I left my house in Hugly, and went in a Budgero a-board ye *Recovery* at Barnagur,[1] a Village rented by ye Duch, where (I blesse God) I arrived in safety about 5 this Afternoon.

This night I received a letter from my Cousin, Nathanael Letter,[2] from Hugly, advising that, just as I was out of sight, he received a letter from my Nephew Hedges to lett him know there was a Horseman sent to ye Factory gate, but could not understand his message. Ye Agent & Councill met immediately, to consult and give him an answer. 'Tis verily believed he was sent by ye Fousdar about Haggerston's business.

December 31.—We weighed anchor, and fell down to Great Tanna, and lay there this night.

[*End of* 1684, *though this date is carried on until Lady Day of* 1685 *in the original manuscript.*]

[1] Baranagar is immediately to the north of the city of Calcutta, on the same bank.—Y.

[2] Apparently not "Letten", as at p. 162. See pp. 177-178.—Y.

JOURNEY HOME *VIA* MUSCAT AND PERSIA.

January 1685.

January 1.—About 7 in y[e] morning we weighed anchor, and fell down a little below Jan Pardo, where we arrived by noone, and there came to an Anchor.

January 2.—We fell downe below Tumbolee[1] River.

January 3.—We anchored at the Channel Trees, and lay here ye 4th and 5th for want of a gale to carry us over to Kedgeria.

January 6.—A gale sprung up, & we gott over to Kedgeria Point, and a little before Sunsett went off in a Budgero, with designe to row round the two Islands of Kedgeria and Ingellee, and meet y[e] Shipp at y[e] entrance of Ingellee River.

A little before it was darke we came to a great Godowne, where Busrook Omed Chan (the Nabob of Pattana), this nabob's Son, has laid in a vast quantity of Salt. Here we found divers great Patellos taking in their lading for Pattana, this being one of the most convenient places in all these parts for that purpose. Our Dandees (or boatmen) boyled their rice, and we supped here. About 8 o'clock we rowed on, and by one or two in y[e] morning (*January* 7) gott round to Ingellee Towne, where we stayed some houres; and having supplyed ourselves with fresh provisions, mett our Shipp about 12 o'clock, newly come to an Anchor over against Ingellee River.

January 8.—This morning by breake of day we weighed Anchor, and by 12 at noon came to an anchor upon y[e] edge, or Entrance, on y[e] Westwardmost Brace, having brought the Salt River Tree to bear North of us; when at low water we

[1] *I.e.*, Tumlook; the river is the Roopnarain.

had no more than 16 Foot, and our Ship drew 15 Foot. At slack water we weighed, and stood downe between the two Braces, steering South and S. by E. about 2 Leagues.

Here we mett with George Herron, ye Company's Chief Pilott, returning to Hugly, who came on board and carryed us over ye Brace, for which I presented him with R. 50. Att first he seemed unwilling to undertake ye business, or so much as afford us ye least advice or assistance, fearing Agent Beard and Councill at Hugly might be soe displeased with him for shewing any kindness to me, as to turne him out of ye Service; but considering, on ye other side, ye promise of soe great a reward, adventured on it.

It hath thus pleased God to deliver me from ye implacable malice of all my Enemies, who have taken greater paines to prejudice me by endeavoring to frustrate my Voyage to Persia, than ever they did to hinder ye Interlopers, whom they have dayly caressed and favored (contrary to the Company's expresse orders) upon all occasions.

This night about 12 a Clock we anchored on ye Westward edge of ye Outward Brace.

January 9.—This Morning early we weighed anchor, and stood into Ballasore Road, steering W. b. N. and W.N.W.; but ye Wind taking us short, we were forced to anchor before we gott to ye Ships.

January 10.—About 8 in ye Morning we gott into Ballasore Road, passing the *Bengall Merchant*, Capt. Goldsborough (who was at Hugly). His Chief Mate, Mr. Hall, sent off his boat to know our Shipp's name, and who was in her (but had not ye manners to give us a Gun by way of Salute). Our Shippe wanting a Pinnace, I desired ye Coxon to tell ye mate Hall I entreated him to lend me his boat to goe on board ye *Defence*, which he very courteously sent me; but Capt. Heath's Chief Mate, Mr. Henry Sharpe, coming aboard, assured me his Captain would send me his Pinnace immediately:

which he performing, I returned Capt. Goldsborough's boat, with many thanks, and gratifying the Crew.

The next Shippe we passed by was the *Ann*, Capt. Browne, who was not so courteous as to give us a Salute; but coming near Captain Heath in y^e^ *Defence*, he gave us 9 Guns. I answered with as many more; he returned thankes with 7, & soe answered each other with 2 lesse, till we came to One Gun.

Capt. Heath sending his boat to me, I went on board his Shippe to give him thanks for his Civility. After halfe an houre's stay on board, as I was going ashore in ye Pinnace, I mett Mr. Fitz Hugh coming off to me in one of ye Company's new Sloopes, with my bales of Goods. I brought Mr. Fitz Hugh aboard with me without going ashore, and having taken my goods aboard, lay for ye Ebb and a Breeze off ye Shore, which springing up about 12 o'clock at night, we weighed anchor, and stood out of ye Road, where I first arrived on ye 17th July 1682, being 2 yeares and a halfe, wanting 7 dayes.

I blesse my God, ye Creator of Heaven and Earth, who has been graciously pleased to carry me through so many troubles and afflictions of divers kinds, to see this joyfull day; maugre all ye Plots and contrivances of my implacable enemies, President Gyfford, Agent Beard,[1] Mr. Charnock, and ye rest of that wicked confederacy, out of whose hands He hath been pleased to give me Deliverance.

About 8 o'clock this night Mr. Archibald, Chirurgeon of y^e^ *Ann*, brought letters aboard to Mr. Fitz Hugh from ye Agent and Councill of Hugly, with a Protest from them against me, Mr. Dowglasse, my cousin Letter, and Mr. Hampton (ye Master of our Shippe), for carrying Mr. Gough & my Nephew Hedges, for all damages to ye East India Company, being a

[1] President Beard, the "Agent" Beard of this Diary, survived to witness the "interlopers" become the "English Company", and the two companies to coalesce, under the style and title of the "United" Company. Mr. Beard died at Madras, July 7, 1706.—Bruce, *Annals*, vol. iii, 602.

Paper stuffed up with most impudent and notorious untruths, for which, if they had the least graine of that Religion or goodness in them which they professe, they would have blushed to subscribe it.

The Copy of ye Protest follows, Verbatim:

"Whereas William Hedges, Esqre., late Agent in Bengall for Affaires of ye Honble. ye Govr. & Company of Merch^nts.^ of London, trading to ye East Indies; Mr. Nathanael Letter, Merch^nt.^, and Mr. Robert Dowglasse, Chirurgeon, late Servants to ye Honble. Company in Hugly, being all Three owners of ye Shippe *Recovery*, and all embarked on her for a Voyage to Persia or Bussora; which Shipp is commanded by John Hampton as Master under them, and is manned with severall English Officers and Seamen, besides the Natives of this country; and Whereas R^d.^ Gough, who came lately out of England as one of ye Agent's Councill for ye said Honble. Company's affaires in this place, & Robert Hedges, late Factor for said Honble. Company's affaires at Rajamaul, both Servants to ye said Honble. Comp^y.^, the latter not having cleared or given any account of his Trust, but is indebted to the said Honble. Comp^y.^ in a very great sum of Money,—both of them, contrary to ye trust reposed in them, and without cause given by Us, have been deluded by the said Wm. Hedges, Esqre., Nathanael Letter, Merch^nt.^, & Robert Dowglasse, Chirurgeon, and others, to run away from the said Honble. Company's Service, and they are now, both of them, run away from ye said Service, and are entertained aboard the said Shippe *Recovery*, by ye said Wm. Hedges, Nath. Letter, Robert Dowglasse, & John Hampton, & Officers and Seamen, to ye great damage of the Govr. & Company aforesaid, & of our selves and others:

"Wee, therefore, the Agent and councill for Affaires of y^e^ Honble. Govr. and Company aforesaid in Bengall, doe, in behalfe of y^e^ said Govr. and Company, and their Successors, and in behalfe of ourselves, and of all and every person or persons herein concerned, make this our lawfull declaration and protest against you, the aforesaid W$^{m.}$ Hedges, Esq$^{re.}$, Nathanael Letter, Merch$^{t.}$, Robert Dowglasse, Chirurgeon, John Hampton, Master, and all the officers and Seamen now serving under them in y^{e} said Shippe, and against y^{e} said Shippe *Recovery*, and her owners & Cargo, and also against the Persons of y^{e} said Richard Gough & Robert Hedges, and against all other persons aiding, abetting, and assisting y^{e} said Richard Gough & Robert Hedges in their soe running away; and Declare all and every one of you, joyntly and severally, liable to make full satisfaction unto y^{e} said Hon$^{ble.}$ Gov$^{r.}$ & Company & their Successors, and to us, and to every other person for said Gov$^{r.}$ & Company concerned, for all such losses and damages as now are, or hereafter shall be, suffered any ways by y^{e} said Governor & Company, or their Successors, or by ourselves, or by any other person what ever, by reason of y^{e} flight of Richard Gough and Robert Hedges aforesaid, or by any other wayes or means whatsoever thereunto belonging.

"Dated in Hugly, this 5th day of January 1684-85.

"JOHN BEARD.
"FRANCIS ELLIS.
"RICH$^{D.}$ FRENCHFEILD.
"EDW$^{D.}$ OXBOROUGH.

"Signed and published in Hugly Factory, this 5th day of January 1684-85, in presence of

"JOHN GOLDBOROUGH.
"JOSEPH TAFFORD.
"SAM$^{L.}$ PINE.
"JOHN BEARD, JUN$^{R.}$

"Signed and delivered in presence of us, at Ballasore Road, 10th January 1684-85,

"WILLIAM FITZ HUGH. "EDW. TENCH.
"CHARLES ARCHIBALD. "EDW$^{D.}$ HULLEY.
"HENRY STANLY."

To which Protest I returned for Answer, that it was a paper stuffed up with notorious untruths, and when it pleased God to bring me into England, I would give an answer to it, and so would the rest of the persons concerned in it.

This night we weighed anchor, and sailed out of Ballasore Road, which (as I am informed) lyes in the Latitude of 21° 35′ N.[1]

January 11, 12, 13.—These 3 days we had little wind, and that Variable, which caused us to steer divers Courses from y^{e} S.S.E. to y^{e} S.W. Latitude by Observation, 20° 35′ N.

January 14, 15, 16, 17.—These 4 dayes continued little Wind, and that Contrary, forcing us much to y^{e} Eastward. Lat$^{de.}$ by Observation, 19° 26′ N.

January 18.—The Wind came up fair at North-East, our course South and South by East. Lat., 18° 32′ N.

January 19.—The Wind continued Fair. Latitude by Obs$^{n.}$, 17° 38′ N.

January 20.—Fair Wind. Course, South. Lat. by Obs., 17° 20′ N.

January 21.—Fair Wind and weather. Course, South. Lat. by Obs., 16° 57′ N.

January 22.—Fair Wind and weather. Course, S. b. W. & S.S.W. Lat., 16° 50′ N.

January 23.—Fair Wind. Course, S. b. W., S.S.W., & S.W. Distance run, 92 miles. Lat$^{de.}$ by Obs$^{n.}$, 16° 7′ N.

[1] The Balasore Buoy, which is as close to the coast as ships can approach, is now in about 21° 25′ 10″, and the Flagstaff is in 21° 28′ N. The "Road" must be considered between these two positions; and the error is probably due to the defective instruments and tables of Mr. Hedges' period—though it is possible his informant spoke of the *town* itself, which is in 21° 29′ 32″ N., a considerable distance up a very winding river.

January 24.—Fair Wind. Course, S.W. b. W. Distance run, 97 miles. Lat. by Obs., 15° 5′ N.

January 25.—Fair Wind. Course, S.W. b. W. Dist. run, 73 miles. Lat. by Obs., 14° 18′ N.

January 26.—Little Wind. Course, W. b. S. Distance run, 35 miles. Lat. by judge[mt.], 13° 50′ N.; horizon hazy; a bad observation.

January 27.—Little Wind. Course, W. by S. Distance run, 36 miles. Lat. by Obs., 13° 40′ N.

January 28. Little Wind. Course, W. b. S. Lat. by Obs., 13° 23′ N.

January 29.—Little Wind. Course, W. b. S. Lat. by Obs., 13° 6′ N.

January 30.—Fair Wind. Course, W. b. N. & W.N.W., having found the Current setting us strongly to y[e] Southward. Lat. by Obs., 12° 30′ N.

January 31.—Fair Wind. Course, W. b. N. and N.N.W. Distance Run, 99 miles. Lat. by Obs., 13° 40′ N.

February 1685.

February 1.—Fair Wind. Course, W. b. N. Distance Run, 87 Miles. Lat. b. Ob., 13° 27′.

The former part of this night shortened Sail, for fear of falling in too close upon y[e] Land. About Midnight we sounded, and had 20 Fathoms Water; then made sail, and came to an anchor in 11 fathoms.

February 2.—This Morning early we saw Fort S[t.] George, about 3 or 4 Leagues to the Northward of us, and S[t.] Thome, bearing N. ½ W. Our Commander was much troubled to find the violence of the Current (which usually setts to the Northward at this time of the Year) had sett him so far to leeward of his Port.

About 10 o'clock this morning 2 Black Fellows on a Cattamaran came off to us with a Note from M[r.] John Stables,

Secretary of ye Fort, desiring to know ye Shipp and Commander's Name; from whence they came, and for what place they are bound.[1]

By ye return of this Cattamaran I wrott to President Gyfford, desiring his Honor to permitt a boat & a Cattamaran to be sent off to me, that I might wait on him ashore.

February 3.—This morning two Musoolas & two Cattamarans came off to ye Shippe, one of each sort for me, and ye other for M^r. Robert Dowglasse and his Lady. About 2 o'clock in ye Afternoon, Mr. Dowglasse & ye Lady and I got into ye Mussoola, when a most unfortunate accident befell us. The Seamen, handing a small Scritoire into ye boat, in which were Gold Mohurs and Rupees to ye value of R. 2036 : 11 for account of M^r. Charles Chamberlan, and R. 3307 : 9 more for account of M^r. Alford of Madras, the said Scritoire dropt into the Sea, striking on ye Shipp's Side, broke ye Scritoire, and the money dropt out into ye Sea.

This unhappy accident, together with ye greatness of ye Sea and Surf ashore, caused us to come aboard again, and defer going ashore till ye next morning.

Being gott on board again, I advised President Gyfford of this mischance, desiring him to send Divers aboard, to search and (if possible) to recover the money—the value of 2036 : 11 for account of M^r. Chamberlan being consigned to his Honor.

We tooke care to sinke downe a parcell of great shott made up in a strong bag, with a rope and a Buoy to it; but notwithstanding all our endeavors whilst I was at ye Fort, no Divers could be found to undertake ye business; so left ye care of ye affaire to Capt. Francis Willshaw, so soone as

[1] This Mr. Stables, when Chief of Vizagapatam in 1689, was killed with four others, and the Company's effects plundered, when Aurungzebe ordered the expulsion of the English from India.—Bruce, *Annals*, ii, 650.

Divers could be procured, & ye Sea growne calme for them to search for the money.

February 4.—This morning by 8 o'clock I went ashore. So soone as we came near ye Surfe, two men leaped into the Sea, and hung at two ropes fastened to the boat's Stern to keep her right before the Sea, and managed their business with so great skill and dexterity, that we came through all the Surfe without any one Sea breaking in upon us. In my Boat were likewise M^r. Dowglasse & his Lady & his Son.

On ye shore we found 3 Palankeens and 3 horses—one Palankeen with 12 Peons, sent by President Gyfford to waite upon me; a second for M^r. Dowglasse; and a 3rd for his Lady and child, sent by D^r. Heathfield, Chirurgeon of ye Fort. The 3 horses were mounted by my cousin Letter, M^r. John Whitmore, & M^r. John Innes, & sent by ye President.

We landed about 8 miles to the Southward of S^t. Thome, and 10 miles from ye Fort. On our way we mett with M^r. Jersey, M^r. Alford, and another Gentleman, who came to meet us. The day before there had been divers more of ye English, who came to Welcome ashore and accompany us to the Fort.

Being gott near ye Fort Gate, I was mett by M^r. Gray, the youngest of Councill, sent to conduct me to ye President, who mett me at his Chamber door, and bade me Wellcome, & drinking to me, fired 15 Guns. His Honor invited me to dinner, and made me promise to sup with him.

After dinner I went to M^r. W^m. Jearsey's, and tooke up my quarters at his house, where I was entertained with so much respect and kindnesse as could possibly be showne to me.

This Afternoon I received divers visits from M^r. Elihu Yale, Mr. Lucas, M^r. Nicks, & M^r. Gray, all of Councill, as also from M^r. Bridgier, M^r. Field, M^r. Griffith, M^r. James Wheeler, M^r. Ramsden, M^r. Fleetwood, and divers others.

Towards evening Capt. Willshaw accompanyed me to the Company's Garden-house, and showed me great part of ye towne. Afterwards he went with me to visit Mr. Littleton & ye rest of ye family.

February 6.—This afternoon I went to see St. Thomas his Mount (about 10 miles from ye Fort), accompanied with Mr. Jearsey, Mr. Dowglasse and his Lady, and my cousin Letter. At ye Mount we mett a Portuguese Fryer, educated at Rome; and speaking Italian, entertained me with great civillity and respect. We returned againe this Evening, having been just 6 hours absent from the Fort.

February 7.—About 5 this Afternoon I took leave of President Gyfford, Mr. Jearsey, and ye rest of my Friends at Madras,—where I was entertained with greater demonstrations of respect and kindness than could be expected, from all persons except ye President, whose commands from Sir Josia Child to be rude and disrespectfull to me (as I am credibly informed), more than his own naturall inclination, caused him to carry himselfe with so clownish and ungentle a behavior towards me,—and gott aboard y^e^ *Recovery* (who was come nearer the Road) before it was darke, Capt. Willshaw doing me ye kindness to lend me his pinnace, and send his son Jonah with me to see me well aboard.

At my coming off the Shore ye Fort fired 15 Guns, & Capt. Willshaw's Shippe, the *Resolution*, fired 9, which were all answered when we came aboard the *Recovery*.

This night we sett sail for Muscatt and Gombroon. God send us a prosperous Voyage.

I have hitherto forgot to note, in its due time and place, that about ye middle of September last, soon after President Gyfford's coming to Hugly, he and his Councill gave orders to Mr. Pownsett to demand of Mr. Charles Crosse of Decca (and in case of refusall to seize and secure by force) all the Letters he had ever received from me, of Publick or

Private concerne; which order being produced and shown to Mr. Crosse (who was well assured violence would have been used in case of refusall), he readily submitted, and delivered up all my letters (in number 52) to Mr. Pownsett, to be conveyed to ye said President & Councill for their perusall, who were possessed with an opinion there lay a greater Juggle (as they were pleased to terme it), or mystery designed, in our correspondence than they were able to apprehend.

Upon perusall of all my letters, nothing was found in them on which their malice could cast the least reflection, save only an expression to this purpose: "That Mr. Crosse should tell James Price (my Vekeel), If ye Nabob should ask him any questions concerning the differences between Mr. Charnock and his Picars and Merchants, he should say, 'he knew nothing of it'. 'That James Price would write to me, and acquaint ye Nabob with my answer.'" Which being condemned for a crime, I shall make this reply:

First. No such question was ever asked by the Nabob, and so no prejudice could arise to ye Company by it.

Secondly. I had no reason to appear in ye business till notice given me of ye Grievance. The fault (if any) was therefore wholly in Mr. Charnock, who, contrary to his duty in all such cases, gave me not the least advice of any difference depending betwixt him and his Merchants—I had it only from general report; nor was it any wise proper for Mr. Charnock (being subordinate to ye Agent and Councill of Hugly) to contemne and despise my authority and character given me by ye Company in so high a degree as not to judge me worthy of being made acquainted with all ye Company's concernes, especially of such vast importance; whereas it is well known (by the Merchants' and said Picars' frequent addresses to me) I could have composed and accommodated ye differences betwixt them for a small expence, now so heightened by Charnock's indiscreet & imprudent management, that it is very improbable it should ever be adjusted with lesse expence than two Lacks of Rupees, together with Mr. Charnock's being dismist ye Company's Service, without which latter the Merchants will never be satisfied.

And as for ye Juggle pretended to be discovered by my letters to Mr. Crosse, I wish those now in power prove no worse Jugglers for ye Company than they have found me during my two years' management in Bengall.

What I principally reflect on is the injustice of Mr. Beard, who thought it an unpardonable fault in me to be privy to the opening of his Letter, but esteemed it no offence in himselfe to seize & peruse 52 of mine.

I cannot apprehend for what reason it comes to be more lawful in him to seize upon and read so many of my letters, than it was in Mr. William Johnson to open one of his, and me to read it, when showne to me, and found my selfe reproached and abused in it: which I humbly submit to ye opinions of better judgements to determine.

February 8, 9, 10, 11, 12, 13.—We continued with little wind; what we had was fair; our course S.S.E. and S.E., sometimes S.E. b. E., the current setting us strong to the Northward, so that in these Sixe dayes past we gott no farther to ye Southward than to ye Latde. of 12° 20′ N.

February 14, 15, & 16.—These 3 days very little wind, but that fair; our course S.E., and Latitude by Observation, 13° 17′ N., so that in these last 3 dayes we have been driven 57 miles to the Northward.

February 17.—These 24 hours a fine fresh gale, and at E. Course, S. b. E. and S.S.E. Latitude by Observation, 12° 45′ N.

February 18.—These 24 hours ye gale continued fresh at E. b. S. Course, S. b. E. Latitude by Obs., 12° 3′ N.

February 19.—These 24 hours fresh favourable gale at E. and E. b. S. Course, S. b. E. and S.S.E. Lat., 11° 16′ N. by Observation.

February 20.—These 24 hours a fine gale. Course, S. b. E. Lat$^{de.}$ by Obs$^{n.}$, 10° 28′ N.

February 21.—These 24 hours a gentle gale. Course, S. Lat. by Ob$^{n.}$, 9° 30′ N.

February 22.—These 24 hours a fine fresh gale at N.E. Course, S. and S.S.W. Distance run, 81 miles. Lat. by Observation, 8° 23′ N.

February 23.—This morning we caught a Dolphin more than 4 foot long: a soft Roe. We have caught divers others with hard roes. The difference of Male and female is plainly distinguished by the make of their heads, the Male's being much more upright and high than that of the Females, by which it is very apparent y^{e} Dolphin is oviparous, and not viviparous, as some Authors have reported.

These 24 hours a fine fresh gale. Wind at N.E. Course, S.W. Distance, 80 miles. Lat. by Obs$^{n.}$, 7° 13′ N. This afternoon saw y^{e} Island of Zeilon.

February 24.—These 24 hours a fresh gale of Wind at N.E. Course from 4 in y^{e} Afternoon till 5 in y^{e} Morning, South; afterwards, till 12 at noon, W.S.W.; then we saw Land againe. Dist. run, 102 miles. Lat. Obs$^{d.}$, 6° 18′ N.

February 25.—These 24 hours a gentle gale of wind at E. and E.N.E. Course, y^{e} former part of y^{e} night, S.W.; from midnight till morning, W. b. S. and W.S.W.; from day light till noon, N.W. Distance run in y^{e} whole, 93 miles. Lat$^{de.}$ by Obs$^{n.}$, 5° 54′ N. No sight of land, by which we judge y^{e} Current has set us farther to y^{e} Westward than we expected.

February 26.—These 24 hours very little wind, and that contrary, at North West; by that we advanced little or nothing more than what y^{e} Current drove us to y^{e} Westward.

About 8 o'clock we saw a Sail standing towards us from Zeilon; by 11 we spoke with her. She proved to be the *Syam Merchant*, from Metchlapatam, whence she departed ye 3rd Instant, freighted by Moors, to Gombroon and Cong.[1] She has on her 106 passengers, men and women, and makes about Rup. 40,000 freight. Her Commander, Capt. Wooldham, dyed the day before she sailed from Metchlapatam. Her Chief Mate, M^r. Clerke, was now her Commander. We promised each other to keepe company, being both bound to ye same Port. Her Commander; M^r. Brough, her supra cargo; Chirurgeon, and Purser came aboard and dyned with us. Latitude by Observation, 5° 40′ N.

February 28.—These 24 hours for ye most part quite calme. Lat. by Obs^n., 5° 40′ N.

March 1685.

March 1.—About 10 o'clock last night there arose a suddaine Storme, accompanyed with much lightning and Thunder, and violent showers of rain, which made us hand all Sailes except ye Foresail. The violence of this Storme was not of one houre's continuance, and ye wind so large as helped us on our way. All the night after little wind. Course, W.N.W. and N.W. Latitude by Obs^n., 6° N.

March 2.—These 24 hours a fresh gale. In ye night it Lightened and Thundered and rained so hard that we handed most of our sailes. Course, W. b. N. and N.W. Distance run, 72 miles. Lat. by Obs., 6° 40′ N.

March 3.—From 12 at Noon till 8 at night the gale continued fresh, all the night after little wind, and so this morning. Course, from ye N.W. to ye S.S.W. Latitude by Judgement, 7° 16′ N.

March 4.—These 24 hours little wind and much rain, with great Thunder and lightning. Course, N.W. The

[1] *Bandar Kongūn*, Cong, or Congo. See notes at pp. 97, 202.—Y.

Sun not shining forth, had no Observation. Lat. by Judg., 7° 30′ N.

March 5.—These 24 hours the wind has been variable and gusty. Lat. by Observ., 6° 25′ N., by which we find ourselves much driven to the S^d.

The *Syam Merchant* came this day under our Sterne to speak with us.

March 6.—This morning, by breake of day, we found ourselves driven within 4 leagues of ye Maldivia Islands, which bore W. b. S., W. b N., and West of us, so forcibly has ye Current carryed us upon these Islands, contrary to our expectation. The weather has been exceedingly variable and gusty. Upon discovery of these dangerous Islands, we tacked, and stood to ye N.E. Lat^de. 6° 2′ N.

March 7.—Last night we stood again to ye N.W. This morning, by peepe of day, we were driven within a mile of ye Maldivia Islands ; the *Syam Merchant* was much nearer ; so that in lesse than an houre more we must of necessity have been cast away upon one or forced to goe through them, as God in his Providence should have directed and disposed of us.

So soone as we espyed them (being all very low land, full of Trees) we tacked, and stood to ye Eastward, when the weather grew so dirty, with violent gusts of rain and Wind, that we could have no observation. We observed by ye stars in ye Night, Lat. 6° 37′ N.

March 8.—Last night it blew hard at N.E., with violent gusts of Wind and raine. We stood off to E. and S.E. till 3 in ye morning, when seeing ourselves again driven near ye Islands with ye force of ye Current, we tacked, and stood N. b. E. and N.N.E., the wind at that very instant favouring of us. We fired 2 Guns and showed two lights (as by agreement), to give our Consort notice of our Tacking : it seems he did not thinke convenient to follow our example, being 4 or 5 leagues asterne of us in ye morning by daylight. We stood on, and made what saile we could, steering North. About 10 this morning we lost sight of the *Syam Merchant*. The Wind blew very fresh at East; and seeing divers Islands ahead of us, which we could not weather, and those to ye Westward standing very open and stragling, not much nearer (in my opinion) than those in ye Archipelago in the Mediterranean Sea, our Captain asked my Councill what course he were best to steer. I advised him (in the name of God) to venture through, and so bore up, steering due West, when we saw the openest passage, having a Man always standing at ye Main Top mast head to direct and con us ye broadest way. By Noon we judged ourselves at least 12 miles within ye Islands. The Latitude by Observation, 6° 40′ North.

March 9.—Yesterday, in ye Afternoon, we sailed neer divers fine, green, pleasant Islands, full of Coco-nutt and other trees; and finding fine, white, gravelly, clean ground between them at 16, 18, and 20 fathoms, thought good (to prevent greater danger in passing in ye night) to drop Anchor, which we did neer one of them, where we saw two boats going into harbour.

We putt out a peece of a Red Ancient, to appear like a Moor's Vessell, not judging it safe to be known to be English, our Nation having lately gott an ill name by abusing ye Inhabitants of these Islands; but no boat would come neer us, though divers rowed and sailed by at a distance to view and make what discovery they could of us.

At the West end of this Island was a Point of Sand and Rocks, which ran out neer halfe a mile, with ye Sea breaking upon it, & so had most of ye other Islands to ye Westward. About 4 or 5 miles to N. Westward of this Island I saw with my Telliscope a Parcell of 15 or 16 houses upon a Sand, which seemed 5 or 6 miles long. The sea broke very high upon it.

This Morning early (no boat coming off to us) we weighed anchor, and perceiving ye fairest Channel lay N.E., steered due North East for some time, and afterwards North. Having gott ye Island under which we anchored asterne, 5 boats putt off from ye North End; 3 of them ran ahead of us, sailing very swiftly; [from] the other two, after great ceremony and caution (all our Europeans hiding themselves except ye Captain, [and] the Mogulls, who were passengers, and Blackmen, only appearing in sight), divers of them came aboard, one of which (having a finer Clout than ordinary about him, and a pretty, neat knife at his Girdle) was a Governor's Son of one of these Islands.

Our Captain telling him there was a person aboard who could speak Arabick, he desired to see him. Notice being given me, I came out of ye Round house, and saluted him in Arabick; to which, not returning a ready and proper Answer, I found he spoke so little of ye Language that no Discourse was to be held with him, so applyed myselfe to a Portuguese mariner who spoke Indostan (ye current language of all these Islands), to which he returned me evasive and unsatisfactory answers, bending his whole discourse to advise our anchoring near his Island this night, & then he would bring us off Wood, Water, and Hens, as much and as many as we should desire. All that I could get of information from him (shewing him ye Compasse) was that, after we had passed those sands and rocks now in sight of us, there was a fair Channel before us to ye North West; and that if we would stay this night, to-morrow morning he would send a Pilott and Boats to sail before us out of the Islands. But the Wind coming up a fine fresh Gale at S.E., I presented the young Governor's Son with a fine Amber handled knife and a bag of Rice, and told him I was resolved to make no further delay, but to make ye best of our way and detayne him no longer; upon which they all got overboard immediately into their boat, seeming to be afraide we should detayne them by force.

Amongst other Questions, I asked them whether they

remembered in what part of these Islands a great English Shippe was cast away about 15 or 16 yeares since. He told me it was upon ye great Sand where I saw the Houses, which were Magazines for ye Cowries that were taken for ye King. These Islands are so full of Inhabitants and boats, that we thought this the chief place from whence the King gets all (or greatest part) of his Cowrees. This Sand is in 6° 40′ Latitude. At Noon we were in Latitude 7° 0′ N. by Observation, and saw no land to ye N.W. of us.

March 10.—These 24 hours a fine, constant, gentle gale at S.E. Course, yesterday in ye Afternoon, N.W. till 4, then steered N.N.W. We saw divers small Islands about 20 miles to ye Northward, but no further; so conclude ourselves in ye 8 degree Channel, whose last Islands are in 7° 10′ N.

Distance run by Log, 50 miles. Lat. by Obs., 7° 40′ N.; and saw no more sight of Land. The most Northerly of these Islands are exceeding full of Coco-Nutt and other sorts of Trees, so very pleasant and delightfull to ye Eyes, that we could not imagine them so unhealthy as those are knowne to be to the S^d.^, especially that on which the King resides; it is said he does it on purpose that none might be in love with his habitation, and dispossesse him of his kingdom. 'Tis believed, with great probability, that those larger Islands (about 17 in number), being between 9 and 12 degrees Lat., are as healthy and fertile lands as most in the World, and would make a most advantageous seat for trade to any part of India.

March 11.—These 24 hours little wind; what we had was at S.E. till 8 o'clock this morning, then it came at ye W.S.W. Our Course, N.N.W., without sight of Land. Latitude by Observation, 8° 7′ N.

March 12.—These 24 hours very little wind. Course, N.N.W. No sight of Land. Lat^de.^ by Obs~n.~, 8° 36′ N.

March 13.—These 24 hours ye winds were very variable, accompanyed with smart gusts of Wind and rain. Distance, run, 37 miles. Course from y^e W. to y^e N.N.W. Latitude by Obs., 9° 2′ N.

March 14.—These 24 hours fine fresh gale. Course from N.N.E. to N. b. W. Distance run, 60 miles. Lat. by Obs., 9° 46′ N.

March 15.—These 24 hours little wind. Course, N. and N. b. E. Lat. by Obs$^{n.}$, 9° 55′ N.

March 16.—These 24 hours little wind. Course, N. and N. b. E. Lat. by Obs., 10° 8′ N. The winds being small and faint, we tacked, and stood W. and W. b. S., sometimes W.S.W., in hopes of meeting stronger winds to y^e Westward.

March 17.—These 24 hours a fine fresh gale. Course, West and W. b. S. and W.S.W. Distance run, 48 miles. Lat. by Obs$^{n.}$, 9° 28′ N.

March 18.—These 24 hours little wind. Course, till towards morning, W. b. S. and W.S.W.; afterwards, N. b. W. till 10 this morning, then W.S.W. again. Lat. by Obs., 9°.

March 19.—These 24 hours little wind. Course, divers, from y^e North to W.S.W., as we could make y^e Ship lye. We judge a great current sets us to y^e Southward. Latitude by Obs., 8° 38′ N.

March 20.—These 24 hours little or no wind. Course from N. to N.W. We hoisted out our boat, and found y^e Current setting more than one mile an houre to y^e Southward. Lat. by Obs$^{n.}$, 8° 6′ N.

March 21.—These 24 hours no more wind than to keepe the Shipp's head to y^e N.W. and N.W. b. W., y^e Current driving us to y^e South$^{d.}$ Lat. by Obs., 7° 48′ N.

March 22.—These 24 hours we have had a fine gentle breeze at N. and N. b. E. Course, W.N.W. and N.W. b. W. Distance run by y^e log, 40 miles. Lat. by Obs. (which was imperfect, y^e Sun being within 2½ degrees of y^e Zenith), 7° 53′ N. In y^e night we observed divers Stars, and found our Latitude upwards of 8° 0′ N.

March 23.—These 24 hours a fine fresh gale at North and

N. b. W. Course, W.S.W. and W.N.W. Distance run, 60 miles. Latitude (taken with an Astrolabe), the Sun being within 2 degrees of our Zenith, 8° 16′; ye Variation, 12 degrees [W. ?].[1]

March 24.—These 24 hours the Wind somewhat abated at N.E. and N.E. b. N. Course, N.W. b. N. and N.W. Distance run by ye Log, 64 miles. Lat. by judgement and observation of ye Stars, 8° 20′ N.

March 25.—These 24 hours a fine fresh gale at N. b. E. and N.N.E. Course, N.W. and N.W. b. N. Variation, 12° 18′ [W. ?]. Lat. by Obs., 8° 41′ N. Dist., 55.

March 26.—These 24 hours little Wind. Course, N.N.W. Distance run, 41 m. Variation, 13° 20′ [probably West]. Lat. by Obsn. of Stars at 2 o'clock this morng., 9° 19′ N.

March 27.—These 24 hours little wind. Course, N.W. and N.W. b. W. Distance run, 54 miles. Lat. by Obs., 10° 0′ N.

March 28.—These 24 hours little wind. Course, N.N.W. and N. b. W. Distance run, 52 miles. Lat. by Obs., 10° 19′ N.

March 29.—These 24 hours little wind. Course, N.N.W. b. W. and N.W. by N. Distance run, 56 miles. Variation, 14° 20′ [W. ?]. Lat. by Obs., 10° 52′ N.

March 30.—These 24 hours little wind. Course, N.W. b. W. and W.N.W. Distance run, 52 miles. Latitude by Obsn., 11° 12′ N.

March 31.—These 24 hours little wind. Course, N.W. and

[1] *Variation of the Compass.*—In Sir Thomas Roe's voyage (1615), the magnetic variation is noted at Socotra as 17° 50′ W., and at Damaun as 16° 17′ W. In the year 1817, Yeates' Magnetic Chart gives the variation at Socotra as 6° 10′ W., and at Damaun as 0° 30′ W. In the year 1870, by Admiralty Chart, the variation at Socotra is 2° W., and at Damaun 1° E., and the Maldive Islands are now (1870) on the "no variation" line. I imagine, therefore, that at the date of this Log (1635), the magnetic variation to the westward of the Maldives, and in latitude 9° N., must have been westerly, as the curves would indicate; but it is curious that an observant man like Mr. Hedges never noted which way it was.—R. F. B.

N.W. b. W. and W.N.W. Distance run, 57 miles. Variation, 15° 28′ [West ?]. Lat. 11° 40′ N.

April 1685.

April 1.—These 24 hours little Wind. Course, N.W.—N.W. b. W. and N.N.W. Distance run, 55 miles. Lat. by Obser. of y^e Stars at 2 o'clock this morning, 12° 0′ N.

April 2.—These 24 hours little Wind. Course, N. b. E. and N.N.E. Distance run, 37 miles. Lat. by Obs. of y^e Stars, 12° 14′ N.

April 3.—These 24 hours little Wind. Course, N. b. E. and N.N.E. Distance run, 31 miles. Lat. by $Obs^{n.}$, 12° 20′ N.

April 4.—These 24 hours a meer calm till 4 o'clock this morning; since, little Wind. Course, N.W. b. N. & N.W. Dist. run, 17 m. Lat. by Obs. of y^e Stars, 12° 57′ N.

April 5.—These 24 hours calm. Lat. by Obs., 13° N. This morning we saw a great Shippe standing Westward; by Sunset she was out of sight.

April 6.—These 24 hours calme. $Lat^{de.}$ by Judgement, 13° 0′ N.

The East India Company having ordered me not to give the least countenance to Interlopers, I shall here relate what passed in discourse this day between me and $M^{r.}$ Dowglasse, who (in presence of $M^{r.}$ Gough, $M^{r.}$ Whitmore, & my Nephew Hedges) told, "That $M^{r.}$ Beard mett and spoke with Capt. Alley and Capt. Read at his house, and had done the like at $M^{r.}$ Littleton's; that $M^{r.}$ Evans, our Minister, did frequently converse and associate with Capt. Alley, and was so intimate with him, that he carried his Wife to sup at Captain Alley's House; that $M^{r.}$ Evans took his leave of Capt. Alley when he was going for England, and, to his knowledge, sent a packet of letters by him, and, he believes, Tokens also." $M^{r.}$ Whitmore says $M^{r.}$ Beard discoursed very kindly and civilly with $M^{r.}$ Davies. $M^{r.}$ Evans kept more

o 2

company with Capt. Alley, Mr. Davies, & Mr. Littleton than he did with those in the Factory.

April 7.—These 24 hours calme. Our Head lay W. and W. b. S. The Sun so near our Zenith, could take no Observation.

This morning we went to allowance of 3 Pints of Water for each passenger, and a Quart for the Mariners, both to drinke & boyle their rice.

April 8.—These 24 hours quite calme. Our head lay N.E. b. N. and N.E. Lat. by Obsn. of ye Stars, 12° 30′ N.; by which we find ourselves driven ½ a degree to ye Southward.

April 9.—These 24 hours a small breeze. Course, N.E. b. E., N., and N.N.E. Distance run, 18 miles. Lat. by Obsn. of ye Stars, 12° 53′ N.

April 10, 11.—Very little Wind, and that Contrary. Course, W.N.W. and E.N.E. Distance run, 24 miles. Lat. by Obsn. of ye Stars, 12° 48′ N. We have driven 8 miles to the Southward.

April 12.—These 24 hours Calme; ye little wind we had for ye most part contrary. Course from ye W. to W. b. S. & to N.E. Distance run, 20 miles. Lat. by Observation of ye Stars, 12° 51′ N.

This day Mr. Rd. Gough told me of an intended Mutiny & Conspiracy of ye Captain against me, when it shall please God to bring us near unto, or in sight of, Gombroon or Cong, in ye Gulph of Persia: which conspiracy, the said Mr. Gough told me, was discovered to him by William Godman, our 2nd Mate, in manner following, with the reasons which (they pretend) induced them to it.

The night before we set sail from Ballasore Road, a Protest was delivered to me by Mr. William Fitz Hugh and Mr. Stanley, from Agent Beard and Council of Hugly, for carrying away ye said Mr. Gough and my Nephew, Robert Hedges, Passengers on this Ship *Recovery*.

Mr. John Hampton, Commander of ye Shippe, tooke this

opportunity to play yᵉ Villaine, and behaved himselfe in a very rude and disrespectful manner towards us in the Voyage, especially since we came from Fort Sᵗ· George, telling us, "When God sent him to Muscatt, he would take no further Charge of the Shippe,"—at which we seemed little concerned; and though Mʳ· Dowglasse was then as much, or rather more, affronted than myself, & made him a sharpe reply, yett it seems all his malice and revenge is bent towards *me*, & not knowing better how to show it, the Divell has put this evill conspiracy and designe into his head, viz.:

"When it Pleased God to bring us to Muscat, hé will not there discover his intentions, because (says he) yᵉ Agent speaks Arabick (yᵉ language of yᵉ Country), and may probably be too hard upon us; but when we come over against Gombroon or Cong, we will stand off with yᵉ Shippe, and not come into port till we have forced him, the said Wᵐ· Hedges, Mʳ· Gough, Mʳ· Letter, & Mʳ· Robert Hedges, to give us good security, and indemnifie us against any pretence that shall be made against us by yᵉ said Agent Beard and Councill at our returne to Hugly in Bengall, by reason of yᵉ said Mʳ· Gough and Mʳ· Robert Hedges going passengers on yᵉ said Shippe." Which evill intention of yᵉ Captain's, if he should continue to put yᵉ same in execution, I apprehend it to be that tresspasse which is called a Barratry of yᵉ Captain and marriners, the said Captain and all his Marriners being hired servants of mine and yᵉ said Mʳ· Dowglasse's, during pleasure, and that all such damages as shall be susteyned by me are to be borne (in proportion) by yᵉ ensurers in England.

April 13.—Mʳ· Gough informs me farther that Wᵐ· Godman told him likewise, Mʳ· Hampton designed to stopp our goods, and give us trouble in Persia; and before he entered into Port, resolved to stand out at sea, and force us to his owne terms before he would bring yᵉ Ship into any Port.

I have now prevailed with Mʳ· Gough to give me the

words in writing (to ye best of his remembrance), as they were related to him by Wm. Godman, our 2nd Mate, a Coppy whereof I have transcribed verbatim, as followeth.

"On board ye Shippe *Recovery*, 11th April 1685.

"This day, between 4 and 5 o'clock in ye Afternoon, discoursing with William Godman, our Second Mate, on the Quarter Deck and in ye great Cabbin (in ye latter place Mr. Robert Hedges was present), he told me that about 3 weeks past he had some discourse with Mr. John Hampton, our Captain, who told him there was a Protest against this Shippe, himselfe, & all ye officers & Lascars (or Mariners), for carrying away one Richard Gough & Mr. Robert Hedges; and that he, ye said Captaine, did not designe to do anything at Muscatt, because Agent Hedges understood ye Arabian Language, and might disappoint him in his designe with ye Government there: but when he came to Gombroon, he would run off with ye Shippe, and seize upon ye Agent's goods, to secure himselfe, &c., for ye damage they were like to come to at their returne to Bengall; and that he would acquaint ye Company's Servants in ye Factory, and the Commanders of ye Europe Shipps, who would assist him in his designe."

Edward Walter (my Servant) declared this morning to Mr. Gough and me that he heard Mr. Hampton say, "He would make ye Divell to doe amongst us when he came to Muscatt."

These 24 hours calme; not any thing upon ye Log; the Lat. by Obs^n.^ of ye stars, 12° 40′ N.; so we conclude ye Current sets us to ye Southward.

Mr. Gough, having further discoursed with Wm. Godman, told me as follows:

"On board Shippe *Recovery*, 13th April 1685.

"This day, between 3 and 4 o'clock in ye Afternoon, I had this further discourse with William Godman, our Second Mate, on the Quarter Deck, when he tolld me y^t.^ John Hampton, our Captain, had a designe when he came to Muscatt to take in more White men aboard ye Shippe; and having 10 White men already aboard, with these, and what more he should there take in, resolved, when he came to Gombroon Road, to run off with ye Shippe, and force ye Agent and all of us to give him and his officers notes under our hands, or obligations, to save him, ye said Hampton, and officers and Shippe, harmless from any damage they were like to come to for carrying me, Richard Gough, and Mr. Robert Hedges away from Hugly; and if we did not thus comply with him, he was

resolved to carry the said Agent Hedges & his Goods back 'again to Hugly: and this ye said W^m. Godman is ready to take his oath, when thereunto required."

April 14.—These 24 hours quite calme. The Shipp's head lay N. b. W., N.N.W., and N.W. b. N. Latitude by Observation of ye Stars, 12° 41′ N.

April 15.—Till nine o'clock last night quite calme; since then a fine small breeze, at S. b. E. and S.S.E. Course, North. Distance run, 21 miles. Latitude by Obs., 12° 50′ N.

April 16.—Till 12 at night quite calme; since that a fine gentle breeze at S. b. E. and S.S.E. Course, N. Distance run, 17 miles. Lat. by Judgement, 13° 20′.

April 17.—From yesterday noon till 9 at night Calme; since that a small breeze. Course, N. Dist. run, 28 miles. Lat^de. by Judgement, 14° 15′ N.

April 18.—These 24 hours calme, and light winds. Course, N. b. E. Distance run, 18 miles. Lat. by. Obs., 14° 45′ N. We find ye current now in our favour.

April 19.—[No entry.]

April 20.—These 24 hours a fine fresh gale at W. b. N., W.N.W., and N.W. Course, N. b. E. and N.N.E. Distance run, 64 miles. Lat. by Obs^n., 16° 30′.

April 21.—These 24 hours the Wind has blowne very fresh at W. and W. b. N. Course, from 8 last night till 4 this morning, N.E. and N.E. b. N., then N. and N. b. W. The Distance run, 76 miles. Latitude by Obs., 18° N.

April 22.—These 24 hours it has blowne as much wind as we could carry; our Topsails a little settled. Wind, W. b. S. Course, N.N.W. From 9 o'clock at night till 5 this morning shortened Sail and went with 2 Courses only, for fear of land. Distance run, 48 miles. Lat. by obs., 19° N.

April 23.—These 24 hours it has blown hard at W.S.W. and S.W. We lay by all night, for fear of land. Between 11 and 12 o'clock this morning we saw Land, which we tooke to be 2 Islands in a Bay to ye West^d. of ye great Island Miserie,[1]

[1] Massera, off the coast of Oman.—Y.

so stood off E. and E.S.E. Lat. by Observation, 19° 50′ N. We saw High Land again, which we took to be Miserie.

April 24.—These 24 hours a very fresh gale. Wind, W.S.W. and S.W. Course various, at E.S.E., E., N.E., and N. b. E. Dist. run, 98 miles. Lat. by obs., 20° 30′ N.

April 25.—These 24 hours yᵉ Wind continued fresh from S.W. to S.W. b. W. We lay by from 8 last night till 5 this morning, then sailed N. b. W. and N. At 9 this morning saw land very plaine on yᵉ Larboard bow and right ahead. Lat. by Obs., 21° 30′ N.

April 26.—These 24 hours a fine gentle gale. From 12 last night till 5 this morning we lay by, then made sail, and by 9 o'clock this morning got within Cape Rasalgate.[1] Lat. by Observation, 22° 42′ N.

April 27.—These 24 hours little wind. Course, N. b. W. & N.N.W. Lat. by Obs$^{n.}$, 23° 21′ N.

April 28.—These 24 hours very little Wind. Course, W.N.W. Lat. by Obs$^{n.}$, 23° 34′ N.

April 29.—About 10 o'clock this morning we arrived at Muscatt,[2] where we found Capt. Edward Say with his Shippe *Welcome*, Capt. Smith, Commander.

Captain Say came aboard and shewed us great kindness and respect. We went all ashore with him to visit yᵉ Governor and Hogea Ishmael. The Governor bad us welcome, and assured us the freedom & Liberty of the Port.

Hogea Ismael has formerly been the only powerfull and eminent person in this place. Lying lately very sick, the King first seized a great part of his Estate, and several of his Factors ran away with the rest; however, he is a person much esteemed and well reputed by yᵉ Governor.

Captain Say tells us Sir Thomas Grantham passed by this

[1] Or Rosalgat, a corruption of the Arab. *Rās-al-Ḥadd*, "Cape of the Limit", or Extremity, being the extreme easterly point of the Arabian coast.—Y.

[2] Muscat is in lat. 23° 36′, long. 58° 40′ E.

way about 3 months since, from Gombroon to Suratt, & that he was very kind and civill to his people here ashore; that y[e] said Sir Thomas Grantham sold Capt. Say's Servants 10 great Guns with their Carriages, and transported 24 horses for [from] that to Suratt, giving them Bills of Lading; that Sir Thomas had taken in divers passengers and great quantity of goods at Gombroon, which he was obliged to carry to Suratt, and would be worth to him a considerable sum of money.

This Sir Thomas Grantham is y[e] Person on whom y[e] Company chiefly relies for taking and destroying of Interlopers; and he has treated those he has mett of them with greater respect than any other of their Commanders.

Capt. Goldsborough, in y[e] *Bengall Merchant*, sailed from this place towards Gombroon on y[e] 25[th.] Ult. During his stay here, which was but 4 or 5 days, he proffered to carry any goods for Interlopers to Persia,—a favour M[r.] Beard would by no means grant to me; though at y[e] same time he permitted M[r.] Dowglasse (a declared Interloper) to lade 6 chests of cloth for his owne account at Hugly.

May 1685.

May 7.—Finding my selfe feverish and indisposed, I left y[e] shore and went on board of y[e] *Recovery*.

May 9.—I returned againe to Muscatt.

May 14.—This day, about Sunsett, I took leave of Muscatt and embarked on y[e] *Recovery*, who rode without y[e] Castles.

May 15.—We waited y[e] coming off of some of our Mariners from y[e] shore, and employed ourselves in y[e] mean time in setting up our Rigging and putting ourselves in a posture to go to Sea.

This evening we sailed from Muscatt.

May 16.—The *Wellcome* (a Shippe Mr. Dowglasse and I hired to carry our goods to Bussora, for fear that we should not meet with a Conveyance at Cong) not appearing in sight, we tacked about and sailed towards Muscatt. About 4 this Afternoon we came up with y^e^ *Wellcome*, and made ye best of our way to Cong, having given them order to keep us company.

May 21.—We got sight of Cape Jasques, and passed by it very early this morning at a great distance, keeping much nearer to the Arabian than the Persian shore.

May 22.—We passed by Cape Muscandon.[1]

May 23.—We came up with the Islands of Ormus and Arack [Larek of Maps]; but having intelligence that a Squadron of 7 or 8 Duch Ships lay before Gombroon, we thought good to sail directly for Cong, and sent Mr. Dowglasse and Mr. Richard Gough in the *Wellcome's* boat to manage our concernes at Gombroon, and to follow us as soon as they could to Cong.[2]

May 24.—This morning by 7 o'clock we saw a Shippe coming out from between Lareck and Ormus Islands, but she could not fetch us up; by 10 o'clock we saw 8 or 9 Shippes at anchor close under ye Island Kishmish [*i.e.*, Kishm], about ye middle of it, where another little Island makes a good Harbour.

May 27.—This Afternoon it pleased God to bring us in safety to Cong Road. I went ashore immediately to Mr. Brough's house (Supra Cargo of ye *Siam Merchant*), and lay there all night.

May 28.—I hired a house for myselfe and the rest of our Company for this Monsoon.

May 30.—It pleased God to visit me with so violent a fever that all men despaired of my recovery. Its rage and fury

[1] C. Massendom, Ar. *Rās Masandum*, the point of Arabia (properly of a small island of the name) marking the entrance to the Persian Gulf.—Y.

[2] From a statement in Bruce's *Annals of the East India Company*, iii, 393, it would seem that in 1677 the Portuguese still kept up some pretence of rights in the port of Cong. But it is apparent, from circumstances mentioned by Chardin (ed. 1735, i, 348), that all foundation for such pretensions had ceased some years before.—Y.

being past, I was taken with a relapse, which continued upon me full 2 months, and reduced me to a most feeble and weake Condition; during all which time I tooke no other sustenance but a little Rice and Water boyled together, which served me both for meat and drink too.

July 1685.

Towards y[e] fine of July, I conceited the great heats of this place caused y[e] continuance of my indisposition upon me, and y[t.] if I could be removed to a cooler Air I should soone recover; in order to which designe I hired 12 stout fellows for Mamoodies[1] 200, and 35 Mamoodies for their Diett money, to carry me as far as Lar,[2] in my Cott (Palankeen fashion), which they performed to my satisfaction.

July 29.—This afternoon my Cousin, Nathanael Letter, and I sett out from Kong towards Spahan, and travelled this night to a miserable poor Village (and a worse Caravan-Sarai) at y[e] foot of y[e] Hill, called "Champa". The Water here very stinking.

July 30.—We rose from Champa, and after an houre or an houre & halfe riding, we ascended an exceeding steep, scragged hill, which yett was not halfe so troublesome and difficult to us as its descent. I judged it the more difficult by reason of the loose Stones. My 12 Palankeen men at once fled all together, and were like to cast themselves and me downe a great precipice. We were not able to reach Obdeen-deen (y[e] usuall Mensill),[3] but lay at a sorry Caravan-Sarai between y[e] hills, called Dellaver Agaring Caravan-

[1] 100 mahmūdis = 1 tomān. The *tomān* at this time was worth £3 6*s*. 8*d*.; hence the mahmudi worth about 8*d*. (See Fryer's *Travels*, p. 211.)—Y.

[2] Lar, formerly an important city, and the capital of a principality of that name, annexed to Persia by Shah Abbas about 1600. It is about eighty miles from Cong, as the crow flies.—Y.

[3] *Manzil* (Pers.), stage, or halting-place.

Saraia, some 3 houres short of Obdeen-deen. Water indifferent good.

July 31.—We rose from Dellaver Agaring Caravan-Sarai and lodged at Char-ber keer—short of Cokeer, ye usuall Menzill. We got a kid at a neighbouring Village. The Water coolest and best I have yett dranke in Persia.

August 1685.

August 1.—We rose from Charber keer, and passing by Kokeer on ye right, arrived at Bustag before Sun rising. Here is plenty of Provision, but no good water.

August 2.—We rose from Bustag, and arrived at Sheack-zur 4 hours before day. Here's store of provisions, and indifferent good water.

August 3.—We rose from Sheack-zur and lay at Possa-Chan, where we found divers of our hired Camels (with their lading) going towards Lar. Here is no want of provisions, but ye Water exceeding bad and Stinking.

August 4.—We rose from Possa-Chan and travelled this night to Nimma. Store of Provisions, but sorry water. Here I bought 5 live Partridges for 15 Cosbys,[1] which is 4 pence ½ English money.

August 5.—We rose from Nimma & gott to Lar about 10 or 11 o'clock at night. We were no sooner arrived, but a Person at the Caravan-Sarai giving notice of my being there, the Gov$^{r.}$ sent a Ser$^{t.}$ to direct me to a house he had ordered for my reception.

August 6.—Our Servants informing us it was customary for y^e English to lodge at y^e Duch house, I removed thither, where the house keeper received me very courteously.

This Afternoon I went to visit y^e Governor, who had ordered us a house for our lodging. I wish we had continued

[1] A small copper coin of obsolete name, called by travellers *Coz*, *Gaaz*, *Cosbeaque*, *Gosbeck*, *Kaz-begie*. The true form appears to be *Ghāz-begi*.—Y.

in it, being much better than that of the Dutch to which we removed.

August 7.—I went to visit the Shabunder; but he was not ashore.[1]

August 8.—The Shabunder came and gave me a visit at my lodging, with expressions of great kindness, and sent me a present of fruit and provisions.

August 9.—I returned ye Shabunder his Visit; when he was pleased to present me with a stately fine horse, valued at 8 tomans; and presented another of lesse stature (a very pretty nag) to my Cousin Letter. The camells with all our goods being gonne towards Spahan, I gave ye Shabunder a note under my hand, promising to present him 4 Bales of Sugar and some pieces of Cloth at Spahan, in recompence of his horse, with which he was well content. My Cousin Letter gave him the like note for 2 Bales of Sugar and some pieces of Cloth.

August 11.—I went to see ye famous Castle of Larr. 'Tis a most pitiful, sorry, ruinous building; the Walls (in many places) ready to drop downe. We past not above 5 or 6 Soldiers in all ye Castle, whose business was chiefly to guard 5 Usbeque (Tartars) prisoners taken in War. They were stout, able-bodied persons, with good countenances; all of them spoke Turkish.

In this Castle of Larr are 5 large brass guns, all taken from y^e^ Portuguese at Ormus, weighing from 31c. to 44c. weight a piece; some of them made Anno 1618 in Goa by y^e^ Vice King, with y^e^ King of Portugall's armes on them. The bore of one of them was inches $9\frac{1}{4}$ Diameter.

August 13.—We sett out from Larr (where we stayed 4 dayes extra for want of mules) and lodged at Kuda-Poi-

[1] Read probably "not *at home*". Lar is 60 or 70 miles from the sea. A *Shah-bandar* was properly a port-officer; but the term was also applied, at inland marts, such as Lar was, to the officer superintending trade and duties.—Y.

cotall, a very large and convenient Caravan-Sarai, well stored with provisions.

August 14.—We dislodged from Kuda-Poicotal and travelled to Beeres, a pretty large Towne, and a spacious Caravan-Sarai, the best I have yet seen on y[e] Road, except that at Larr. Very bad Water, but plenty of Provisions.

August 15.—We rose from Beeres, and passing through Benarroo, lay at Bocktearee, a pretty well seated village, where our Chief Muleteer lived, who invited and entertained us at his house very courteously. This Place is well watered (a rarity in this Country) with a fine running stream (the first and only one I have yet seen in this barren Country), conveyed to them by an Aqueduct under ground.

August 16.—We lay here (being Sunday) all day, and accepted of our Muleteer's entertainement.

August 17.—We rose from Bocktearee and travelled this night to Mowueseer, an old, ruinous Caravan-Sarai; and sorry Water.

August 18.—We rose from Mowueseer and lodged at Chatalkee, a spacious Caravan-Sarai, with plenty of good fresh water and provisions.

August 19.—We rose from Chatalkee between one and two o'clock in y[e] Afternoon, having divers steep scraged Hills, which required five hours' time at least (we made it more than 6) to pass over,—'twas most convenient to be done by day light,—and arrived at Jarroon a little within night. This is a great towne, and affords plenty of all things for y[e] use of a traveller in these parts.

August 20.—We rose from Jarroon and lodged at Moocack Sookta, a large, convenient Caravan-Sarai; good water, and no want of provisions. Here we had y[e] best musk melons that ever I saw of y[e] growth of Cossir.

August 21.—We rose from Moocack Sookta, and went 4 Farsanges or leagues out of our way to see Dottiuan, situated in the most pleasant and fruitful plaine (as reported) in all Persia, where we lodged this night in a garden belonging to ye Duch (the same affording no Caravansarai), near a small rivulett that runs through it. The Gardener gave us store of Figgs (ye least, but as good as I have seen), Grapes, Pomegranetts, Peaches, and Wall-nutts, all very good of their kind. The towne is full of Gardens, all plentifully watered with Cutts out of a River running by it, out of which we had brought us two good dishes of Fish, which cost but 1 Mamoodee: 2 of them were 20 inches long apiece. This is the most pleasant, fruitfull place I have yet seen in Persia. We are promised a guide on our way this Afternoon (God willing) to Cossir, who will show us certain great Vaults under ye Rocks, large enough, some of them, to hold 1000 men.

August 22.—We rose from Dottiuan, & passing by Cossir, lodged at Agatakee.

August 23.—We rose from Agatakee and lay at Mussaferee, a good Caravan-Sarai. Store of Water in a great plain.

August 24.—We rose from Mussafferee and lodged at Bobba Hadgee, in a fine plaine, well watered and stored with provisions. This is a long Stage. We satt out early, and travelled hard to be here 3 hours (or more) within night.

August 25.—We satt out by 1 o'clock in ye afternoon from Bobba Hadgee, and arrived at Shirash about Sunset, and lodged at the English house.[1]

August 26.—I went to see ye Bazaars and public Buildings of ye City, which were most of them handsome, rich, and convenient for the heats of this Country.

This Afternoon Padre Agathangelo, a Carmelite Fryer, formerly resident for many years at Bussora, came to give

[1] We have not found an accurate detailed itinerary of this road from Lar to Shiraz, whereby to identify all the names in Hedges' orthography; but Pā-i-Kotal, Berez, Benārū, Jahrūm, Chāh-i-talkh ("Bitter Well"), Maghāk Sokhta, Āga Tākī, and Bābā Hājī, are recognisable. Dottiuan is the *Dadivan* of Tavernier (Bk. V, ch. xxii), "one of the most delicious situations in all Persia."—Y.

me a visit. I delivered him a letter from Padre Marc Antonio Santucci, chief of ye Jesuits order in Bengall, and he gave me another from himselfe to ye Superior of his Order in Spahan.

August 27.—This morning I rode about ye City of Shirash, to see divers parts that I had not seen yesterday; and returned ye Padre's Visit at their Convent, where I was most courteously entertained by them.

August 28.—I went to see ye King's garden, and that of ye old Khan of Shirash, who tooke ye Kingdome of Ormus from ye Portuguese in ye time of ye great Shah Abbas.

This evening, at Sunset, we set out from Shirash and lodged at Zurgoon, a large and exceeding pleasant village, situated on the side of a high hill, overlooking a well watered plaine, full of vineyards stored with excellent good grapes, which the villanes carry every night to sell at Shirash.

This Village is in the way to Cheker-Minar (commonly called Chil-minar), the road to Spahan parting from it about 2 leagues distance from ye Village.

August 29.—We set out from Zurgoon, and passing over a very large plaine with a river running through it, over which we rodd on a Bridge of 4 Arches, we arrived 2 hours within night at Emer-Cascoon (a towne within ¾ of a mile of Cheker-minar), and lodged there all night.

August 30.—We rose very early this morning, and went to see ye Ruins of Cheker-Minar[1] (which signifies 40 Pillars in ye Persian Language), antiently judged to be ye Palace of ye once famous Persepolis; and leaving Meer Cascoon, travelled this evening towards Moyeen (in a great plaine), where we arrived about 2 o'clock in the morning. This is a pretty Village, well watered, and stored with provisions.

August 31.—We sett out from Moyeen: an hour within night we passed by Imaum Zade, a pretty Village, and lodged at Woo-John. Between these two townes is a very high hill.

[1] *Chihal Minār* ("Forty columns") is a well-known name of the ruins of Persepolis.—Y.

September 1685.

September 1.—We set out from Woo John and lodged at Assapos, a place well stored with good water.

September 2.—We set out from Assapos and lodged at Coskezar.[1]

September 3.—We set out from Coskezar and lodged at Deregherdoo.

September 4.—We set out from Deregherdoo and lodged at Yes-de-gas, a good Caravan-Serai, built in a vast great ditch, where ('tis credibly reported) formerly ran a river.

September 5.—This morning early a horseman met me with a present of Wine, strong waters of Rushia, Oyle, Achars,[2] Rose Water distilled with muske, sugared Biskett, Caviare, and divers sorts of excellent good fruit, sent from Spahan by Signr. Zacharia, the Armenian Father.

This Zacharia is a Merchant, who came passenger on ye *Recovery* with me from Bengall, and was entertained by me and Mr. Dowglasse to assist us in ye management of our business & concerns at Cong and Spahan.

We rose this morning from Yesdegas and lodged at Macksood Beigh, a sorry old ruinous Caravan Serai, and bad water. There is a good new Caravan Sarai within halfe a mile of it, but not much frequented, for want of provisions.

September 6.—We rose from Macksood and lodged at Comesha.

September 7.—We rose from Comesha and lodged at Moyar.

September 8.—We rose from Moyar, and about 10 at night got to a Caravan Sarai in ye Suburbs of Spahan.

September 9.—We entered the Citty of Spahan and went to ye English house, where I was kindly entertained (for a few dayes, till I could provide myselfe with a more convenient

[1] For this and preceding names: Zargūn, Mīr-Khāsagūn, Mayin, Aūjan, Aspās, Khushkī-zard, Yezd-i-Khāst, Maksūd-Begī, Kum-i-shāh, Mayār.—Y.

[2] A kind of pickle.

Lodging) by my old friend, Mr. Daniel Edwards, at present (by ye death of Mr. Darnelly) Chief for ye Honble. East India Compys Affaires in Persia.

September 10.—I received visits from the two Orders of the Carmelites & Dominican Fryers, and likewise from divers of ye French Nation, as Jewellers and Watchmakers (some of them my acquaintance in Constantinople), Servants to the King of Persia.

September 11.—I went to see Julfa, where all Armenians live. In our way we passed over a large handsome Bridge. In this towne (for more conveniency) I tooke a house for 3 months, and Warehouses for my goods, in ye Queen mother's Caravansarai, called Gidda.

September 12.—I returned a visit to ye Padri Carmelitani. They have a handsome large Convent, with a pretty Chappell, and Library well stored with books, amongst which were divers in English, with an English Bible.

This Afternoon Sigr. Fabricius, ye King of Swedeland's Envoy, gave me a visit. He was born in Holland, and bred a Soldier in Sweden. He is a most courteous, civill, ingenious person, and gave me divers invitations to his quarters.

September 14.—This afternoon Sigr. Van Havell, ye Duch Commissarius, as he is called, gave me a visit, excusing himselfe, with many compliments, that he had not done it sooner. He was well attended by divers persons well mounted: a Trumpeter riding, and 2 Soldiers in Crimson Velvet coats going before him, with Musketeers. He has lived 15 yeares in Persia.

September 15.—This morning I removed, for better conveniency and management of my business, from ye Company's Factory in Spahan to ye house I had taken in Julfa, but left my goods at Gidda Caravansarai in Spahan, except 86 Bales of Sugar, which were brought hither.

September 17.—I returned visits to ye Dominican and Augustine Fryers.

September 18.—I went to see yᵉ King of Persia, Sha Soliman,[1] ride abroad to take yᵉ aire. The person that gave me intelligence not coming in time to see his Majestie take horse, I waited at yᵉ Bridge foot (where he was to passe) till his returne. I was advised to salute him by pulling off my hatt, after the European manner, which he expects from all Franks. So soon as the King saw me, he turned to yᵉ Vezier to know who I was, not having seen me before. The Vesier not being able to informe him, the King sent one of his Shatirs,[2] or Footmen, to Monsieur Sein (a French Jeweller who has served this King and his Father many years), standing near me, to enquire who I was. The Monsʳ· made him answer, I was an English gentleman lately come to towne from India to see yᵉ Court. He looked very chearfully, and gave me a gentle nod, telling me in Turkish "I was Wellcome",—which is esteemed an exceedingly great honor; indeed, the generality of mankind here are more respectfull and civill to Strangers than they are (for the most part) in any Citty in Christendome.

September 20.—I received a Visit from yᵉ Emperour's Ambassador (a learned, grave Bishop). He lived many yeares at Legorne, and was well acquainted with divers of our Nation there.

September 23.—I received a Visit from yᵉ Pope's Nuncio, Monˢʳ· Sampson, a French Priest.

September 24.—I returned a Visit to yᵉ Emperor's Ambassador.

September 27.—I mett yᵉ Compte De Soria, the King of Poland's Ambassador, on yᵉ Bridge at Spahan. After divers compliments, he desired yᵉ favour of a Visit, which I promised him.

[1] Shāh Sulaimān, great-great-grandson of Shāh 'Abbās, reigned from 1668 to 1694.—Y.

[2] *Shātir*, "a courier, a footman."—Y.

September 30.—I visited ye King of Poland's Ambassador, who received and entertained me with great Courtesy and respect.

October 1685.

October 2.—I returned a visit to Mons^gr. Sampson, ye Pope's Nuntio.

October 10.—Sig^r. Fabricius, the King of Sweden's Ambassador, gave me a Visit.

October 20.—I met the King of Persia in ye Choar Bog, or Long Walke.[1] I satt a horseback till he past by. Seeing me salute him, [he] returned me a courteous nodd.

October 27.—I visited Sig^r. Fabricius, ye Swedes' Ambassador.

October 30.—Monsr. Varine, a French watchmaker, carried me to see the King of Persia's Pallace, built by Sha Abbas ye Great & Sha Sefee, his Successor.

November 1685.

November 6.—Monsr. Varine accompanied me to see ye Pallace built by this King of Persia, Sha Soliman, called Hesti-be-hest.[2] Some days before, Hogea Kiragoos shewed my cousin Letter and me ye King's great garden, called Hazar-jerib.[3]

[1] The *Chahār Bāgh* (lit. "Four-Garden"), the great public garden or square; but the name was also applied to the long avenue which led to it.—Y.

[2] Kaempfer says: "The garden *Bulbul* . . . has been so improved and adorned by the multitude of promenades, avenues, palace-buildings, and works of topiary and hydraulic artists, that it is said nothing so beautiful is to be found in the whole kingdom, especially since the last master-touches have been put to the palace in the middle of it . . . . and from the king himself it has received the magnific name of *Hêste behest*, *i.e.*, of the Eighth Paradise." (*Amœnitates Exoticæ*, 190-191.) *Hasht-bihisht*, lit. "The Eight Paradises."—Y.

[3] *Hazār-jarīb*, "One thousand (square) chains". I do not know how much the Persian *jarīb*, or square chain, was.—Y.

December 1685.

December 1.—I hired 125 Camells to carry mine and Mr. Robert Dowglasse's Bales, at Mahmoodies 80 for 100 Maunds Tauris, to Bagdat, and 13 mules to carry our luggage, at Mahmoodies 90 per 100 Maunds Tauris.[1]

December 13.—This day I left Spahan, and began my journey towards Aleppo, by way of Bagdat.

I came out in company with Mr. Dowglasse, my Cousin Nathanael Letter, and my Nephew Robert Hedges. Mr. Daniel Edwards (then Chief for ye Honble. Compy's affaires in Persia) and Mr. Henry Lawrence (another of ye said Compy's. Servants) favored us with their good company to Mahmoot-Alli-Beig's Caravan-sarai, about 2 hours' riding from Julfa. Divers French Protestants (Servants to ye King of Persia) obliged us likewise to [? let them] come with us to this place, viz., Monsr. Sein, M. Letuall, M. Varein, M. Jurt, M. Pere Grange, M. de Fino, M. Teudor, and one Frenchman more, whose name I cannot call to mind.

December 14.—This afternoon Mr. Edwards took his leave of us and returned to Spahan. We lay here till our Camell and Mulemen had discharged all their debts at this place and at Spahan.

December 15.—We rose from Mahmoot-Alli-Beig's Caravan-sarai and lay at Challisea, where ye present Veseir, Sheck-Alli-Chan, is building a new large Caravansarai. Here we we were forced to compound with ye Rattaree-men[2] for ye

[1] The *Mann* (or maund) *Tabrīzī* is called by Fryer = 6½ *lb.* English; and Prinsep gives it at 6 *lb.* 5 *oz.* 7.2 *dr.* Mr. Wollaston, however, in his *English-Persian Dict.*, gives "from 7¼ to 7½ *lb. avoird.*" For the *mahmūdi*, see p. 203.—Y.

[2] *Rāhdārī.* A transit duty collected on the pretext of protection afforded to traffic, but often very arbitrary, and little better than black-mail.—Y.

Dutys on our goods, which, for all our Mules and camels, cost us 85 Mahmoodies. This Manzeill is 7 houres riding.

December 16.—We rose from Challisea and lay at Deha[1]: 9 houres. All good way. About an hour short of this place we passed by a large town and a good Caravansarai. On y[e] road I received letters from Aleppo and Bagdat.

December 17.—Our Camells not coming up with us, we lay this day at Deha.

December 18.—We lay still at Deha.

December 19.—We rose from Deha and lay at Deharaban: 9 houres riding.

December 20.—We rose from Deharaban and lay at Cogga: 6 houres. This day one of our Camells fell downe and broke his leg, which caused us to lye here 2 dayes.

December 23.—We rose from Cogga and lay at Macliana: 6 houres riding.

December 24.—We lay at Mecliana.

December 25.—We rose from Mecliana and lay at Bog: 6 houres. A good large Caravansarai, & y[e] best water I have drank in Persia.

December 26.—We rose from Bog and lay at [ ]: 7 hours.

December 27.—We rose from [ ] and lay at Saroo: 5 hours.

December 28 & 29.—We lay still at Saroo, upon a hill, at a good Caravansarai: ye weather exceeding cold.

December 30.—We rose from Saroo and lay at Deezabad: 5 hours riding.

December 31.—We rose from Deezabad and lay at Nana: 8 houres.

[1] Challisea and Deha appear in Dupré (*Voyage en Perse*, i, 288, 287) as *Tchallisié* and *Dehak*. He mentions a great caravanserai at the former, but ascribes the building to the munificence of the grandmother of Futteh 'Ali Shâh, then reigning.—Y.

January 1686.

January 1, 2, 3, 4.—We lay at Nana, occasioned by the vast quantity of Snow that fell all these 4 days without intermission.

January 5.—We rose from Nana and lay at Faraspa: 10 houres riding. One of our Camel men, being sick, rode upon a Camel, and was found dead. We judge he was frozen to death.

January 6.—My Nephew Hedges and I rose from Farespa (leaving M^r. Dowglasse and my Cousin Letter with ye Camels) and lay at Kengauar.[1] On ye road we were overtaken with a letter from my Cousin Letter, advising, since my departure they were robbed of all their money, to the sum of 4 Tomauns, and one Bale of Luckarees[2] opened, out of which 36 Peices were stolen.

January 7.—We rose from Kengauar and lay at Sohana: 7 houres riding.

January 8.—We rose from Sahana and lay at Bisetoon, ye best Caravan-sarai I have seen in Persia, near a very fine large fountaine issuing out of a Rock: 5 hours riding.

January 9.—We rose from Bisetoon and lay at Kirmansha.

January 10.—This morning, 2 hours before day, I despatched away Hogea Bureat with 5 Tomans, to meet

[1] We have now got into the direct route from Hamadān to Baghdad, and it is more easily followed. This is *Kangāvar* (Kongaver, etc.), a place of old note, the Κογκοβὰρ of Isidore of Charax. The next stage is *Sahāna*, and then *Bisutūn* (*Bihistūn*, *Bāghistān*, "the place of gardens", Βαγίσταvov or Βαγίσταvη of the Greeks), the site of the famous spring, and of the rock-inscriptions in cuneiform, with which the name of Rawlinson is for ever associated. The next stage is the well-known city *Kirmānshāh*. Then *Pul-i-Shāh* ("King's Bridge"), *Māh-i-dasht*, *Hārūnābād*.—Y.

[2] We find *Laccowries* among piece-goods of Bengal in Milburn's *Or. Commerce*. Possibly stuffs dyed with *lac*.—Y.

Mr. Dowglasse and my Cousin Letter, and to hasten them hither.

January 11 *to* 22.—We lay still at Kirmansha, occasioned by the tyrannical and abusive useage of ye Governor, Coole-Sha-Kan, Sheih Alli Har's Son, who caused divers bales of our goods and chests to be opened for Gold or Silver, which is forbid to be exported out of ye Country. To prevent his doing us greater mischief, we were forced to present him and his Servants to the value of 15 Tomans in money and goods.

January 22.—We rose (with much joy) from Poolesha (near Kermansha) and lodged at Moydasht: 6 hours riding.

January 23 & 24.—We lay at Moydasht.

January 25.—We rose from Moydasht and lay at Harnawar.

January 26, 27, & 28.—We lay at Harnawar, where ye Aga of the Village carried us a Coursing, & killed 2 Hares.

January 29.—We rose from Harnawar & lay at Aslan Chesmesi, not being able to reach Gamber-Chesmesi by reason of the great depth of Snow, that made ye Road unpassable with Camels.

January 30.—We lay at Aslan Chesmesi. Here I saw Bread made of Acorns and Barley.

January 31.—We rose from Aslan Chesmesi and lay at Gamber-Chesmesi: an hour & halfe Riding.

February 1686.

February 1 & 2.—We lay at Gamber Chesmesi.

February 3.—We rose from Gamber Chesmesi and lay at Mansoor, in the open fields, then covered with snow, under an oake.

February 4.—We rose from Mansoor and lay at Gilan.

This day we passed over a very great steep Mountain : 7 hours riding.[1]

February 5 & 6.—We lay at Gilan, under a black haire tent, as we had done divers nights before.

February 7.—We rose from Gilan and lay at Chamsura, a pitifull, poore Village: 8 hours riding. The first 3 hours passed over a great Mountaine; ye latter part exceeding dirty.[2]

February 8 & 9.—We lay at Chamsura, a pittiful Village of haire cloth tents.

February 10.—We rose from Chamsura, and were forced to take up our lodging halfway our Stage, where it rained all night. This day we passed between ye Mountains over divers violent rapid torrents; one of them carried away two of our Camells, with their loads, and we were in great danger to have lost both goods and Camells. An Asse was carryed away and immediately drowned. A mule, laden with a chest of wrought Silke Stuffs, for account of Mr. Daniel Edwards of Spahan, and a bale of my best goods, were carried 2 miles down the river; and had it not been for ye great diligence of one of my Servants, they had both been lost.

February 11.—We rose from ye side of this rapid river and lay at Sambur, ye last town belonging to ye Persians.

February 12.—We rose from Sambur, accompanied with 6 or 7 Soldiers, who brought us to their bounds on ye top of ye hill, and tooke their leaves; and we lay at Mandali, ye frontier town under ye Turks.

[1] This is a pass across Mount Zagros, sometimes called the Pass of Allah Akbar, some 20 miles to the S.W. of the more usual pass between Kirmānshāh and Baghdad, by the Tāk-i-Girrāh, or Gates of Zagros. Rennell supposed it to be the pass ascended by Alexander, identifying Gīlān with the Kelonæ of Diodorus; but this Rawlinson rejects. In the latter's famous paper in *J. R. G. S.* (ix, 44) will be found interesting particulars about Gīlān. He speaks of the direct passes between Harūn-ābād and Gīlān (viz., as followed by Hedges) as very difficult.—Y.

[2] This pass is over the Ānārish mountain to *Jamsūri*, where the roads from Baghdad by the Gilān and Tāk passes diverge.—Y.

February 13 & 14.—We lay at Mandali.[1] Here we paid Rattarree: an Abassee and 8 Cosbies for every Camell, an 1 Mahmoodies and 4 Cosbies for each mule.

February 15.—We rose from Mandali, accompanyed with ye Governor or Aga, and 10 Soldiers with 2 Colours. We were not able to reach Belad-il-roos (our Manzil), and lay in ye open fields.

February 17 & 18.—We lay at Belad-il-Roos.[2]

February 19.—We rose from Belad-il-Roos and lay at Bookoroos.[3]

February 20.—We ferried our goods and Camels over ye River Deala.[4] We rose about sun set, and lay at an old ruinous Caravansarai: 3 hours riding towards Bagdat.

February 21.—We rose from ye Caravansarai, and arrived about 12 o'clock this day at Bagdat (God be praised), all in good health, having been 71 dayes on our Journey from Spahan to this place.

We were this night most courteously invited and entertained by Padre Georgio Di Vandosme, Superior of ye Capuchine Fryers at this place.

February 22.—We lay at ye Convent.

February 23.—We removed to a house in ye towne, where we had large and convenient accommodation for ourselves, goods, and horses.

Here I mett with an Imperial Command, procured at Constantinople by Mr. Samuel Lannoy, and forwarded to me by my Cousin, Robert Wakeman of Aleppo, directed to ye Pasha, Janizary Aga, Customer, & all other persons of Public employment in this Citty, to be treated with respect and kindness, and to have no more exacted from me than was

[1] Sambur and Mandali are *Saūmār* and *Mendālī* (still the Turkish frontier-town) of Rawlinson (*J. R. Geog. Soc.*, ix, 46).—Y.

[2] *Bela-Droz* (?) of Rich.—Y.

[3] *Beheruz*, of P. della Valle (*Letter I* from Ispahan).—Y.

[4] Diyālah.

allowable by our Capitulation with y^{e} Grand Sig$^{r.}$ However, y^{e} Chief Customer here (as at all places in y^{e} Empire where they are able) took the advantage of my great distance from y^{e} Port, and forced me to pay 5 per cent. Custome for all my goods ; besides, he was so unjust as to overrate all things so much, that in truth I paid 8 or 9 per cent. for ye whole, one with another. But, to make me some kind of amends and satisfaction for this oppression, to give him his due, he was otherwise very kind and respectfull to me, not suffering any other person to be ye least injurious to me. Besides ye Chief Customer (by ye force of presents), I had ye favour of ye Shabender, a person in great esteem, especially amongst Merchants; being properly a Judge of all differences and disputes that happen betwixt them; and one that appears for them before ye Pasha, or Mufti, or Caddi, when they are opprest by ye Government. These two persons, the Chief Customer and Shabender, accompanyed me to ye Pacha's Seraglio a-horseback, where I was received in ye kindest manner, sitting before the Pasha (all other persons standing), being entertained with Coffee, Shirbet, and Pirfumes. I paid well for it by ye rich presents which I gave him; but, without this means and manner of addressing, with ye helpe of the Turkish Language, I judge it next to an impossibility for a Franke to passe this way with so considerable an estate, without being eaten up and ruined by ye Government. Here we sold a great quantity of Indian Cloth, &c., to defray our charges, not suffering any of our Gold to be seen which we brought from Spahan, for fear of being killed for it, but carryed it on with me to Aleppo.

Bagdat stands on ye Chaldean side[1] of ye Tigris, ye River washing one side about a quarter part of ye Citty. It is a most pleasant, fruitful, healthfull situation, in ye degree of 33½. It rarely snows in this place, and when it does, it never lyes many hours on ye ground. It's almost ye same

[1] *I.e.*, on the left or eastern bank.

Latitude as Spaha, our course being due West all the way. Yet, by reason of ye great height of ye country and ye vast mountains we pass over in Persia, it is there exceedingly much colder in ye Winter than ever I felt it in England.

We had a robust, hardy Camel man that fell sick: & being forced to ride upon a Camel, between ye Bales, was frozen to death, between Nana & Farossa, ye 5th Ultimo. We thought it convenient to alight and walke two or three times in a morning, to prevent the freezing of our toes, fingers, & faces.

In Bagdat I fitted myselfe with store of provisions (as Biskett, Rice, Butter, Spice, Coffee, Shirbett, &c.) for the continuance of my Journey to Aleppo.

I bought two large tents with 2 Posts apiece to cover my goods, and a Kitchin Tent for ye Cooke and servants. I had a very stately large tent for myselfe, which I brought out of Bengall, with ye Walls that stood about it high enough to prevent a horseman's looking over: 'twas as much as two Camels could well carry.

March 1686.

[*No entry whatever in this month. Remaining at Baghdad.*]

April 1686.

April 11.—I left my lodgings in Bagdat and lay in my tent, pitched on ye Mesopotamia side of ye River Tigris.

April 13.—The Caravan rose and pitched at Emam-Zade, about 3 hours' riding towards Moosul or Ninave.[1]

April 14.—The Caravan lay still, and M^r. Dowglasse, M^r. Letter, my Nephew, and I went to see a great Tower called Nimrod, built of Sun-burnt bricks,[2] about 2 hours' riding from

[1] Nineveh.

[2] The great ruin 11 miles west of Baghdad, called 'Akarkūf, also known as *Tel-Nimrūd*, *Minār-an-Nimrūd*, and *Kasr-Nimrūd* ("The Tower, or Mound, or Palace of Nimrod").—Y.

Emam Zade; & this morning I returned to Bagdat Bridge, where I mett Padre Georgio di Vandosme, from whom I received a packet of letters from Consul Nightingale and my Cousin, Robert Wakeman of Aleppo. About 9 o'clock we sett out from ye Bridge, and arrived at our Caravan, lying at Tangoos, near ye River Tigris.

April 16.—We set out before day and travelled to Mansura: 6 houres.

April 17.—We set out by 5 o'clock and travelled through cornfields, and lay amongst them.

April 18.—We travelled 6 hours, and lay a little beyond Deegill.[1]

April 19.—We sett out by break of day and travelled 6 hours, and pitched by Usire-Beig's Tents, a Prince of ye Arabs, who commands ye country between Bagdat and Moosul; him we hired for P. 550 in money, and divers considerable presents, to conduct us with 50 horsemen to Moosul.

April 20.—We sett out a little after 4 o'clock and travelled till 11, and pitched upon ye banke of ye Tygris.

April 21.—We travelled 5 hours, and lay upon ye banke of ye River.

April 22.—We travelled 2 hours to Tigrett.[2]

April 23.—We travelled 5 houres. These 4 last dayes journey was most of it through Cornfields.

April 24.—We rose very early, and travelled 3 houres through the highest and finest meddows of 3 leaved grasse that ever I saw, intermixt with some thicketts of Tamarisk trees. It rained hard all the way. We pitched near an old Caravansarai.

April 25.—We rose before day, and travelled 9 houres to a place called Fina Su, which in Turkish signifies "Bad

[1] Sumeichah, or *Dujeīl*, 36 miles north of Baghdad, on the banks of an ancient canal bearing the latter name="Little Tigris". (See *J. R. G. S.*, ix, 444.)—Y.

[2] *Tekrīt*, on the Tigris.—Y.

Water",[1] taking its name from the brackishness of the water.

April 26.—We sett out by 3 o'clock and travelled 9 hours. We passed over a mountaine of exceeding white Marble, and pitched in a most pleasant, fruitful valley, near the river.

April 27.—We sett out by 5 this morning, and travelled over a most fruitful meadow of Rye Grasse, 3 leaved grasse, and sanfoin.

April 28.—We sett out at 3 o'clock and travelled 7 houres. About Sunrising we passed a Valley covered with a thick, Bitumenous substance of ye consistence of Pitch, of a strong Sulphurous Stench. About a muskett shot from hence we passed a small Rivulet; ye Water looked of ye colour of Brimstone. We judged it came from a mine of that nature.[2] We pitched in a plaine opposite to ye mouth of ye River Zarbe.[3]

April 29.—We sett out at 4, and travelled 7 hours over ye most pleasant, fertile Valley that we have yet seen, far exceeding any of ye former, being full of 3 leaved White, Red, and Yellow Honeysuckle grasse. We pitched our tents in another plaine, about a mile beyond ye hot baths, which proceed from these Sulphurous mines. Divers of our Company went into ye baths. Upon ye topp of ye Water (like a Scum) they take off great quantity of a Black, Pitchy substance, which ye Natives chew in their mouths to fasten their teeth & for Wantonesse, which they call black Mastick.[4]

April 30.—We arrived at Musul; its Latitude is 36° 15′.[5]

[1] *Fanā sū.*—Y.

[2] These are the asphalt springs at *Al-Kayyāra*, or "The Pitch place", briefly described by W. Ainsworth in *J. R. G. S.*, xi, 3.—Y.

[3] Zab.

[4] These are the baths called *Hammām 'Ali*, south of Mosul, also noticed by Ainsworth, *ibid.*, p. 2.—Y.

[5] True lat., 36° 25′.

This Citty stands on Mesopotamia side of ye River Tigris, the River washing about a quarter part of its Walls. It is finely situated in a most fruitfull soile. The Citty is of large extent, about 3 miles in compasse; the walls, formerly very strong and thick, with a broad, dry ditch about them, fortified after ye old fashion, full of towers. On ye other side of ye River are to be seen vast Ruines of Buildings, which ye Natives say was Old Nineveh: this is on ye Caldea side. 4 miles (or thereabout) Westward of Musul stands a great old Church, to which ye Christians of this Citty, most of them of ye Nestorian Opinion, resort every Saturday, in ye Afternoon, and lye in ye Church, on carpetts, all night, to be early at their devotion in ye morning,—who are poor, ignorant creatures, for ye most part have little more knowledge of Christian Religion than ye strict observation of Lent, and their other fasts and festivals. Here is an honest, poor Capuchin Fryer, a Frenchman, to whom we were much obliged for his civill respect to us, and information of all things remarkable in these parts.

Here our Arab Prince Usire tooke his leave of us, after he had consigned [us] to ye Pasha of Musul; and here we remained till ye 26th May, preparing ourselves for the prosecution of our Journey to Aleppo.

May 1686.

May 12.—My Cousin, Nathanael Letter, having received letters from his Father, the same day he departed from Bagdat, to returne for Bengall in India. He came thus far with us on our journey, having provided all things necessary for that purpose, which could not be conveniently separated from ours till we came to stay at this place. Here he hired passage for himselfe and two servants for P. 15, on a Killet, which is a frame of wood buoyed up by a great number of goat-skins, blowne up as Bladders with wind, and fastened to the frame: with these devices they carry and transport to

Bagdat vast weights and great store of goods, with a small draught of water, and, the River being very rapid, performe their Voyage in 2 dayes and a halfe, which we were 15 days coming up by land. I tooke leave this evening about sunsett of my cousin Letter, upon his Killet, wishing him a prosperous Voyage for Bengal, and returned to my tents, about halfe a mile out of ye Citty.

May 15.—I went to see the Nestorian Church, an hour's riding distant from Musull, where we were most courteously entertained by ye Christians.

May 17.—The Caravan of Camels (our Carryage was of Mules) pitched at ye North Gate of ye Citty.

May 18.—A new Mussellim[1] (a Pasha's Deputy) arrived at Musul, to whom we thought good to give some small presents, to prevent him doing us any mischief.

May 20.—The Mansoold[1] (or displaced) Pasha of Kirkooke[2] (a Citty in Chaldea) arrived over against Musul, and pitched his tents there, to take ye opportunity and advantage of our Company, being on his returne for Constantinople.

May 26.—We left Musul, and ferryed over ye Tigris with all our goods very early in ye morning, and pitched on ye Chaldean side.

May 27.—We set out by 4 in ye morning, and travelled 6 hours over a fertile, good Country, full of grasse and cornfields, and pitched by a towne inhabited by Koords and Ezeedees.[3] These people are said to worship the Devil.

May 28.—We travelled 6 hours over a most delicious

[1] "Mussellim" is *musallim* used for *mutasallim*, "a lieutenant to a governor, sent before to take possession for his superior", but commonly used for a governor of a certain rank. "Mansool'd" is a quasi-English participle, made from *ma'zūl*, "displaced or superseded."—Y.

[2] *Kerkūk*, 60 to 70 miles east of the Tigris, the seat of a Pashalik, and famous for the great naphtha springs near it.—Y.

[3] Ainsworth describes a visit to the Yezīdīs near Mosul, in *J. R. G. S.*, xi, 21, *seqq.*; and Layard does the like in *Nineveh and its Remains*, I, ch. ix.—Y.

country, and pitched on yᵉ top of a hill, near a delicate, large fountaine.

May 29.—We set out at 3, and travelled till 9 o'clock, through a pleasant and fruitful country, having passed over a small but exceeding rapid river.

May 30.—We rose by 2 in yᵉ morning, and travelled over a great Plaine, 5 houres, to yᵉ foot of a Mountain, where yᵉ usual stage is for Caravans to repose; but our Mulemen, knowing yᵉ straightness and difficulty of yᵉ Passage, by reason of yᵉ scraggedness of yᵉ Rocks, thought good to pass all difficulties this day, and lodged on a plaine halfe way over yᵉ mountaine.

May 31.—We sett out early, and passed yᵉ rest of yᵉ mountaine, on yᵉ skirts of which were many Arab Tents, and pitched at Zacloo,[1] on yᵉ banks of the lesser river Caboor, in yᵉ Bey of Amadee's territories, who is a Christian Prince of yᵉ Nestorian Religion,[2] and is able to bring 20,000 Coords, all able Soldiers, into yᵉ field, for his own defence.

June 1686.

June 1.—We rose at break of day and passed yᵉ bridge over yᵉ river Caboor, for which we paid 2 Bagdattees and ⅛ for every horse, mule, or asse in our Company. About 3 hours after we passed this bridge we forded over the river Chissell, a very rapid stream.[3] This river divides the country of Amadee and Gizra. We pitched near a Village wholly inhabited by Nestorians.

June 2.—We rose by 3 in yᵉ morning, and travelled 6

[1] Read *Zachoo*. Zākhū is on the (Kurdish) Khābūr, about 50 miles E. by S. of Jazīra. See Badger, *Nestorians*, i, 70.—Y.

[2] '*Amādiya*, formerly a great centre of the Nestorian or Chaldæan Christians, and seat of a hereditary Pashalik, about 60 miles N.W. by N. of Mosul.—Y.

[3] The *Heizel*, or *Khisel*, joins the Kurdish Khābūr a little below Zākhū. (See *Ritter*, ix, 716.)—Y.

hours, having the Mountaines of Coordistan on ye right hand and ye Tigris on ye left. On the top of one of these Koordistan Mountains[1] the country people say Noah's Arke rested. We pitched in a rich plaine, full of all sorts of sweet Herbes and Mulberry trees.

June 3.—We set out by 3 in ye morning, and travelled over a hill which brought us in sight of ye City Gizra,[2] where we arrived about an hour after Sunrising. It stands on an Island in ye Tigris, over which, from ye Caldean or Assirian side, you are conveyed by a Bridge of boates to ye Citty, and on ye Mesopotamian side by a Stone bridge without Arches, over which are loose boards layed, to be taken up on a suddaine, to prevent ye incursion of Arabs. The City is walled, but now gone much to decay: here we payed a dollar for every load of goods; besides considerable presents to ye Governor and Customer. We were here refreshed with plenty of fruit, as Apples, Apricots, Cherrys, & black and white Mulberries. We continued several dayes at this place.

June 6.—We crossed the river and pitched on Mesopotamia side. This evening we went to see some pleasant Gardens on ye side of a Hill to ye Westward of ye Citty, watered with divers large Fountains of excellent good water, full of water-cresses.

June 7.—We sett out early, and travelled over a stony, mountainous Country full of springs, which, notwithstanding the stones, makes it full of grass; and in divers places are to be seen large fields of rice. This evening newes was brought us that we must returne to Gizra: Mehmet Usire (who commands ye whole country between Moosul and Diarbekir), a Prince of Arabs, having sent a menacing letter to

[1] *I.e.*, on *Jibal Jūdī*, a range of great height, 80 miles nearly due north of Mosul, generally believed by the Mahomedans to be the resting-place of Noah's Ark.—Y.

[2] *Jazīra* (or *Jezīreh*), *i.e.*, "The Island", sometimes called *Jazīra-Ibn 'Omar*, on the Tigris, 90 to 100 miles above Mosul.—Y.

yᵉ Bey of Gizra, "if he permitted us to pass through his country that way, and came not downe towards Nisibeen to pay his duty which he demands of all Caravans, he would destroy all yᵉ subjects of Gizra, and villages belonging to them": to which command we thought it our safest course to yield obedience, after we had spent much money and loss of time to no purpose.

June 8.—We returned to Gizra againe. This night, Phettee Chellibea, a Nestorian, brought me assurance from Mehmet Usire (whom he had been to visit) that I should have safe passage through his country, and be kindly used by him.

June 9.—We sett out with yᵉ Pasha of Kirkooke (being upon his returne to Constantinople from his government on Caldea side), with some merchant subjects of yᵉ Grand Seignor that came in his company. Our Caravan now consisted of above 1000 Camells and Mules, with about 300 horsemen, and lodged always in the fields as near as we could where we might have yᵉ greatest plenty of Water.

June 10.—We sett out very early, travelling through a pleasant country well watered with small rivulets, and grasse to ye horses' bellies. This day, yᵉ Pasha of Kirkooke, seeing me on yᵉ road, sent a person desiring to speak with me. I rode with him about 2 hours, discoursing of divers parts of yᵉ world, especially of the East Indies: he is an ingenious, civill person, Nephew to yᵉ famous old Vezier Cuperlee.[1]

June 11.—We rose early and travelled 8 hours over a pleasant country, as was that of yesterday. This day we met with Mehmet Usire, the Prince of yᵉ Arabs governing this part of yᵉ Country. We pitched near his tents. He was accompanyed with about 200 horse, and 40 or 50 footmen with long guns. I went to wait on him, and a great carpet being

[1] Küparli, Pasha of Damascus, made Vizír by Mahomed IV in 1656, when already eighty years of age; a strong, sagacious, and merciless man; died in 1661, and was succeeded by his son.—Y.

spread, we sat down and drank Coffee, and were entertained with yᵉ usual ceremonies and civilities of the Country. These 2 days last past we had yᵉ Mountain Sanjar in sight to yᵉ Southward of us, out of which arises yᵉ River called yᵉ Great Caboor, which empties itself into yᵉ Euphrates above Ana.[1] The Arabs say Noah's Arke was built in this mountaine, and that it struck first in this place, and rested afterwards on yᵉ mountaine in Koordistan (before mentioned) called Gibbal Jeude.[2] This night we made our present to Mehmet Usire, yᵉ Arabian Prince.

June 12.—This morning Mehmet Usire, out of some particular designe to enhance our dutys, caused us to raise our tents and pitch them againe about 2 hours' riding from yᵉ Pasha of Kirkooke. All this day was spent in capitulating with yᵉ Arabs about payment of our dutys; but night came on before they could be adjusted.

June 13.—We were detained till 2 in yᵉ afternoon by Mehmet Usire before we could make an end with him, and then were forced to pay him P.[3] 1800 in money and goods. The Villaine would not permitt us to sett up our tents all this day, but forced us to lye broyling in yᵉ Sun all this day to afflict us. Having procured his permission to depart, we made all possible haste to reach Nisibeen, where it pleased God to bring us in safety an houre within night.

A little before we rose this afternoone, Mehmet Usire, like a perfidious Thief, ordered his brother, with a party of 25 Horsemen, to goe before and lye in a convenient place undiscovered, a little distance from yᵉ road, on purpose to assault

[1] The Khabūr, anc. *Chaboras*, joins the Euphrates at the site of ancient *Circesium*, a long way above Anah.—Y.

[2] See p. 226.

[3] The symbol in the copy is obscure, but seems to mean *Piastres*. The Turkish piastre struck in 1757, was worth 1*s*. 10½*d*. In Hedges' time it probably meant a larger sum, but it is difficult to ascertain.—Y.

me and drive away my Sisanall,[1] or Sumter Horse, with as many of my laden Mules as he was able to procure. But it having pleased God to put it into my thoughts to make greater haste than ordinary to reach and pass a Bridge over a good large River about 2 miles short of Nisibeen, to avoid ye crowd of mules which many times would force us to wait halfe an houre for an opportunity to pass over, coming to ye Bridge, notwithstanding ye great haste I made, a parcell of laden mules were got before me. I then ordered my Servant that led ye Sisenall to ford the River, which he scrupeling, not knowing its depth, I tooke ye Sisenall in my owne hand and got safely over: which I had no sooner done but I heard a great noise, and 2 or 3 guns fired, and was presently told ye Caravan was assaulted by 25 Horsemen commanded by Mehmet Usire's Brother, who, missing of me in ye hurry (by Divine Providence), sett upon a Turk Merchant's goods, of Aleppo, and carryed away 2 mules' lading of fine Indian Cloth, and a Sisenall of provisions and other necessaries, which they supposed to be mine, and missed of their designe but a few minutes, I being providentially got over the river before the Spie[2] employed by them could give them intelligence of my being got so near ye bridge.

The Turke Merchant that was robbed returned ye next day to Mehmet Usire, and lamentably complayning at his unjust and unkind usage (having paid him all his duties, and being fairly dismissed by him), the perfidious Arab told him he was exceeding sorry for his misfortune, his Brother's designe and his being only to take 2 or 3 mules' lading of *my* goods and Sisenall with Sapetts,[3] which he thought were full of

[1] There is a Pers. word *Sāïskhāna*, a beast of burden, a bat-horse. And in Bianchi's Dict. (*Turc-Français*), 1835, we find that this in Turkish is commonly made into *Sāïsnè* (or *Sāïsna*). This must be the word used by Hedges, though we cannot account for the termination.—Y.

[2] *I.e.*, *Spāhī*, horseman, same word as *sipāhi*, or sepoy.—Y.

[3] Qu. *sabad*, "basket"?

money; but seeing he was so unfortunate, he should have all his goods restored to him: which he fully performed, save only a few trifles to a small Value taken by his brother,—so maliciously bent are these villainous Arabs to y[e] destruction of Europeans.

June 14.—We sett out by 4 o'clock and travelled to Cara-Derry,[1] 6 houres, where we saw y[e] ruines of exceeding costly and sumptuous buildings, well described by Mons[r.] Tavernier. It is now a small town with pretty gardens on y[e] back side of y[e] hill, out of sight of travellers. Here we were mett by y[e] Customer of Diarbekeer, who tolled our loads, and tooke y[e] custom & dutys of all the 3 places of Nisibeen, Mardeen, & Diarbekir.

June 15.—As we were setting out early this morning by breake of day, we were overtaken by our Turke Merchant who was robbed of his 3 mules' lading of goods near Nisibeen; he came to us starke naked, with one person more in y[e] like condition, having been robbed of his horse and stripped to his skin by 12 Arab horsemen, which he counted, and believes them more, who told him they came thither on purpose to surprize and set upon me as I was rising, but, meeting with him in y[e] very nick of time, lost their opportunity to put their intended designe into execution, being informed by their Spie that I was mounted and following the caravan in so good order that they durst not adventure to assault me: so mercifully has it pleased God to shew himselfe in preferring me this second time. For both deliverances I beseech him to make me truly thankful.

[1] Kara Darah, or Dāra, the site of the famous *Daras*, or *Dara*, fortified first by Anastasius, and then by Justinian, as a barrier against Persia; taken, after a siege of five months, by Chosroes (*Naushirvān*). See *Gibbon*, chs. xl and xlvi. Tavernier, in the passage which Hedges refers to (Bk. II, ch. iv), calls the place Karasara. It is said, in the *Dict. of Gr. and Rom. Geog.*, s. v. *Daras*, that "D'Anville has tried, but we think in vain, to find any town or ruins which may mark the site of *Daras*." But see *Ritter*, xi, 398, *seqq.*; and see Niebuhr, *Voyage*, ii, 372; Dupré, *V. en Perse*, i, 85; Ainsworth, *J. R. G. S.*, x, 526.—Y.

June 16.—This day we travelled 6 hours to a small Christian Village under Merdeen,[1] which Citty stands upon a steep Hill, and ye Castle upon ye top of it.

We rose about half an hour after 3 o'clock, not without apprehensions of some danger, being credibly informed 30 horsemen lay privately on the road to surprize us before we entered ye hills. I provided for them the best I could by keeping my servants in good order (expecting little or no helpe from the Caravan), but, God be praised, saw none of them. We lay in a pretty little valley between ye Hills. On the top of one of them was a vast rock, out of which were many great Grottos, curiously cutt out, with vast expence, and divers cisterns for water, besides great ruines, which caused us to believe it had been a most stately building.[2]

June 17.—We sett out at 3, and travelled 8 hours over divers small rising Hills and fine, pleasant, well-watered Valleys; ye Hills covered with Oaks, and the Valleys with plenty of grasse and corne. We passed by a pretty town, ye greatest part of it cut out of a Rock, called Sheck Zooly.[3]

June 18.—We sett out at 3, and travelled 2 hours over hills and valleys, and then came into a pleasant Downe 3 hours farther, and pitched in sight of Diarbekir.

June 19.—We travelled 4 hours, and pitched near a Christian Village called Alli Punar, about half an hour from Diarbikeer, which lies in ye Latde. of 38° N.[4]

June 20.—I went into ye City of Diarbikeer to visit ye

[1] Mr. Ainsworth (1840) also "had intended not to go up the hill to Mārdīn, but await at *Gōl, a Christian village on the plain* S., a little W., of the city" (*J. R. G. S.*, x, 524).—Y.

[2] The place seems to be the *Shech Chan* of Niebuhr, *Voyage*, ii, 323.—Y.

[3] *Sheikh Zuli*, in Otter, quoted by Ritter, xi, 385.—Y.

[4] "On a icy de l'eau en abondance, en partie de la petite rivière *Ali poar*, et en partie des fontaines" (*Niebuhr*, ii, 326). His route-map shows the village of *Ali poar* about half a German mile west from Diarbekr.—Y.

French Padres of ye Order of St. Francis, who received and entertained me with great civility and respect.

June 21.—I went to visit and present ye Voyvode & Musellim of Diarbikeer, ye latter of which is ye most insolent, proud fellow that ever I saw in Turkey, or any other part of ye world where I have travelled. Here we continued till ye 6th of July.

Diarbikeer is a large, well-built Citty, as full of Inhabitants as any in these parts, situate upon ye banks of ye Tigris, on Mesopotamia side, in a most fruitful valley.

July 1686.

July 2.—This morning, a little before day, my two Muffrages,[1] or large Portmanteaus, wherein my bedding was carryed, with all my wearing apparell, Sword, Pistols, Gold Watch, Yamerlook, and divers other necessaries, together with my two Servants' cloaths, were stolen out of my tent, as near as could be to my Bed's head, 6 or 7 Servants then lying round about me. So soone as I missed them in ye morning I gave notice of it to ye Voyvode, who commanded all my Servants before him. After strict examination he chose out 2 persons: the Chout,[2] an Armenian, who had charge of watching my tent that night; and my Mossalagee,[3] or person who carries ye light before me in ye night: these two he sent to ye Massellim, who presently clapt them in chaines. This afternoon a Stranger that had been seen for two nights past to associate with ye said Mossalagee, and entertained by him, was taken upon suspicion, and also clapt into Irons; and this night, I hear, were severely drubbed to confesse; but no discovery being made, are continued still in prison.

[1] *Mifrāsh*, "a travelling bag".—Y.

[2] Should apparently be *chous; i.e.*, T. *chāūsh*.—Y.

[3] *Mash'alchi*, a torch-bearer, a word of very common use in India, where the servant so called is, however, usually a kitchen-drudge.—Y.

July 4.—This Stranger, being yᵉ 3rd person clapt in prison, not discovering who stole my Muffragees, I caused them to be all taken out of chaines, which cost me, all charges, P. 40. The Mussellim was advised to drub yᵉ Christian Chout[1] to death, assuring himselfe that would be a means to bring him in 2 or 3 purses of money to satisfie the Grand Seignor for yᵉ death of his Subject,—such is yᵉ Tyranny and Injustice of yᵉ Turkish Governors in these parts.

July 6.—About 4 o'clock this morning we sett out from Diarbikeer, and, travelling 6 houres, pitched near a fountaine of good water, in good pasture for our horses.

July 8.—I was taken with so violent a paine on yᵉ inside of my thigh that it put me into a great fever.

July 9.—We arrived at Severick,[2] a small towne near yᵉ ruines of an old Castle. The Aga of this place takes P. $\frac{3}{4}$ on every load of goods, besides a present to his satisfaction. The 4 last dayes journey from Diarbikeer to this place are the most stoney and troublesome for cattell to passe that ever I saw, almost as inconvenient as yᵉ steep hills of Cong in Persia. The pain of my thigh, and fever, continuing violent and strong upon me, I hired a Chamber in yᵉ towne, to lye out of yᵉ noise of yᵉ Caravan.

July 10.—My thigh began to swell, yᵉ paine and fever continuing.

July 11.—The swelling of my thigh increased and my Fever something abated. I am now assured my fever is occasioned by this excessive great paine in my thigh; and *that*, I conceive, may proceed from the growing of one of those dangerous Wormes which are bred by drinking those putrid and corrupt waters at Cong (two of our Company being afflicted with those kinds of Wormes at this present); or else I apprehend it has pleased God to strike me with a

[1] See p. 232.

[2] *Severek; Söverek* of Niebuhr (ii, 329), half-way between Diarbekr and Orfa.—Y.

Plague Sore. His Gracious Will be done in all things: a little more patience will discover what it is. Blessed be God for so much strength and intermission as I enjoy at present, to sitt up and write this account of it. I have bespoke, and am promised, a Horse Litter to carry me (if God gives me life) as far as Anlab.[1]

July 12.—The last night I took two large doses of Sal Prunello (in two hours' time), which caused me to sweat so freely that before morning it carried off my Fever (God be praised for it); but the swelling and paine of my thigh rather increased than any wise abated. This morning I got into my horse litter, and travelled 6 hours to ye side of a Hill, near a pretty little river, where we had store of good grasse for our horses. The swelling and paine of my Thigh, as also my fever, increased now to that degree that I was able to write no longer in my Journal, and, despairing of recovery, thought it impossible for me to hold out so long as to goe to Aleppo; however, contrary to my expectation, it pleased God so far to enable me that I arrived at Aleppo on ye 29th July 1686, being the very day 12 Months that my Cousin Nathanael Letter and I set out of Cong in Persia.

August 1686.

August 2.—My thigh was lanced by my fellow traveller, Mr. Robert Dowglasse, who performed ye Operation with great judgement and dexterity. There issued out near a Pint of Corruption, and continued running very much till ye latter end of September.

September 1686.

[*No diary.*]

October 1686.

October 26.—I set out of Aleppo towards Scanderoon,

[1] This must mean Aleppo (*Halab*).—Y

accompanied with Consul Thomas Metcalfe and late Consul Gamaliel Nightingale, together with most of ye English Nation. The French Consul, Monsr. Julian, did me the honor likewise to send out 6 of his Nation to attend me, who came all together to a baiting place about 2 houres riding out of Aleppo, where we parted (after ye usual manner) with our Aleppo Friends, and lay this night at Hangear, in comp^y.^ with my Cousin, Robert Wakeman, Mr. Arthur Browne (at whose house I lay at Aleppo), and Mr. Darly.

October 27.—Mr. Browne and Mr. Darly returned to Aleppo. My Cousin Wakeman, Nephew Robert Hedges, and I continued our Journey, and lay this night at ye Coordeen Village, in ye Plaines of Antioch.

October 28.—We lay at Byland,[1] 7 miles short of Scanderoon.

October 29.—About 9 o'clock this morning we arrived at Scanderoon. Mr. Fisher, ye Vice Consul, and divers French Merchants mett us about a mile out of town. Here I was most courteously invited by Capt. Spence, Commander of the *Levant Merchant*, and lay aboard his Ship.

October 30.—Capt. Spence invited Mr. Fisher, Mr. Peter Renouf, Mr. Dowglasse, and my Cousin Wakeman aboard his Shippe to a noble entertainement.

October 31.—The same Company were all invited by Capt. Renouf, and dined aboard his Shippe, *James ye Second*.

November 1686.

November 1.—This afternoon my Cousin Wakeman took his leave, and returned to Aleppo. My Nephew Hedges and I, in a short time after, went aboard the French Shippe, in whom we designed to take our passage for Marseilles, called y^e^ *Nostra Dama della Guarda*, commanded by Captain Corraill, of that Port.

[1] Beilān.

November 2.—The Wind blowing fresh at South West, we continued in Scanderoon Road.

November 3, 4, 5.—The weather continuing very stormy, with great gusts and violent Showers of raine from ye mountaines, we lay in Scanderoon Road. This day, 5th, ye Shippe *Charles* imported[1] from Leghorne, consigned to Mr. Peter de Leau & Mr. Darly of Aleppo. The wind blew so hard this night that it broke one of our Cables, and had very near driven ye *Charles* ashore.

November 6.—The weather cleared up, and ye *James ye Second* & our Capt. Corraill set saile together about sunset for Cyprus.

November 8.—We arrived at Cyprus.

November 9.—Capt. Renouf arrived at Cyprus. This morning I went ashore at Solinus. Monsr. Balthazar Sauuan (Consul for ye English, French, and Dutch Nations) sent me his horse to carry me to Larnica, where I was received and entertained with the greatest respect and civility imaginable till ye 15th ditto.

November 15.—This evening I went aboard of Capt. Corrail. The Commander of ye *Hollands* Convoy did me the favour to carry me first aboard his owne Shippe, and after Supper sent me on board ye French man.

This night Captain Renouf sett sail for England; but our Commander, finding ye wind contrary, and like to be dirty weather, waited for a more seasonable opportunity.

November 18.—We sailed this morning from Cyprus.

November 20.—We lost sight of ye Island of Cyprus.

December 1686.

December 7.—Being Tuesday, we had a violent Storm at North and N.E. off ye west end of Candy, which put us into so great a terror that we broke and threw overboard our least

[1] Mr. Hedges uses this word for "came into port". See again under January 3rd, 22nd, and 23rd, 1687.—Y.

boat, all our empty Water casks, and whatever else lay in yᵉ mariners' way upon the deck. It began about noone; yᵉ Violence of it continued till Midnight, and then abated. We steered W. b. N. and W.N.W., under a Fore Course reefed and lowered halfe Mast. [?!] Most of yᵉ Shipp's crew, as well as yᵉ Passengers, gave themselves up for lost. God be praised for this deliverance.

December 13.—This day about Noon we discryed yᵉ Island of Sicilia.

December 15.—About Sunset we saw Cape Bono, and came up with it before morning.

December 16 & 17.—Little wind, and that contrary.

December 18.—It continued all day calme, scarce so much wind as to govern the Ship. In yᵉ morning we had sight of Sardinia at a great distance.

December 19.—We came up with Sardinia, but yᵉ Wind blowing fresh at West and W.S.W., were forced to saile on yᵉ East side of yᵉ Island. The wind increased this night to a Storme, but continued not above 2 or 3 houres, and then grew calme.

December 20.—We came up and spoke with a French Settee[1] of Marseˡᵉˢ·, wanting two months from Smirna: we spared them some bread for their relief. By breake of day this morning we discovered a small Shippe lying under the land, with her sails hauled up, which she soone let fall and stood up to us. We displayed our Colours, and she putt out English Colours, but standing in againe close to yᵉ shore. We took her to be a Corsaire.

December 21.—We came up with yᵉ Island Corsica. In yᵉ afternoon a Shippe lying close under yᵉ shore stood out towards us, and perceiving she got much upon us, we hauled up our Main sail and Fore saile and stayed for her. Coming

[1] "A single-decked Mediterranean vessel with a long and sharp prow, without topmasts, and carrying lateen sails" (Adm. Smyth's *Sailor's Word-book*).—Y.

up with us, she proved an Argiers man of war of 20 guns and 150 men. Having peace with France, she only wished us a good Voyage, and stood towards Sardinia. She told us ye ship we saw yesterday was her Consort, belonging to Argiers. This night it blew very fresh, and carryed us about half the length of Corsica.

December 22.—By 6 o'clock this morning it blew a most violent Storme at North, insomuch that for divers hours we could carry no more than a little stay sail to keepe the Ship before the Wind; after some time they got out a little part of our Mainsail, which was all we were able to carry this day and all the night following.

December 23.—The Storme continued without ye least intermission perceivable till towards 2 or 3 in ye afternoon. We continued our course due South; but fearing before day we might be driven upon ye Africa Shoare, lay by with part of our Fore saile. It pleased God that all this night ye wind was so favourable that we were able to lay our head to the weather.

December 24.—About break of day the storme returned to its former Violence and Rage; and being no longer able to lye by, bore up before it, making all ye sail we could to recover the Port of Tunis, which, by God's great mercy to us, we obtained, and anchored in ye Road (5 miles short of ye usual place of riding) before it was quite so darke that I could not see my hands—for which great Deliverance I beseech y^{e} Lord to make me truly thankful.

December 25.—The wind blew so hard that we could not send our boats ashore.

December 26.—Our boat set me ashore at y^{e} Castle of Goletta, where I hired a horse and Guide for P. 1¼ to conduct me to y$_{e}$ English Consul at Tunis, Thomas Goodwyn, Esq$^{re.}$, who received me with demonstrations of y^{e} greatest respect & civility that could be showne. He went with me to visit y^{e} King, who made us sitt downe by him, and entertained us with Coffee, enquiring after y^e affaires of Turky and Christendom. Having taken leave of y^e King, we went and saw all ye Castle, which is well stored with excellent good Gunns of Brasse and Iron.

December 27.—We continued at Tunis till our Scrivan, or purser, had made "Consolato" for ye damage done ye Shippe and goods in ye two stormes we have had since we left Cyprus. We mett here in Port ye ship *Neptune*, Capt. Milborne commander, and ye Ship *Francis*, Captain Fore commander. At ye Consul's house was Capt. Wickers, a person who came to seek employment.

December 28.—I took leave of Consul Goodwyn. Capt. Milborne did me the favor to lend me his boat, and accompanyed me himself to Goletta, and thence aboard his Shippe, where I was nobly entertained, and saluted with 13 Guns at our going off, ye Captain himself accompanying me on board of our Shippe, Capt. Corrail, who immediately weighed anchor and sett sail for Marseille, being about 4 o'clock in ye afternoon, with a fair wind; but as soon as we gott without ye Cape of Porta Ferine ye Wind chopped about and blew hard at North and N.W.

December 29.—We returned and anchored in ye Bay of Tunis, over against ye watering place, nearer ye Shipps than we lay before.

[*No further entry till January* 3.]

January 1687.

January 3.—The last night and all this day it hath blowne a very great Storme at North and N.N.W. About Noon a Ship imported with French Colors.

January 4.—The Storme continued exceeding violent all ye last night; our long boat at ye Sterne was filled full of water. About 12 at Noon ye rage of ye Wind and Sea somewhat abated; but ye waves ran still very high and violent, the Sky continuing much clouded.

January 5.—The Storme being much abated, Consul Goodwyn wrote me a most kind letter, and sent me a noble present of fresh Provisions by Capt. Milborne's boat, on which I went ashore ye second time to ye Consul's house at Tunis, accompanyed with my Nephew, Robert Hedges, Monsr. Ainesse, a Frenchman, and Sig^r.^ Clockner, a Hollander.

January 6, 7, 8, & 9.—The Wind blew a great Storm at W. and N.W. by W.

January 10.—The Wind coming up fresh at East and S.E., I tooke my leave of Consul Goodwyn, and came down in a Towne boat to the Castle at Goletta. The sea ran so high that the Boatmen would not adventure to carry us over the Barr; but Capt. Milborne discovering of us with his prospective Glasse, sent his Pinnace to bring us aboard; which it pleased God they performed, though with ye greatest hazard & difficulty imaginable, the Seamen being all, except ye Coxon, in ye Water as high as their Armepitts, to force ye boat & run her upon ye sand through ye Waves, which were very furious and lofty, as usuall upon Barrs. Capt. Milborne, perceiving ye Hazard, came off in his Yall to our assistance & see us safe aboard ye French Shippe, designing himselfe to goe ashore this night (if possible) to Tunis.

January 11.—The Storme increased to a great Violence all this day and ye night following.

January 12.—This morning it rained hard, and ye Wind very much abated.

January 13.—The wind increased last night to a greater degree of Violence than it hath done since we came into this port; and this day it has cleared up to a calme from 8 o'clock this morning.

January 14.—The Wind came up a faire and gentle gale at E. and E.S.E., as faire a Wind as could blow; but because it rained a small drizling shower our Hen-hearted Provinsalls, would not putt to sea till they saw the Weather better settled.

This Afternoon Captain John Cobbold, commander of a great Fly Boat[1] (who had been 8 yeares a Slave in Argiers) [Algiers], came aboard to give me a visit, and presented me with 2 Hens, halfe a Holland Cheese, and 4 English Neatt's Tongues,—all y[e] provisions y[e] poor man had aboard, which added exceedingly to y[e] Obligation; besides, for my sake, he spared our Captain a Butt of Water and a parcell of wood, which we very much wanted, and it was of great use to us.

January 15.—The wind coming about last night at 12 o'clock to y[e] N.E. and N. b. E., our Captain did not think fitt to weigh his anchor, but lay still in y[e] port of Tunis. The Winde this day being pretty moderate, Capt. Cobbold came aboard and dyned with us, and invited me to dine with him to-morrow aboard his Shippe, y[e] *Numidia*.

January 16.—The Wind springing up at E. b. N. this last night, we weighed Anchor, and set sail about halfe an hour after 10 o'clock this morning. Being got as far out of y[e] Bay of Tunis as y[e] Point of Porta Ferine, the Wind encreased to a Storme, and so continued all night. Our course, W.N.W.; Winde at East and E. b. S.

January 17.—By 8 in y[e] morning we saw the Island of Sardinia. By 10 this morning y[e] Wind encreased to a violent Storm. We bore away before it all y[e] breadth of Sardinia, and before night anchored near y[e] Island Palma de Sol, on y[e] West side of Sardinia, in a good harbour.

January 18.—We lay at anchor; wind at S.E., as faire as can blow; but our dastardly mariners durst not adventure to Sea, for feare it should blow as hard abroad as it did yesterday.

January 19.—We gott under saile this morning by breake

[1] "A large flat-bottomed Dutch vessel, whose burden is generally from 300 to 600 tons. It is distinguished by a remarkably high stern, resembling a Gothic turret, and by very broad buttocks below" (Smyth's *Sailor's Word-book*).—Y.

of day, but seeing the weather a little more overcast (which soon passed over, with a small shower of raine), our Mariners' hearts fainted, and we returned to anchor near ye same place from whence we weighed, and had steered N.N.W., ye due course for Marseilles.

January 20.—A French Settee sailed by us ye last night, and anchored near ye bottom of ye Bay. She came from Toulon, and bound for Tunis. Our boat went ashore this morning to fill water and bring what provisions they can procure from ye inhabitants. About noon ye Winde came up fresh at N.W. At Sunsett the Settee sailed for Tunis.

January 21.—Our boat went ashore to buy provisions. Wind at N.E. A great Shame that we are not at Sea, to make ye best use of it. About noon a Settee coming from ye Eastward anchored at ye mouth of ye Harbour.

January 22.—This last night proving very clear and faire Weather, our Captain for mear shame weighed anchor, and sett sail by daybreake, passing by ye Settee that imported yesterday: she spared us a Kintall of Biskett. She wanted 4 dayes from Marseilles, and is bound for Candia. Being gott without ye Island Palma, we found the Wind N. and N. b. W—a fresh gale; and so returned and anchored before Noone in ye Gulf of Palma, where another Settee spared us a kind of Biskett & some salt Fish—provisions being very scarce with us.

January 23 & 24.—We lay in ye Bay of Palma with very faire weather. A Tartan[1] that imported ye 22nd Instant from ye Levant sett saile about Midnight; we conceive her bound for Marseilles. About 2 o'clock this afternoon a gentle gale sprung up at West; yett our Block-headed Captain and Mariners did not think fitt to Sett saile.

January 25.—The Wind coming up in ye night at West, we got under Saile this morning before day; by Noon y^e^

[1] A small, one-masted, lateen-rigged coasting vessel.—Y.

Wind veering to ye N.W., and shrinking so fast upon us that we were forced to our old Harbour of ye Gulf of Palma. This is our 3rd returne. God send us better fortune ye next departure.

January 26.—The wind blew exceeding hard all ye last night, and continues soe to do this morning at West. Our Captain is of opinion it is ye greatest Storme we have had since we came to sea. God be praised, we are in a very good Port.

January 27.—Yesterday, towards evening, ye Wind came about to ye N.W. and N.N.W., and blew most violently ye greatest part of last night till towards this morning, when it abated with a great Showere of Raine, and continues still at N.N.W.

January 28.—Last night it blew very hard, and this morning early it encreased to an exceeding great Storme, insomuch that our Captain and Mariners (who ought to have had more courage) despaired of saving their lives, and gave all for lost, betaking themselves wholly to their prayers. The chief occasion of their fears was the Shipp's driving towards ye Shore, though we had 3 anchors ahead, and at least 2 miles' drift.

About 2 o'clock in ye afternoon our Captain and mariners grew into great disorder and confusion ; most were for cutting the Cables, and running ashore in the best Creeke we could find ; others for cutting down ye Mainmast ; and some few for riding it out and expecting God's providence—which latter course had been ye best ; but it determined in cutting downe ye Mainmast, which was done about halfe an hour after two, when ye Storm began to abate, and before Sunsett we had little Wind.

We then wisht againe (but too late) for our Main mast. Our boat was sunke at our Sterne in ye morning, by neglect, for not throwing out ye water. In this distraction the Mariners threw every thing overboard that lay in their sight upon deck, so much as a few sticks of Wood to dresse our Meate, and a Top Gallant Mast or something like it. I remember I entreated hard to save ye boat's Grapplin.

God Almighty's Name be praised for thy great deliverance! & grant I may never be necessitated to take my passage upon a Provinsall. They are certainly ye most despairing, low spirited Mariners in ye World when they are brought to any extremity.

January 29.—It was calme all ye last night, and this morning we began to weigh our Anchors and clear our boat of ye Water, intending to saile downe to ye bottom of ye Bay to refitt ye Shippe. God knows how long that may be.

At 9 o'clock this morning, observing two Settees sailing out of this Bay, I prevailed on ye Captain to make a Weft of his Antient and fire a Gun, in hopes that one of them at least (seeing our distresse) would come on board, pretending to send a letter to some Port of Italy or France. It pleased God that this designe tooke its desired effect. The best of ye Settees, bound for Mayorke,[1] without lading, having only 2 Spaniards, passengers, aboard, came to our side, with whom I agreed for P. 325[2] to carry my Nephew and me, with ye rest of our passengers (we paying P. 200 of ye said money), to Marseilles. We would have embarked on ye Settee immediately, but her commander, Capt. Guiran, was not then willing to receive us, pretending he would first clear his Cabbin of ye Spaniards, and (Wind & weather permitting) come to us ye next morning.

January 30.—The Settee came to us according to her Commander's promise, and having taken leave of Capt. Corrail (by whom I was most respectfully treated, and saluted with 7 Guns at my departure), I went on board ye Settee, who sett sail immediately, and arrived at Porta Scolie, a small village

[1] *I.e.*, Majorca.

[2] Piastres, but *what* piastres? Probably Sp. dollars.—Y.

with a Tower for its defence, on ye island of Sardinia (over against S^t. Peter's Island), about Sunsett, to putt ashore ye two Spaniards, who had no mind to goe with us to Marseille.

January 31.—This morning early we put ye Spaniards ashore, and by 8 set saile for Marseilles. By 3 in ye Afternoon (finding ye wind contrary at Sea) returned and anchored at S^t. Peter's Island, and by Sunsett (ye Wind coming up at East again) we sett saile ye second time for Marseilles.

February 1687.

February 1.—The Wind coming up last night about 12 o'clock at N.W., and blowing hard, we lay by all night, and before 10 this morning anchored againe, in a Storme of Wind, under S^t. Peter's Island.

February 2.—About 12 o'clock noone, came into this road a small fly-boat with English Colours, who had lost all her Masts. My Nephew and I went aboard with our Captn. to see what she wanted in this miserable condition. She is called y^e *Providence*, Daniel Morley, Commander, belonging to M^r. James Denn of Marke Lane, London, laden with salt from Juasy, bound for Villa Franca. She mett with the Storme on ye 24th and 25th Ultimo, which was so violent that ye first day it carryed away her Foremast and Boltsprit, and ye next day her Main and Mizen Masts, leaving her like a Wrack. The Sea frequently running over her Poope, it once ran so high as to wash and endanger ye carrying away a man from off ye Main Yard. It broke and washt away her two boats, strongly lashed in 9 places, and carryed away her Sheet Anchor from her bow. I knew her Gunner, one Jeremy Bascum, formerly servant to M^r. Nathanael Letter in London.

February 3.—This morning, by breake of day, ye Shippe *Providence* ran aground, her Commander designing to go between ye Islands Sardinia and Palma de Sol, where y^e

English Platts and Wagones[1] make a large passage; but in truth there is none, the said two Islands being joined together by a Bridge. The right passage is between Palma and St. Peter's Island. Ye shippe had been there undoubtedly lost, and ye men in great hazard of their lives (if any had escaped), had it not been for ye great Diligence and Industry of Capt. Guiran, who (for my sake) went off to her in his boat, and carryed out her anchors (her owne boats being all lost in ye Storme), and helped to throw out 5 tons of her salt to lighten ye Vessell, by which means she got off into 5 fathoms of Water.

Our Captain likewise lent her Commander, Capt. Morley, P. 50, not having any money to buy him provisions in this his extremity (for which I was his Security), and gave his bill for ye Sum on Messrs. Goodwin & Martin, in Marseilles.

February 4.—We lay in Harbour.

February 5.—We sailed about 3 o'clock this morning with a very bare wind, & by 11 o'clock at night anchored in ye Bay of Oristan (in our Platts called Napoli), a most excellent good harbour, sufficient to containe 500 sail of Ships. Its entrance is 10 miles at least. We mett here a French Shippe wanting 20 dayes from Cyprus. She has lost ye head of her Boltsprit, and cracked her Fore Topmast in foul Weather: she has lain here 17 dayes for a fair wind to Marseilles.

February 6 & 7.—We lay in the Bay of Orestan [Oristano].

February 8.—This morning, by 3 o'clock, ye wind coming up at S.S.E., our Captaine sett saile. Without ye Port we found ye wind freshen upon us on ye same Point, and con-

[1] *I.e.*, Charts and Sailing Directories. But the second word should be *Wagoners*, from the famous Dutch author on Navigation, Lucas Tansz Waghenaer, whose work, *Spieghel der Zeevaert*, was translated, and popular in the English marine, under the name of the *Mariner's Mirror*. See Mr. Tiele's Introduction to Dr. Burnell's Linschoten, p. xxvii (Hak. Soc., 1885), and Smyth's *Word-book*, s. v. *Waggoner*.—Y.

tinued a strong gale all ye day. Our Course, N.N.W. and N.W. b. N.

February 9.—The gale continued fresh all ye last night. This morning at Sunrising the weather began to grow dirty and foggy, with frequent showres of raine. About 11 we discovered ye Isles of Aires [Hyères], near Toulon, which we had no sooner done, but on a suddaine the wind came about contrary at S.W. and then N.W., so that we had some trouble and difficulty to get into the said Harbour of ye Isles of Aires, where we anchored about 2 o'clock this afternoone. At Sunsett we weighed again, and ye wind increasing to a Storme with a N.W. wind, put into Toulon before morning.

February 10.—I went into ye Citty of Toulon, and thence into ye Lazaretta.

February 18.—I was visited in ye Lazaretta by Capt. Say, Capt. Gibson, Commander of y^e^ *George*, Mr. Packston, & Mr. Sandland, this latter accompanying Capt. Say to ye East Indies by way of Aleppo.

February 19.—This morning ye Officer of y^e^ *Sanita* gave me Prattick. I went ashore in Captain Gibson's boat, accompanyed with Capt. Waters, Comman^r.^ of [ ], and dined with them in Toulon. I was invited to supper by Monsr. Sabatory, an eminent French merchant, and to bear me company he invited likewise Monsr. Bidau, a Captain of one of the King of France's Men-of-War.

February 20.—I left Toulon at 7 o'clock in ye morning (being carryed in a litter), and arrived at Marseilles about 7 at night, and lay at Mr. Hastings' house till ye 28 Instant.

February 28.—This Morning my Nephew, Robert Hedges, & I sett out in a litter from Marseilles towards Lyons. We dyned at St. Port, and lay at Lambase [*i.e.*, Lambesc].

March 1687.

March 1.—I dyned at Orgone [*i.e.*, Orgon] and laye at Avignon.

March 2.—I dyned at Orange (from whence y$_e$ Prince of Orange takes his title) and laye at Boulene [Bollène].

March 3.—I dyned at Mountilimar [Montelimart] and lay at Lorioll.

March 4.—I dyned at Valience & lay at St. Valie [St. Valier].

March 5.—I dyned at Le Poige de Rosilion [? Péage de Rousillon] and lay at Vienne.

March 6.—I arrived by 11 in ye morning at Lyons, and lay this night at ye 3 Kings—a good Inn. Here I discharged our Muleteer, having paid him Livres 66, or P. 22,[1] and hired 2 Places in ye Diligence for Paris, for which each person is to pay 22 Crowns, Diet included.

March 7.—We departed from Lyons in a boat, and lay at Mascoon [Maçon].

March 8.—We embarked again very early, and about noon arrived at Challoon [Chalons]. Here we took coach (paying 6 Sols per pound for our Portmanteaus, except 10lb. presented), and lay at Shane [? Chagny].

March 9.—We sett out at 4 in ye morning, dyned at Arnay le Duc, and lay at Essolio [? Saulieu].

March 10.—We dyned at Busele Forgis and lay at Vermonton [Vermenton].

March 11.—We set out at 3 in ye morning, & at 8 dyned at Osser [Auxerre], & lay at Villeneuf-le-Roi [*i.e.*, V. sur Yonne].

March 12.—We dyned at Vilneuf le guerre [Elguiard] and lay at Melun.

March 13.—By 10 in ye Morning arrived at Paris, and lay at ye Ville d'Anjoy, in the Dolphin's Street.

March 26.—About 10 o'clock this morning my Nephew Hedges and I tooke Coach for St. Denis, and there took post towards Callis.

[1] The Fr. Livre at that time was = 1s. 6d. nearly; therefore 1 P. = 4s. 6d. And this confirms the supposition in note at p. 244.—Y.

March 29.—This morning I arrived in Callis, and lodged in ye Golden Dragon—a good Inn.

April 1687.

April 3.—About 2 o'clock this afternoon I embarked on ye Packet boat at Callis for Dover.

April 4.—At 1 this morning I arrived (praised be God) at Dover, and lay this night at Canterbury.

April 5.—This Evening I mett my Cousin, Dr. Charles Hedges, my two Brothers Vanacker, Mr. Webster, Mr. Sussex, Mr. Mayres, & Mr. Wallopp, at Rochester.

April 6.—My brother and Sister, Sr. Jeremy Sambroke & his Lady, Mr. William Johnson and his Lady, my Cousin Tresser, my Sister Newton, and my 3 children, did me the honor to meet me at Blackheath and accompany me to London, where I arrived (blessed be God) in good health this Evening.

April 7.—I waited upon my Lord High Chancellor Jefferys, accompanyed with Sir Robt. Clayton & Sir Jeremy Sambrooke. His Lordship was pleased to bid me welcome home, and to tell me (amongst other discourse) he did not care if all ye E. India Compy. knew he had a greater kindness and respect for me than he had for Sir Josia Child.

July 1687.

July 21.—I marryed Madam Anne Searle, ye Widow of Col. John Searle of Finchly. The Office was performed by Dr. John Tillotson, Deane of Canterbury, in Bassishaw Church. We dyned at my Uncle Anthony's house in Coleman Street, and went to Finchly in ye Evening.

March 1688.

March 6.—This Afternoon his Majtie. King James was pleased (as a marke of his Royall favour) to confer on me ye honr. of Knighthood in his Bedchamber.

[*Here the Journal ends abruptly, without any signature. The remaining half of the page is blank, as also the "over leaf"; then eight leaves, which may or may not have been manuscript, have been roughly torn out; then follow twelve blank leaves, and on the fly leaf at the end of the book* (*a folio* 14 *inches by* 9) *are some memoranda as follows*:]

The removall of Agent Dacres (being greatly favoured and beloved by y[e] King of Bantam), together with M[r.] Arnold White's rude and uncivill carryage towards him at his first Arrivall, is judged to have been the cause of the losse of Bantam.[1]

Sept. 24, 1685.—I presented y[e] Calenter (or Chief of y[e] Armenian Merchants) of Giulfa with a bag of Sugar of Okes 35, and another Bag to Hogea Kiragoos, his Brother, of Okes 39½.

The Citty of Lar in Persia lyes in y[e] Lat. of					27° 44′ N.
,,	Shiras	,,	,,	,,	29° 40′ N.
,,	Spahan	,,	,,	,,	32° 40′ N.

From Gombroon	to Lar	are Leagues	42=	miles	126	
,, Lar	,, Shiras	,,	64=	,,	192	
,, Shiras	,, Spahan	,,	73=	,,	219	
		,,	179=		537	miles.

[1] The English were expelled from Bantam on August 30th, 1682.—Orme's *Hist. Fragments*, p. 118; Bruce's *Annals*, ii, p. 486.

END OF HEDGES' DIARY.

INDEX TO VOLUME I.

(THE DIARY OF W. HEDGES.)

THE END.

THE END.